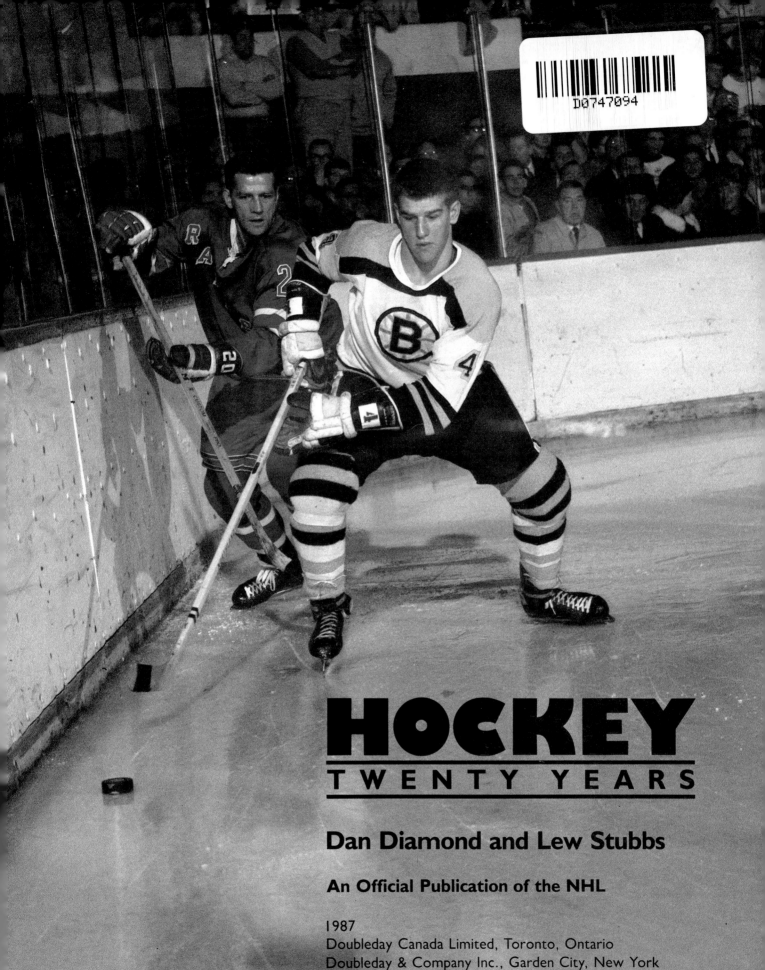

# HOCKEY
## TWENTY YEARS

### Dan Diamond and Lew Stubbs

**An Official Publication of the NHL**

1987
Doubleday Canada Limited, Toronto, Ontario
Doubleday & Company Inc., Garden City, New York

ISBN 0-385-25120-3
CIP data: see page 212

# Contents

# Introduction

I recall, sometime around 1965, watching a television comedy about a World War II soldier discovered still guarding his remote Pacific outpost some twenty years after the war had ended. He knew nothing of the armistice nor any events of the intervening years. Holding those who stumbled upon him at gunpoint, skeptical at their insistence that his war was long over, in thick Brooklynese he questioned the "enemy" trying to trick him into surrender: "If youse guys is Americans," he implored, "tell me what city da Dodgers play in?" Of course they answered "Los Angeles," and the soldier cocked his rifle.

Since then, I've often wondered how a hockey fan, after a 20-year hiatus, might react to some of the infinite changes — both monumental and trival — that have taken place in the game of hockey. Imagine a latter-day Rip Van Winkle awakening at 2:15 a.m. on Easter Sunday morning, 1987. A few minutes ago, Pat LaFontaine whacked a puck past Bob Mason and ended the longest and — at least in terms of quantity — most entertaining hockey game in my lifetime, allowing the New York Islanders to defeat the Washington Capitals in the Patrick Division Semi-final for the right to play the Philadelphia Flyers in the Patrick Division final, the winner advancing to the Wales Conference Championship, and, ultimately, the Stanley Cup final. What would our sleepy-eyed hockey fan think?

He'd certainly recognize overtime. But just who, he'd wonder, are the New York Islanders? The Washington Capitals? The Philadelphia Flyers? The Patrick Division or Wales Conference? And what would he make of plastic skate blade holders, aluminum sticks, plastic helmets, transparent visors and Mikko Makela?

If he was to read just a bit about our sport today, how would he react to 21 NHL teams, Rendez-Vous '87, the Hartford Whalers, the New Jersey Devils or Wayne Gretzky? And when trying to fill in the gaps, he'd have to confront Alan Eagleson and the NHL Players' Association, the World Hockey Association, the Summit Series of 1972, the California Golden Seals, the Atlanta Flames, Bobby Orr, Dave Shultz, Gordie, Mark and Marty Howe and the Stastny brothers. To borrow an apt phrase that came into currency around the time Rip went out of circulation, it would "blow his mind."

The NHL Rip would remember was a closely-knit six-team affair, employing 120 players, most of whom seemed to stay in the NHL year after year, playing well into their thirties and traveling between New York, Boston, Montreal, Toronto, Detroit and Chicago almost exclusively by train. They were usually coached by former stars and needed summer jobs to make ends meet. Almost all came from Canada. Almost none went to college. The wings skated up and down their lanes, the defenseman rarely ventured much past the offensive blueline. If you were lucky, you could see one game a week on television. It seemingly had been that way for decades and no one was in a hurry to change it.

But North America's appetite for sports had grown insatiable. New teams — even new leagues — appeared in various sports and hockey, the game that was so successful in six cities, was coveted by many more. There were large national television packages to be won with large national television dollars to be awarded, and — it was believed — a large national television audience out there waiting to be converted to the new game in town. And with would-be stars stacked up in minor pro leagues around the continent, there was a talent pool that could support it all.

The NHL answered this clamor by launching the most ambitious expansion ever undertaken by an established professional league. What had once been the most stable of sports institutions doubled its size to 12 teams for the 1967–68 season. New franchises stretched the NHL map past New York to Philadelphia and Pittsburgh, and beyond Chicago, not merely to Minnesota and St. Louis but all the way to San Francisco and Los Angeles. The Pullman sleeper had given way to the jetliner, but no one on the aircraft foresaw the turbulence that lay ahead.

As a veteran hockey observer at the ripe age of 16 years old, and a fortunate (albeit chauvinistic) resident of one of the original six cities, I was skeptical about the possibilities of expansion's success until one Saturday night early in the initial expansion season of 1967–68. While nodding off on my grandmother's couch with the TV on, a sold-out St. Louis Arena jolted me from my nap as the Blues overtook the Rangers. I had never fallen asleep watching a hockey game before (it was a Central Time Zone game, I later rationalized, and I had had a tough day) and the fans in St. Louis, of all places, had administered an aural spanking. Their cheers made me a believer. Had it not been for them, I might have slept for 20 years too.

Expansion meant colorful new hockey sweaters to see and stars to wear them in each new city: "Cowboy" Bill Flett in L.A., Bernie Parent and Doug Favell in Philly, Gord "The Red Baron" Berenson and the Plager brothers in St. Louis. Bill Goldsworthy danced the "Goldy Shuffle" after each of his North Star goals while Les Binkley in Pittsburgh proved he should have been an NHL netminder all along.

The new teams celebrated their maiden voyage by winning or tying one-third of their contests with the established clubs — better than the one-fourth NHL president Clarence Campbell had predicted. It was an impressive start.

Still, the biggest stars shone in the East: Hull, Howe, Beliveau, Gilbert, Mahovlich, Ullman, Esposito, Worsley, Mikita, Giacomin. And there was a new star who was about to change the face of the game.

Defensemen before Bobby Orr had rushed the puck, but none had his incomparable combination of skill and speed — and none did it in front of international television audiences. As a result, no hockey player was ever more imitated or made a more lasting impact. When you look down the rosters of NHL teams today and see the United States-born players and graduates of the burgeoning American collegiate hockey scene, you are seeing Bobby Orr's legacy.

If you loved hockey — even if you hated the Bruins — you had to love Bobby Orr. The Europeans did — especially the Soviets. Soon, although we in North America were hardly aware of the process, European hockey produced numerous players who approached Orr's calibre. We would learn in 1972 in that first classic confrontation between NHL stars and the Soviet Nationals.

Within a few years, the NHL began luring European stars to play in the best leagues in the world. An ever-lengthening line of fascinating international matches, tournaments and series continues to demonstrate the value of a cross-pollenization unlike any other in professional sport.

Of course, not everything about expansion was an immediate success. One franchise (San Francisco-Oakland-California-Cleveland) was never to be successful. But the majority persevered and the demand for expansion continued. The future looked bright with Buffalo and Vancouver joining in 1970 and Long Island and Atlanta in 1972.

Then suddenly there was the WHA, a whole new league that exploded onto the scene for the 1972–73 season with 12 new teams of its own. It would reach 14 teams two seasons later with a freewheeling brand of hockey that not only attracted fans in both new and established hockey markets, but also lured NHL stars and near-stars with mega-buck contracts.

The drain on bankrolls and the talent pool became too much. With 30 major-league hockey teams by 1976 (the NHL had added Kansas City and Washington in 1974, thus tripling its original size in seven years) the product became diluted. Finances were uncertain and the whole structure began to totter. Ownerships changed with increasing frequency. National TV networks in the United States lost interest in what their ratings told them was a regional sport.

In 1976, NHL franchises relocated for the first time since 1934. In 1978, the number of franchises decreased from the season before for the first time since 1942. The roller coaster that had climbed to its peak a few seasons earlier now rocketed downward.

Through it all, there was some pretty damn good hockey and some important indications that expansion had, for the most part, succeeded. Philadelphia became the first expansion team to win the Stanley Cup in 1974. A year later they won again, beating Buffalo in the first all-expansion final. Los Angeles emerged as a mid-decade power, with standouts like Rogie Vachon and Marcel Dionne bringing notoriety to the ice sport in sunny

California. Pittsburgh benefited from good drafting and trades, coming up with the likes of Pierre Larouche, Syl Apps, Jr., Jean Pronovost and others to flourish in the mid-70s as well. Atlanta began a string of playoff appearances in 1975–76 that remains uninterrupted in Calgary. The Islanders began to establish a never-say-die franchise character on their way to building a dynasty.

So many images from the period gave hope that hockey's problems could be overcome: Guy Lafleur with his blond mane, tireless Bobby Clarke, Phil Esposito parked in front, the Sabres' swirling French Connection, Don Cherry waving his arms, Ken Dryden leaning on his stick, Bill Smith wielding his to clear the crease, Ed Giacomin wiping away tears as Ranger fans salute him following a trade to Detroit.

With so much going for it, hockey needed only (only!) to become a solvent business again. A change in the presidency of the NHL — from Clarence Campbell to John A. Ziegler, Jr. — signaled a more business-like approach to the league's problems. The direction from the NHL's Board of Governors was clear — make peace with the WHA and build upon the league's strengths.

It did not happen overnight, but happen it did. The NHL Players' Association (whose working relationship with the league is unique in sports) acknowledged its stake in the game's future and made some concessions that helped the league through tough times in the 1970s. The California-Cleveland franchise merged with the Minnesota North Stars. Kansas City-Colorado migrated east, settling in New Jersey's Meadowlands Arena. The Flames flew from Atlanta to Calgary and the Blues had to be tossed the life preserver a few times. It seemed that every year another major problem had to be tackled.

Finally, in 1979–80, four WHA teams were absorbed into the NHL. It is a tribute to the WHA that, seven years later, those four teams (Edmonton, Winnipeg, Hartford and Quebec) are all serious contenders for the Stanley Cup.

In place of a big American network television contract, the NHL has made good use of changing TV technology, using new sports cable systems to cover games both nationally and in regions where hockey is strongest in the United States. In Canada, two networks now deliver games throughout the country.

The result? A popular sport and, once again, a successful business. And new images for the next 20 years: Mario Lemieux turning a checker inside-out, Mats Naslund darting through enemy defenders, Kirk Muller working his heart out, Al MacInnis unleashing his slapshot, Denis Savard dancing toward the goal with the puck on his blade, John Vanbiesbrouck clamping down on a rebound, Wendel Clark storming up and down his wing, Michel Goulet picking the corner, Ray Bourque's smooth skating, Dale Hawerchuk steaming toward open ice, Ron Hextall's stick rat-tat-tatting the goalposts, Kevin Dineen's *kamikaze* rushes. Tony Tanti, Doug Gilmour, Dino Ciccarelli, Pat LaFontaine, Jimmy Carson, Luc Robitaille, Steve Yzerman and, of course, Wayne Gretzky — new stars for a new era.

It's getting late. I'd better get some rest. Don't let me sleep too long.

—Stu Hackel

*Stu Hackel is editor of GOAL Magazine.*

# YEAR BY YEAR

For coaches and managers of new NHL teams, expansion equaled frustration for their first few seasons in the NHL. Here Red Sullivan, coach of the first-year Washington Capitals, feels the pressure of coaching a club that won only eight of 80 games in 1974–75.

# In the Beginning
## by Lew Stubbs

In an undeniable concession to aging, I find myself prefacing a lot of my sentences with, "When I was a kid. . . ." Well, when I was a kid, only six hockey teams played in the NHL, a scant 120 jobs were available in hockey's elite circuit and the pay was so low that minor-league professionals were an endangered species. The junior and juvenile hockey programs financed by the six NHL teams were graduating players ready for professional hockey, but prospects of top-rung jobs in the field looked sufficiently bleak to discourage many talented athletes from continuing with the game. Low incentive for promising young players was one of several factors in favor of expanding the NHL.

A further spur to expansion was the prospect of a lucrative television contract with one of the big three American networks. National television coverage in Canada every Saturday night had generated significant revenue for the Toronto Maple Leafs and the Montreal Canadiens since the early 1950s. In fact, the 1959 Stanley Cup final, which featured the Leafs and the Canadiens and was televised by the Canadian Broadcasting Corporation, broke all Canadian ratings records. Hockey's popularity with the Canadian viewing public was so great that a second network, CTV, started showing games on Wednesday nights. The four US-based teams benefited from games televised by local affiliates in their individual markets, but could not attract national sponsorship or coverage because the sport was perceived as being of interest only in the northeastern and midwestern states.

Hockey was a strong box office attraction through the mid-1960s, as 93 per cent of all tickets to NHL games were sold. The Boston Bruins, who finished out of the playoffs for eight consecutive years beginning in 1959–60, consistently sold more tickets in the same arena than the perennial National Basketball Association champion Boston Celtics.

The NHL felt that there was a surplus of good hockey players and that hockey was popular with the public, but recognized that in order to be perceived as a national major league in the United States, hockey needed a presence in big cities outside of the northeast and midwest. It all added up to expansion.

The two owners most responsible for bringing about expansion were Bill Jennings of the New York Rangers and David Molson of the Montreal Canadiens. Their efforts paid off when, on June 25, 1965, NHL president Clarence Campbell announced that the league was expanding to cities "of major-league status in the United States and Canada." Backers of each new franchise had to pay the NHL an entry fee of two million dollars and have access to a well-maintained arena with a seating capacity of at least 12,500. Recognizing that the "Original Six" teams would be better than the new clubs in the first few years after expansion, the NHL adopted a plan to admit six new franchises, which would form a new division. With the exception of a limited number of regular-season games against the teams from the other division, the new teams would compete against each other for four playoff berths. The ensuing playoff rounds would determine the champion of the new division. The division-winning club would then play the winner of the other division in the Stanley Cup finals. This approach was designed to foster intra-divisional rivalries. It was decided that the new teams would begin play in the 1967–68 season as the West Division. The "Original Six" would play in the East Division. Clubs would play each of their divisional rivals ten times and each of the teams in the other divison four times, for a 74-game schedule.

On February 8, 1966, after much deliberation, Clarence Campbell announced that franchises had been granted to groups from Los Angeles, Minnesota, Philadelphia, Pittsburgh, St. Louis and the San Francisco-Oakland Bay area. Unsuccessful applicants included Baltimore, Buffalo, Vancouver and Washington, DC.

The NHL was particularly optimistic about its prospects in the San Francisco Oakland Bay area. This relatively small territory was felt to be a sports hotbed, supporting baseball's San Francisco Giants and, beginning in 1968, the Oakland A's as well as football's Oakland Raiders and San Francisco 49ers. Barry van Gerbig, the man responsible for the franchise bid, was well versed in the game of hockey. He had played goal for the Princeton University Tigers and was the back-up netminder to Jack McCartan on the upset Gold Medal US Olympic team of 1960. Van Gerbig and his partners aligned themselves with the Shasta Corporation, which controlled the on-ice variety show known as the Ice Follies. They also bought a controlling interest in the San Franciso Seals of the Western Hockey League. Once Van Gerbig's group secured its NHL franchise, they bought out the Shasta Corporation and paid $450,000 compensation to the Western Hockey League for the liquidation of its San Francisco team and the rights to the Bay area. The new owners decided that the old San Francisco Cow Palace was an inappropriate home for an NHL team, and moved across the bay to the new Oakland Alameda County Coliseum Arena. This impressive glass-walled structure had a seating capacity of 12,500.

This move to Oakland upset other franchise owners, who felt that the city of Oakland didn't have a sufficiently big-league image to sell tickets on the road. As a compromise, the team started the season as the California Seals. Even the team logo — a stylized seal holding a hockey stick encircled not by an ''O'' for Oakland, but by a ''C'' for California — ignored the club's Oakland home.

There was a further problem: who would coach the team. In their final Western Hockey League season, the San Francisco Seals hired former Chicago Blackhawks coach Rudy Pilous as coach and general manager. Pilous took the position with the understanding that he would retain these responsibilities if the organization were able to move up to the NHL. Because of what he felt was a firm deal, Pilous turned down an offer to coach the Boston Bruins, who instead hired Harry Sinden. A month prior to the expansion draft, Van Gerbig fired Pilous. Instead, Bert Olmstead was chosen to be behind the bench when the Seals, resplendent in their green, blue and white jerseys, took to the ice.

Minnesota, home of the new North Stars, was one of the great hockey areas in the United States. Its cold winters and proximity to the Canadian border made the grass-roots growth of the game natural for the state. The NHL's lone American-born player at the time, Tommy Williams, was from Duluth, Minnesota, and the state had also produced some of the country's top college hockey teams. The Minneapolis-St. Paul area was enjoying rapid growth and a new big-league status was reflected in the arrival of baseball's Minnesota Twins and football's Minnesota Vikings earlier in the 1960s.

California became home to two NHL teams in the 1967 expansion from six to twelve teams. The Seals were based in Oakland and the Kings in Los Angeles. L.A.'s Sheldon Kannegiesser heads up-ice in this 1975 photo of a match played in the Kings' home rink, the ''Fabulous Forum'' in Inglewood.

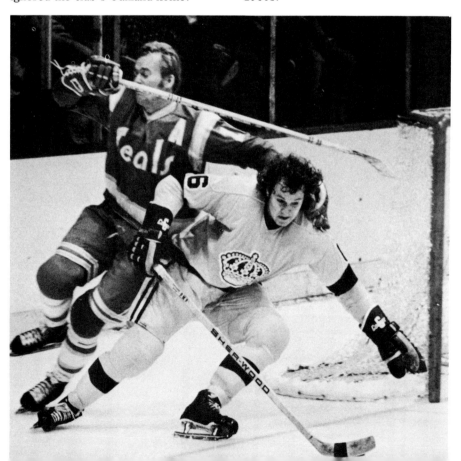

Attorney Walter Bush, Jr., construction executive Gordon Ritz and communications magnate Bob McNulty pooled their initiative and resources to gain the franchise. The major stumbling block they faced was the lack of a suitable arena. With an eye to not alienating fans residing in either city, a new arena with a seating capacity of 15,000 was built in suburban Bloomington, equidistant between Minneapolis and St. Paul and adjacent to Metropolitan Stadium, home of the Twins and Vikings. The natural rivalry between the two cities was encouraged in a competition to see which community could sell the most season tickets. By opening day, they had sold 5,800. The North Stars wore green, yellow and white uniforms.

Walter Bush, Jr. had a hockey background, as a college player and as the coach and co-owner, along with Ritz and McNulty, of the Minnesota Bruins of the Central Hockey League. The three owners hired Wren Blair to be their coach and general manager. The 42-year-old Blair had been the Bruins' director of player personnel since 1960. His crowning achievement had been discovering Bobby Orr—a gangly 14-year-old prospect in Parry Sound, Ontario, who would

go on to singlehandedly change the way defense in the NHL was played and lead the Bruins from last place to the Stanley Cup.

The Pittsburgh franchise entered the NHL on a winning note: the Pittsburgh Hornets of the American Hockey League captured that league's Calder Cup championship in the spring of 1967. The team played its games in the Pittsburgh Civic Arena, a state of the art facility featuring a partially retractable roof and a seating capacity of 12,508. The white, dome-shaped roof of the arena resulted in it being nicknamed "the Igloo," which undoubtedly contributed to the controversial decision to name the team the Penguins. In an effort to build fan enthusiasm, the team obtained a real penguin named Pete who would totter around the ice on tiny skates. Poor Pete, missing the Antarctic, caught pneumonia and died in mid-season.

The Pittsburgh franchise was owned by a consortium of local residents headed by Peter H. Black and Pennsylvania State Senator Jack McGregor. Jack Riley was convinced to leave his post as president of the American Hockey League to become the Penguins' first general manager. George "Red" Sullivan resigned as the Rangers' chief scout to take the Pittsburgh coaching job. Sullivan had NHL coaching experience, having coached the Rangers from 1962 to 1965. The team's colors were light blue, dark blue and white.

Philadelphia's entry into the NHL resulted from efforts headed up by William R. Putnam. Putnam had helped Jerry Wolman finance the Philadelphia Eagles' NFL franchise. So Putnam, Wolman and Eagles' vice-president Ed Snider secretly joined forces to pitch for a spot in the NHL. Secrecy was crucial because the city of Philadelphia lacked a proper arena to house an NHL club. A lot of research was required to locate an appropriate piece of real estate for an arena. Eventually several acres of property at the intersection of Broad Street and Pattison Avenue were chosen, positioning the arena next to the John F. Kennedy Memorial Stadium, home of the annual Army-Navy college football game. Groundbreaking ceremonies for the Philadelphia Spectrum took place on June 1, 1966.

Norman "Bud" Poile, a veteran manager from the Western Hockey League, was hired to run the new Philadelphia franchise. Poile hired another WHLer, Keith Allen, as coach. Allen had been coach and general manager of the Seattle Totems in the WHL. A name-the-team contest established the squad as the Flyers and orange, black and white were chosen as the team's colors. A stylized winged "P" was used as the team logo.

Los Angeles was the city in which the competition for ownership of a new NHL franchise was most hotly contested. Jack Kent Cooke, a prominent Canadian entrepreneur and owner of basketball's Los Angeles Lakers, won the franchise over Dan Reaves, owner of the Los Angeles Rams football club. In addition to his involvements in sports, Cooke was a communications magnate with interests in radio, television and newspapers. For his initial foray into hockey, Cooke assembled a high-profile board of directors, including fellow Canadians Lorne Greene and press baron Lord Thompson of Fleet as well as prominent American trial lawyer Edward Bennett Williams. Cooke opted to build his own arena, which was located in Inglewood and became known

as the "fabulous Forum." Its seating capacity was 16,000. To manage his new team, the Kings, Cooke hired former NHL player Larry Regan. Regan won the Calder Trophy as NHL rookie of the year in 1956–57 and finished his playing career as playing coach of the AHL's Baltimore Clippers. The Kings livened up the NHL's expansion meetings by naming 20-year NHL star Leonard "Red" Kelly as their coach. Kelly had demonstrated his still-considerable talents on the ice as part of the Toronto Maple Leafs' Stanley Cup-winning team the previous spring. The Leafs had planned to protect Kelly in the expansion draft, but hadn't counted on him joining an expansion franchise as a coach rather than a player. The Kings planned to wear the royal colors of purple and gold with a crown as their logo.

The St. Louis franchise was granted to Sid Solomon, Jr. and his son Sid Solomon III. The Solomons had their work cut out for them in St. Louis. For four million dollars, they purchased the only suitable existing facility — the dilapidated St. Louis Arena — from Chicago Blackhawks owners James Norris and Arthur Wirtz. The Solomons went to a member of one of hockey's royal families when they hired Lynn Patrick as their general manager. Lynn was the eldest son of Lester Patrick, a hockey legend who was a vital part of the NHL's much earlier expansion to the United States in 1926. Lynn had coaching experience in both New York and Boston. Most recently, he had been coach and general manager of the Los Angeles Blades of the Western Hockey League. Patrick selected 33-year-old William "Scotty" Bowman as his assistant. Bowman had been director of personnel in the Montreal Canadiens' extensive minor-league system.

Despite an infringement of copyright, the Solomons called their club the St. Louis Blues, hoping that any resulting litigation from the owners of the musical score of the same name would translate into good publicity and increased fan interest. Two million dollars were spent on refurbishing the St. Louis Arena and the team uniforms were designed around a dark blue and yellow color scheme with a musical note as the logo.

NHL president Clarence Campbell oversaw the expansion of the league from six to twelve teams in 1967–68.

# The Expansion Draft

Elmer "Moose" Vasko was an Expansion Draft selection of the Minnesota North Stars. Vasko had retired after ten successful seasons on defense with Chicago. Like other veteran players, he came out of his brief retirement to help one of the NHL's new clubs in its big-league debut.

An NHL expansion draft was held on June 6, 1967, at the Queen Elizabeth Hotel in Montreal. The six expansion clubs were given the opportunity to select players from the development systems of the original six. This draft guaranteed each new team 18 skaters and two goaltenders. The original six clubs were entitled to protect one goalie and eleven skaters. All junior-age players signed the previous year were exempt from the draft. Because of this exemption, Boston did not have to protect 19-year-old Bobby Orr.

The first stage of the draft involved goaltenders. Here the expansion teams had a chance to select some quality players, as each established club could only protect one netminder. Upon having a goaltender chosen by an expansion franchise, an established team could protect an additional goalie.

The draft of defensemen and forwards consisted of 18 rounds. Everytime an established team lost a player to an expansion club, it was permitted to protect one additional player. This one-for-one format made up the first two rounds. For rounds three, four, and five, the established teams weren't permitted to add players to their protected lists. The final thirteen rounds reverted to the one-for-one format. Though a number of established NHL stars moved to expansion franchises, the format of the inaugural draft created six new club rosters that were of a lower standard than the original six. To accelerate the development of the new clubs, league president Clarence Campbell announced that in 1968 and 1969 each of the 12 teams would be allowed to protect only two goalies and 14 skaters. This would be of little consequence to the new teams, but because there was far more depth on most of the established teams' rosters, being allowed to protect only fourteen skaters in the intra-league draft was bound to leave some fine players available to the new teams.

Jack Kent Cooke dropped a bombshell the night before the draft: at a press conference, he announced that he had purchased the Springfield Indians of the American Hockey League from former Boston Bruin star Eddie Shore. This gave Cooke's Los Angeles Kings an edge on the competition in the Western Division, because the Kings would be the only new franchise with its own farm system. The move sent shock waves through the other expansion organizations. Philadelphia wasted little time in striking a deal to buy the AHL's Quebec Aces.

Several back-room deals were struck, as the established teams offered packages of players in return for agreements from new teams to not select certain unprotected players. Because the established clubs owned well-stocked minor-

Terry Sawchuk, instrumental in the Toronto Maple Leafs' Stanley Cup victory in 1966–67, joined the new Los Angeles Kings for 1967–68. In L.A., he played in 36 games, recording a 3.07 goals-against average.

league systems, it was beneficial for the "upstarts" to honor these verbal deals. One such arrangement saw the Minnesota North Stars use the first pick in the draft to take utility forward Dave Balon instead of Claude Larose from Montreal. Larose was generally regarded as the best forward available in the draft. Shortly thereafter Montreal packaged up Andre Boudias, Mike McMahon and Bob Charlebois and sent them to the North Stars for cash and future considerations. The rest of the first-round choices saw Bob Baun leave the Stanley Cup champion Leafs to play for his old teammate Bert Olmstead in Oakland; Earl Ingarfield left Madison Square Garden and the Rangers to become a Penguin and play in the Igloo; the Kings took Gord Labossiere from the Montreal organization, while St. Louis took one of the Habs' best penalty killers, Jimmy Roberts. Philadelphia took defenseman Ed Van Impe from

Chicago.

Five of the six new clubs drafted goaltenders with previous NHL experience. Terry Sawchuk was chosen by the Kings from Toronto. Bernie Parent left Boston for Philadelphia. St. Louis took a chance and claimed retired Vezina Trophy winner Glenn Hall from Chicago. Minnesota selected Cesare Maniago from New York and Charlie Hodge left Montreal to play for the California Seals. Pittsburgh chose Joe Daley, a Detroit farmhand who had played 15 games for the AHL Pittsburgh Hornets in 1966–67.

Of the established clubs, the Toronto Maple Leafs were the hardest hit by the expansion draft. In addition to losing two top defensemen—Kent Douglas and Bob Baun were both drafted by California—the Leafs lost the services of veteran Red Kelly, who retired as a player to coach his Toronto teammate Terry Sawchuk in Los Angeles.

# 1967–1968

The most ambitious expansion in sports history was set to begin with the 1967–68 NHL season. The league achieved one of its objectives when CBS agreed to televise a national game of the week. The deal called for $3.6 million over three years, with 14 weekend afternoon games to be televised during the 1967–68 season. The first game featured the Los Angeles Kings and the Philadelphia Flyers on December 30, 1967 and marked the long-awaited opening of Jack Kent Cooke's Los Angeles Forum. CBS also planned coverage of Stanley Cup playoff games.

The first meeting between an established team and one of the new clubs saw the Montreal Canadiens play the Pittsburgh Penguins on October 11, 1967. A crowd of over 9,000 saw two of the game's great veterans notch important goals.

Jean Beliveau, the Canadiens' popular centerman, netted the 400th goal of his career early in the second period to give the Habs a 2–0 lead. Another great veteran, Andy Bathgate, scored the Penguins first-ever NHL goal. The game was a good one, with Montreal winning by a 2–1 score.

There were two blockbuster trades. Prior to the season, the Boston Bruins obtained Phil Esposito, Ken Hodge and Johnny McKenzie from the Chicago Blackhawks for Gilles Marotte, Pit Martin and Jack Norris. This trade enabled Boston to secure a playoff spot for the first time in the 1960s. Detroit and Toronto, two teams destined to finish out of the playoffs, also swung a multi-player major trade late in the season. Scoring ace Frank Mahovlich took his considerable talents to the Red Wings along with Garry Unger, Pete Stemkowski and the rights to Carl Brewer in exchange for Norm Ullman, Paul Henderson and Floyd Smith of Detroit.

From early on in the season, it was apparent that the California Seals were not attracting fans. Partway through the season, the club name was changed from "California" to "Oakland" in an attempt to increase local enthusiasm for the team, but the fans still stayed away. Bert Olmstead became the first coach to step down that season as the Seals limped through their inaugural year in last place. The club needed loans totalling $850,000 to make it through the season.

Tragedy struck in January 1968 when

The new on the old and the old on the new: Montreal rookie Serge Savard and veteran St. Louis players goaltender Glenn Hall and right winger Dickie Moore in the first post-expansion Stanley Cup final.

Gump Worsley posted 11 victories and a 1.88 goals-against average en route to the Stanley Cup. Montreal won the 1968 finals in four straight games, but each was a one-goal victory. Larry Keenan wears number 18 for the Blues.

Minnesota's Wayne Connelly led all expansion team players with 35 goals. His 14 power-play goals led the NHL in 1967–68.

Bill Masterton became the first NHL player to die as a result of injuries sustained during a game. Unable to win a regular NHL job in the days of the six-team league, Masterton had been out of hockey for four seasons. While playing center for Minnesota in a game against Oakland, Masterton dumped a pass to right winger Wayne Connelly, when he was hit by Oakland defenseman Ron Harris and crashed into Larry Cahan of the Seals. Masterton fell backward, striking his head on the ice. He died later, suffering from a brain injury. Masterton's death brought about an outcry for protective headgear and many players adopted helmets for a brief time. Though most eventually discarded them, Chicago's Stan Mikita stated he would never play another game without a helmet.

The Philadelphia Flyers had to wonder if Mother Nature was lining up with the opposing teams when a fierce windstorm ripped open a part of the Spectrum's roof on March 1, 1968. The facility was declared unsafe and the Flyers had to play their remaining home games on the road. The club was forced to give refunds to its disappointed fans. The Flyers played one of their home games in Madison Square Garden and another in Maple Leaf Gardens before moving to Quebec City, which was the home base of Philadelphia's AHL farm team. They managed a 3–2–2 record under these trying conditions and overtook the Los Angeles Kings to finish first in their division.

The Montreal Canadiens worked magic in the second half of the season, moving from worst to first with a 14-game unbeaten string in the five weeks following Christmas. Not surprisingly, the East Division had 86 wins, 40 losses and 18 ties against the new expansion teams. Red Kelly's LA Kings fared best against the established teams, with a record of 10 wins, 12 losses and 2 ties. Kelly's former teammates in Toronto fell from playoff contention largely because of a 10–11–3 record against the West. The New York Rangers were able to grab second place with a fine 17–4–3 result against the new teams.

The New Year saw Bobby Hull pot goal number 400 on January 7. The Blues' Glenn Hall, in the midst of an astonishing season, recorded his 70th career shutout on January 3. Veterans Ron Stewart of the Rangers and George Armstrong of the Leafs played in their one-thousandth NHL games.

An injury deprived Bobby Hull of a 50-goal season and, although he had 31 goals in his first 39 games, he had to settle for a league-leading 44 markers. His teammate, Stan Mikita, duplicated his achievement of the previous year by win-

Garry Unger, one of hockey's all-time "iron men," was a promising rookie traded from Toronto to Detroit as part of a major six-player deal in 1968. He went on to play in 914 consecutive games from 1968 to 1979; a league record that stood until Hartford's Doug Jarvis surpassed it in 1986.

ning the Art Ross Trophy as the league's top scorer, the Hart Trophy as the most valuable player and the Lady Byng Trophy for gentlemanly conduct. In his acceptance speech, Mikita referred to his family's immigration from Czechoslovakia by commenting, "not bad for a little DP." Boston's third-place finish was due in large part to the emergence of two players. Bobby Orr established himself as the game's premier defenseman and Phil Esposito stepped out of the shadows of Hull and Mikita to finish as the second-leading scorer in the NHL.

With Boston matched against Montreal in the East Division semi-final, many felt that the rugged Bruins, playing in the confines of the small Boston Garden, would upset the Canadiens. In the first game of the series, Boston jumped to an early lead and seemed to have momen-

tum in its favor, but Montreal's John Ferguson took on Boston tough guy Teddy Green in an encounter that seemed to deflate the Bruins. They lost the crucial first game 2–1 and were swept in four games. The Chicago Blackhawks spotted the Rangers the first two games in their series before rebounding to win four straight. In the East Division final, Montreal had too much firepower, eliminating Chicago in five games. Rookie Jacques Lemaire fired the series-clinching goal in overtime.

The West Division playoffs were much more competitive, as both semi-finals went the maximum seven games. St. Louis, backstopped by Glenn Hall, eliminated Philadelphia, while Minnesota defeated Los Angeles. The West final went the full seven games as well, with no less than four of the encounters requiring

# TWENTY TRENDS THAT SHAPED MODERN HOCKEY

## 1. The Slapshot and the Curved Stick

The slapshot—that obliterative drive that delights play-by-play broadcasters and terrorizes goaltenders—goes back to the 1930s when Frank Boucher, a seven-time winner of the Lady Byng Trophy, made effective use of it as a center with the New York Rangers. Bernie "Boom-Boom" Geoffrion of the Montreal Canadiens popularized the shot by being its first proponent in the era of televised hockey. Geoffrion scored a record-tying 50 goals in 1960–61 and, in so doing, became a hockey hero whom young players tried to emulate. When Bobby Hull, who also favored the slapshot and was the most glamorous of the NHL's superstars of the 1960s, scored 50 the following season, players throughout the NHL and all other levels of hockey jumped on the slapshot bandwagon.

The merits of the slapshot coming from the sticks of Geoffrion, Hull or other gifted hockey players could not be denied. But once the slapshot became fashionable down to youth hockey levels, players often worked on their slapshots to the point of neglecting their skating skills. By the 1970s, when NHL expansion and the creation of the WHA had diluted the hockey talent pool, a number of lumbering skaters found a place on big-league rosters largely on the strength of their heavy shots. In today's hockey, a hard slapshot is almost a requirement for significant advancement in the sport, but

it must be combined with skating, puckhandling or defensive skills to earn regular employment in the NHL.

At the time the slapshot first became popular, Andy Bathgate of the New York Rangers was experimenting with the effect of curving the blade of his hockey stick. From hockey's earliest days, players had imparted a modest curvature to their sticks by jamming the blade beneath a door and elevating the handle, but the effect of this small curve was largely confined to making the puck easier to cradle while skating.

Stan Mikita and Bobby Hull, the two top scorers on the Chicago Blackhawks in the 1960s, are credited with popularizing the curved blade, The two players began to curve their sticks first by using the under-the-door method and then by ordering custom-built sticks from the Northland Ski Manufacturing Company of St. Paul, Minnesota, which supplied hockey sticks to most players on the four US-based NHL teams.

Hull opted for a very exaggerated, continuous curve to his blade while Mikita preferred a single, drastic bend

about one-third of the way along the blade from the heel of his stick. Hull found that the curved blade allowed him to pull in the puck and shoot all in one motion. Depending on his follow-through, he could make a curved-bladed shot rise or drop on the way to the net. The innovation sparked controversy in the 1960s as some felt that the curved blade inhibited a player's ability to receive a pass and shoot on the backhand. Ranger goalie Ed Giacomin concurred, saying that Hull didn't have much of a backhand, but that since he had shattered Rocket Richard's 50-goal record for goals in a single season with 54 in 1964–65, he didn't really seem to need one anyway. Mikita still retained an effective backhand shot with his curved stick and, by winning three Art Ross Trophies as the NHL's scoring champion, had demonstrated his ability to give and receive passes.

By the expansion of 1967–68, the curved blade and the slapshot were in wide use throughout the NHL as pucks flew faster, harder and less accurately than they ever had before. Both innovations were effective in the hands of skilled players, but spread throughout professional and amateur hockey to the detriment of basic skill development. Stick curvature had become so extreme by the early 1970s, that the NHL imposed a half-inch limit on the allowable amount of curvature in a stick blade. This combination of the slapshot and the curved stick compelled every goalie in hockey to wear a mask.

The first year of the NHL's new West Division saw virtual parity between the new clubs. Six points separated first from fifth place. Philadelphia finished on top with 73 points. Minnesota finished fourth with 69. All three playoff series in the West went seven games.

overtime. St. Louis finally advanced to the Stanley Cup when Ron Shock lit the lamp at 2:50 of the second overtime period.

Little was expected of the first post-expansion Stanley Cup final series. St. Louis' top player, Red Berenson, had been the property of the Montreal organization and had not been able to win a regular job with the club. Four Blues, Glenn Hall, Al Arbour and late-season acquisitions Dickie Moore and Doug Harvey had been talked into coming out of retirement to play with the club. But the Blues gave the Canadiens excellent competition in the series opener, losing 3–2 in overtime. Once again, rookie Jacques Lemaire netted the winner.

Game two was scoreless into the third period when Montreal rookie defenseman Serge Savard scored the game's only goal to put Montreal ahead by two games. Game three was another overtime encounter, with Bobby Rousseau emerging as the hero for Montreal. Game four saw the Habs score two third-period goals to win the cup in four anything-but-easy games. Glenn Hall played so well that he was awarded the Conn Smythe Trophy as playoff MVP despite being on the losing team. Montreal Canadiens' coach Toe Blake chose to leave hockey on a winning note, retiring after 13 seasons behind the bench and eight Stanley Cup championships.

# YEAR                             1967–68

**Stanley Cup Champion**          Montreal Canadiens
**Prince of Wales Trophy Winner**  Montreal Canadiens
**Clarence Campbell Bowl Winner**  Philadelphia Flyers

## Final Standings

### East Division

| Team | GP | W | L | T | GF | GA | PTS |
|------|----|----|----|----|----|----|----|
| Montreal | 74 | 42 | 22 | 10 | 236 | 167 | 94 |
| New York | 74 | 39 | 23 | 12 | 226 | 183 | 90 |
| Boston | 74 | 37 | 27 | 10 | 259 | 216 | 84 |
| Chicago | 74 | 32 | 26 | 16 | 212 | 222 | 80 |
| Toronto | 74 | 33 | 31 | 10 | 209 | 176 | 76 |
| Detroit | 74 | 27 | 35 | 12 | 245 | 257 | 66 |

### West Division

| Team | GP | W | L | T | GF | GA | PTS |
|------|----|----|----|----|----|----|----|
| Philadelphia | 74 | 31 | 32 | 11 | 173 | 179 | 73 |
| Los Angeles | 74 | 31 | 33 | 10 | 200 | 224 | 72 |
| St. Louis | 74 | 27 | 31 | 16 | 177 | 191 | 70 |
| Minnesota | 74 | 27 | 32 | 15 | 191 | 226 | 69 |
| Pittsburgh | 74 | 27 | 34 | 13 | 195 | 216 | 67 |
| Oakland | 74 | 15 | 42 | 17 | 153 | 219 | 47 |

## Leading Scorers

| Player | Club | GP | G | A | PTS | PIM |
|--------|------|----|----|----|----|----|
| Mikita, Stan | Chicago | 72 | 40 | 47 | 87 | 14 |
| Esposito, Phil | Boston | 74 | 35 | 49 | 84 | 21 |
| Howe, Gordie | Detroit | 74 | 39 | 43 | 82 | 53 |
| Ratelle, Jean | New York | 74 | 32 | 46 | 78 | 18 |
| Gilbert, Rod | New York | 73 | 29 | 48 | 77 | 12 |
| Hull, Bobby | Chicago | 71 | 44 | 31 | 75 | 39 |
| Ullman, Norm | Det., Tor. | 71 | 35 | 37 | 72 | 28 |
| Delvecchio, Alex | Detroit | 74 | 22 | 48 | 70 | 14 |
| Bucyk, John | Boston | 72 | 30 | 39 | 69 | 8 |
| Wharram, Ken | Chicago | 74 | 27 | 42 | 69 | 18 |

## NHL Award Winners

**Hart (MVP)**                       Stan Mikita
**Art Ross (Leading Scorer)**        Stan Mikita
**Calder (Rookie of the Year)**      Derek Sanderson
**Vezina (Lowest Goals-Against)**    Gump Worsley, Rogatien Vachon
**Lady Byng (Gentlemanly Conduct)**  Stan Mikita
**Norris (Top Defenseman)**          Bobby Orr
**Conn Smythe (Playoff MVP)**        Glenn Hall
**Patrick (Service to US Hockey)**   Thomas F. Lockhart, Walter A. Brown,
                                       Gen. John R. Kilpatrick
**Masterton (Perseverance)**         Claude Provost

**World/Olympic Champions**          Soviet Union

**AHL Calder Cup Champions**         Rochester Americans
**Memorial Cup Canadian Jr. Champions**  Niagara Falls Flyers

**NCAA Champions**                   Denver University

**Canadian College Champions**       University of Alberta

# 1968–1969

Record-shattering performances highlighted the 1968–69 season. The West Division teams, anxious to attract fans, demanded more games with the star-laden East Division clubs. Two games were added to the regular season, making the schedule 76 games long. Each club would play the teams in its own division eight times and those in the other division on six occasions. While realizing that they could not perform on even terms with the established teams, the expansion clubs wanted the gate receipts guaranteed by a visit from the Howes, Hulls, Beliveaus and Orrs of the original six.

Five new coaches paced behind NHL benches. In Montreal, Claude Ruel, 29, became the NHL's youngest head coach. Two former star players, Bill Gadsby with Detroit and Bernie Geoffrion with New York, got a look at life from the other side of the bench. Oakland had a new ownership group led by Potter Palmer. The same group also owned the Harlem Globetrotters. They added a new vice-president, Bill Torrey, made Frank Selke, Jr. general manager and hired Freddie Glover as coach. When the season started the Seals' roster included only three skaters and two goaltenders from their 1967–68 roster. This revamping paid dividends: the Seals finished in second place, despite a continued poor showing at the gate.

As season opened, goaltending great Jacques Plante came out of retirement to work in tandem with Glenn Hall in the St. Louis nets. Dissatisfied with the contract offered him by Blackhawks' management, Bobby Hull announced his retirement. He returned when the Hawks offered him a three-year deal worth $100,000 per season. Hull became hockey's first six-figure salaried player and was quick to justify it by smashing his own record for goals in a season with 58 tallies. Two NHL veterans left California and headed for Detroit: Terry Sawchuk quit the Los Angeles Kings and Bob Baun the Oakland Seals to play for the Red Wings.

Gordie Howe, showing no signs of slowing down in his 23rd season, scored his 700th regular-season goal in a game against the Penguins on December 4, 1968. Doug Harvey, who came out of retirement at the age of 43 to join the St. Louis Blues, recorded his 450th assist on February 26, 1968, an NHL record for

Opposite page, top: Chicago defenseman Pat Stapleton led NHL rearguards with 50 assists including six in one game. He and Montreal's Bobby Rousseau fight for the puck in front of netminder Dennis DeJordy. Right: Montreal goaltender Rogie Vachon allowed just 12 goals in eight playoff games as Montreal won its second straight Stanley Cup.

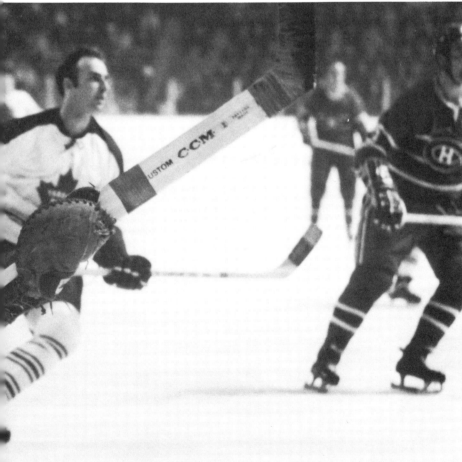

a defenseman. The Blues' Red Berenson scored six goals in a single game in an 8–0 triumph over Philadelphia, which equaled a record set 24 years earlier by Syd Howe. The Blues' owners, the Solomon family, were in the habit of giving a $750 watch to any Blue who scored three goals in a game. For his six, Berenson received not only a watch but a station wagon with a canoe on top and a shotgun inside. Berenson's 35–goal season equaled the mark for a player in the West Division set by Minnesota's Wayne Connelly the previous season. Chicago defenseman Pat Stapleton's six assists in a 9–5 victory over Detroit equaled the record set by Toronto's Babe Pratt in 1944.

The real assault on the record book came in the form of single-season achievements. Pat Stapleton's 50 assists established a record for defensemen, as did Bobby Orr's 64 points and 21 goals. Two West Division rookies, Minnesota's Danny Grant and the Seals' Norm Ferguson, tied Nels Stewart's rookie scoring mark of 1925–26, when both scored 34 goals. Grant's 65 points established a new record for freshman skaters. The Rangers' pair of hot rookies, Brad Park and Walt Tkaczuk, equaled the rookie record for assists in a game with four each.

The Boston Bruins went on a scoring binge led by Phil Esposito's record-breaking 126-point season. His 49 goals established a record for centers as did his 77 assists. The line of Esposito, Hodge and Murphy collected 263 points, surpassing the previous record for points by a forward line by 37. Boston scored more goals, 303, and added more assists, 497, than any team before it. The team also established a record for penalty minutes in a season with 1,297.

The game's two biggest names also surpassed the 100-point plateau, as Bobby Hull finished second in the scoring race with 107 points, followed by Gordie Howe with 103. Howe set a record for assists by a right winger with 59 and, along with linemates Frank Mahovlich and Alex Delvecchio, established a record for goals with 118.

East Division leader Montreal disposed of the New York Rangers in four straight games in the semi-finals. The second-place Bruins were so convincing in their

## 2. The Two-Goaltender System

Goaltenders were hockey's ironmen in the years preceding expansion. The top goaltender on an NHL team usually played every minute of every game unless injured. Prior to 1965–66, back-up goaltenders weren't even dressed for each game. If the starting goalie were injured, either a skater would don the goaltender's pads and play in net or an emergency goaltender watching the game from the stands would dress and take to the ice. Glenn Hall played goal in 502 consecutive games for Detroit and Chicago from 1955 to 1962. If, with only 120 roster spots, it was difficult for skaters to make an NHL team, consider the task facing a young goaltender, with only six possible job openings. Charlie Hodge was the understudy to Jacques Plante in Montreal during the Canadiens' powerhouse years of the 1950s, but didn't get a chance to play regularly in the NHL until 1963–64 when he recorded a 2.26 goals-against average and won the Vezina Trophy as the league's top goaltender. That year also marked the last occasion that one goaltender handled all of his team's play as Eddie Johnston played all 70 games for the sixth-place Boston Bruins.

In 1964–65, back-up goaltenders played in more than twenty games on four of the league's six teams. The Toronto Maple Leafs, who had hired Terry Sawchuk to share the job with Johnny Bower, split the workload in two,

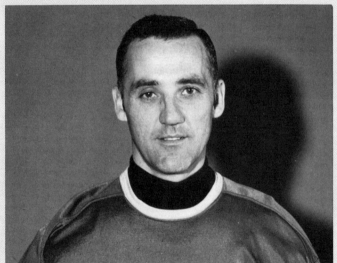

Glenn Hall (top) and Jacques Plante won the Vezina Trophy as the NHL's top goaltending duo in 1968–69.

with Sawchuk playing in 36 games and Bower in 34. Their fine play resulted in the first shared Vezina Trophy award for lowest goals-against average. The six-team NHL stressed defense as the leading goaltenders of those years finished with goals-against averages of less than 2.50. With only five different opposing teams and a very gradual introduction of new talent to the league, goalies could keep accurate track of the style and shooting prefer-

ences of each opponent. Expansion doubled the number of opposing shooters, reduced the number of games played against each club and brought with it the popularization of the slapshot and the curved stick. Subsequent growth in the NHL resulted in younger, bigger, hard-shooting players coming into the game. Additional games were added to the regular season and the number of playoff contests more than doubled. A two-goalie system made sense

and teams became known for the goaltending tandems. Glenn Hall and Jacques Plante for the Blues, Ed Giacomin and Gilles Villemure for the Rangers and Gerry Cheevers and Eddie Johnston for the Bruins were three of the most successful pairings.

The 1967 expansion allowed younger goaltenders to play in the NHL. Tony Esposito won the Vezina Trophy for Chicago in 1969–70 with a goals-against average of 2.17 and a remarkable 15 shutouts in 63 games. Ken Dryden came up from the minors to be the hero of the Stanley Cup playoffs for Montreal the following season. Many of these new younger stars went against the trend and played the majority of their clubs' games. Bernie Parent appeared in 73 games in 1973–74 and in 68 games the following year, posting goals-against averages of 1.89 and 2.03 as the Flyers won two Stanley Cups.

Through the 1970s and into the 1980s, scoring has reached new heights in the NHL and two or three goaltenders have played regularly on most clubs. Twenty of the NHL's 21 teams used their back-up goaltenders in more than 25 games in 1986–87. The pressure on goaltenders in today's hockey has become so great that most clubs have found it worth the expense to carry a third goaltender, though this player is not in uniform during games. In 1981, Montreal won the Vezina Trophy with three goaltenders — Richard Sevigny, Denis Herron and Michel Larocque — sharing the award.

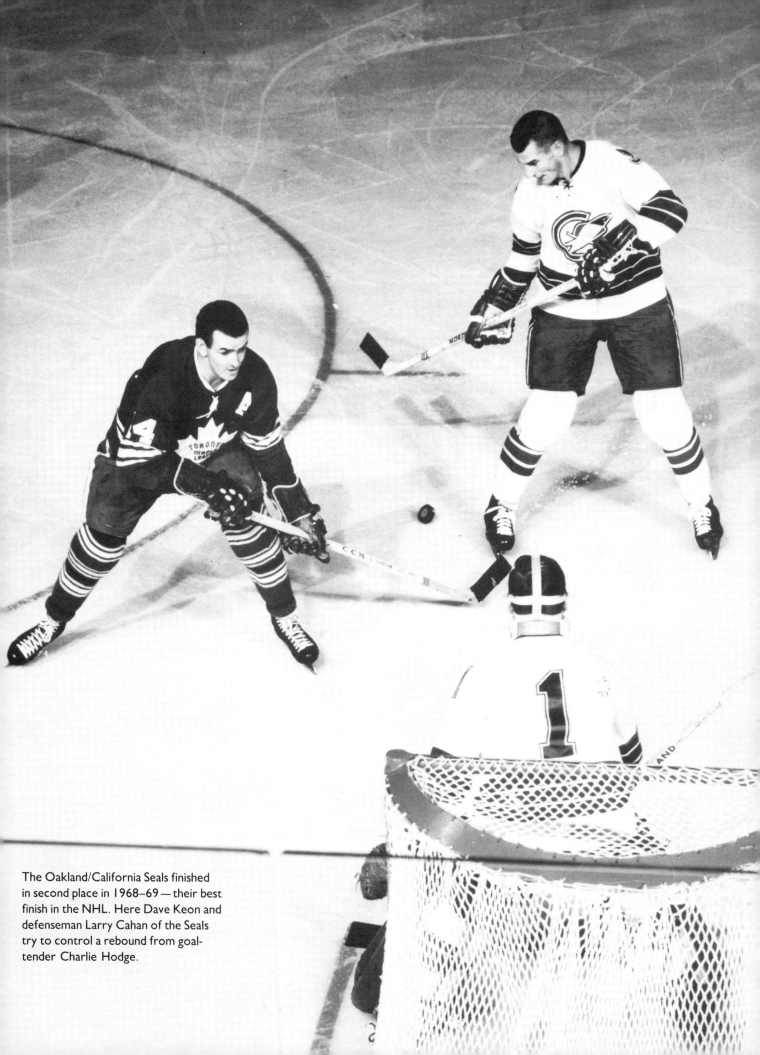

The Oakland/California Seals finished in second place in 1968–69 — their best finish in the NHL. Here Dave Keon and defenseman Larry Cahan of the Seals try to control a rebound from goaltender Charlie Hodge.

thrashing of Toronto that Punch Imlach was removed as coach and general manager of the Leafs. Montreal then met the high-scoring Bruins in the East Division final. The two teams did not disappoint their many fans, as Boston put on an exemplary performance in the Montreal Forum, only to drop both games in overtime. The Habs needed a goal with 56 seconds left in regulation time to force the first game into overtime. Ralph Backstrom netted the winner at the 42-second mark. Game two was a virtual carbon copy of the first match as the Canadiens needed a goal from Serge Savard with 69 seconds left in the final stanza to force extra time. Mickey Redmond scored at 4:55 of overtime to win it for the Habs. The goal was timely, as CBS was just in the process of transferring coverage to the Masters Golf Tournament. Game three shifted to the Boston Garden and saw Bruins convincingly defeat Montreal 5–0. Boston took the fourth game 3–2 to deadlock the series. Behind the acrobatic performance of Rogie Vachon in the nets, Montreal

registered a 4–2 victory in game five. Vachon shut out Phil Esposito on every occasion, kicking out 26 shots in the second period. Jean Beliveau scored one of the many big goals of his career when he ended the series at 11:28 of the second overtime period in the sixth contest.

In the West Division, the Blues were showing the form that enabled them to finish 19 points ahead of the second-place Seals during the regular season. St. Louis's remarkable goaltending duo of Hall and Plante won the Vezina Trophy for the league's best goals-against average. Hall's eight shutouts coupled with Plante's five equaled the modern NHL record of 13 in a minimum 70-game schedule. Plante recorded his 11th and 12th playoff shutouts as the Blues swept Philadelphia in four straight. In the other semifinal, Los Angeles and Oakland played for the bragging rights to California. Apparently this state championship didn't mean much to fans in Oakland as only 5,449 showed up to the first-ever home playoff game.

The Kings' Ted Irvine sent the small

Opposite, top: Bobby Hull's 58 goals established an NHL single-season record. Goaltender Vachon looks determined to get back in position before Hull gets the puck. Opposite, bottom: Rangers' goaltender Eddie Giacomin led the NHL with 37 wins. Here two team captains, Bob Nevin of the Rangers and Jean Beliveau of the Canadiens look to control a bouncing puck. Right: Ted Hampson of the Oakland Seals was the second winner of the Masterton Trophy as the player who best exemplifies perseverance, sportsmanship and dedication to hockey.

crowd home unhappy when he scored the winner in a 5–4 game at 19 seconds of overtime. Oakland prevailed in the next two games, but Los Angeles bounced back to take the series in seven. The rigors of the seven-game semi-final took their toll on the Kings as St. Louis swept Los Angeles in four straight games, earning the Blues their second consecutive appearance in the West Division championship.

The 1969 Stanley Cup final proved more of a foregone conclusion than the matchup of 1968, as the Canadiens easily handled St. Louis, winning four straight. It was a testimony to the Toronto police force that there was a Conn Smythe Trophy available for recipient Serge Savard to accept as playoff MVP. Prior to the semi-finals, thieves made off with a number of trophies from the Hockey Hall of Fame on the Canadian National Exhibition grounds. The booty was discovered in a vacant house in the Toronto suburb of Etobicoke. In addition to the Smythe, the Hart and Calder trophies were also recovered.

# YEAR

## 1968–69

| | |
|---|---|
| **Stanley Cup Champion** | Montreal Canadiens |
| **Prince of Wales Trophy Winner** | Montreal Canadiens |
| **Clarence Campbell Bowl Winner** | St. Louis Blues |

### Final Standings

**East Division**

| Team | GP | W | L | T | GF | GA | PTS |
|---|---|---|---|---|---|---|---|
| Montreal | 76 | 46 | 19 | 11 | 271 | 202 | 103 |
| Boston | 76 | 42 | 18 | 16 | 303 | 221 | 100 |
| New York | 76 | 41 | 26 | 9 | 231 | 196 | 91 |
| Toronto | 76 | 35 | 26 | 15 | 234 | 217 | 85 |
| Detroit | 76 | 33 | 31 | 12 | 239 | 221 | 78 |
| Chicago | 76 | 34 | 33 | 9 | 280 | 246 | 77 |

**West Division**

| Team | GP | W | L | T | GF | GA | PTS |
|---|---|---|---|---|---|---|---|
| St. Louis | 76 | 37 | 25 | 14 | 204 | 157 | 88 |
| Oakland | 76 | 29 | 36 | 11 | 219 | 251 | 69 |
| Philadelphia | 76 | 20 | 35 | 21 | 174 | 225 | 61 |
| Los Angeles | 76 | 24 | 42 | 10 | 185 | 260 | 58 |
| Pittsburgh | 76 | 20 | 45 | 11 | 189 | 252 | 51 |
| Minnesota | 76 | 18 | 43 | 15 | 189 | 270 | 51 |

### Leading Scorers

| Player | Club | GP | G | A | PTS | PIM |
|---|---|---|---|---|---|---|
| Esposito, Phil | Boston | 74 | 49 | 77 | 126 | 79 |
| Hull, Bobby | Chicago | 74 | 58 | 49 | 107 | 48 |
| Howe, Gordie | Detroit | 76 | 44 | 59 | 103 | 58 |
| Mikita, Sam | Chicago | 74 | 30 | 67 | 97 | 52 |
| Hodge, Ken | Boston | 75 | 45 | 45 | 90 | 75 |
| Cournoyer, Yvan | Montreal | 76 | 43 | 44 | 87 | 31 |
| Delvecchio, Alex | Detroit | 72 | 25 | 58 | 83 | 8 |
| Berenson, Red | St. Louis | 76 | 35 | 47 | 82 | 43 |
| Beliveau, Jean | Montreal | 69 | 33 | 49 | 82 | 55 |
| Mahovlich, Frank | Detroit | 76 | 49 | 29 | 78 | 38 |
| Ratelle, Jean | New York | 75 | 32 | 46 | 78 | 26 |

### NHL Award Winners

| | |
|---|---|
| **Hart (MVP)** | Phil Esposito |
| **Art Ross (Leading Scorer)** | Phil Esposito |
| **Calder (Rookie of the Year)** | Danny Grant |
| **Vezina (Lowest Goals-Against)** | Jacques Plante, Glenn Hall |
| **Lady Byng (Gentlemanly Conduct)** | Alex Delvecchio |
| **Norris (Top Defenseman)** | Bobby Orr |
| **Conn Smythe (Playoff MVP)** | Serge Savard |
| **Patrick (Service to US Hockey)** | Bobby Hull, Edward J. Jeremiah |
| **Masterton (Perseverance)** | Ted Hampson |
| **First Overall Draft Selection** | Rejean Houle |
| **World/Olympic Champions** | Soviet Union |
| **AHL Calder Cup Champions** | Hershey Bears |
| **Memorial Cup Canadian Jr. Champions** | Montreal Jr. Canadiens |
| **NCAA Champions** | Denver University |
| **Canadian College Champions** | University of Toronto |

# 1969–1970

In May, 1969, a Canadian government taskforce chaired by Federal Health Minister John Munro tabled a report that questioned the legality of the NHL's reserve clause. This clause, which was a standard part of NHL player contracts, bound a player to his club for the season following the one covered by his contract. Though the reserve clause left room for salary negotiation and offered binding arbitration by the league president if the club and player could not agree, under no circumstances could the player sell his services to another NHL club. The taskforce favored terms of employment similar to those used by the National Football League. Under these terms, a player had the right to "play out" his option year at a ten per cent reduction in salary and then negotiate with other teams.

June 1969 saw the start of a universal amateur draft whereby all junior players of 20 years of age were eligible to be drafted by any club. This new draft ended the old system of territorial picks and letters of intent that, in some cases, determined the NHL affiliation of hockey players as young as 13 years of age.

Through behind-the-scenes trading, Montreal general manager Sam Pollock obtained the first two selections, which he used to draft Rejean Houle and Marc Tardif.

Plans were announced to shift the Chicago Blackhawks to the West Division for the 1970–71 season. The league also drew up plans to add new franchises in Buffalo and Vancouver. Despite Vancouver's Pacific location, both new teams would skate in the East Division beginning in 1970–71. Chicago recruited three US college players, bringing up Keith Magnuson, Cliff Korall and goaltender Tony Esposito from the University of Denver. The team also picked up defenseman Bill White and netminder Gerry Desjardins in a trade with Los Angeles. The Blackhawks looked to be in serious trouble when Bobby Hull sat out until November in another contract dispute. But instead of folding, the Hawks followed coach Billy Reay's blueprint of defensive hockey to perfection, winning the East Division. Tony Esposito performed like a seasoned veteran, winning the Vezina Trophy with 15 shutouts. The Hawks'

Montreal center Jacques Lemaire upset by defenseman Jim Dorey behind the Toronto net.

A long drought ended for the Boston Bruins with a Stanley Cup win in 1969–70. Johnny Bucyk accepts the trophy from NHL president Clarence Campbell. Bobby Orr won the Hart, Norris, Ross and Smythe Trophies while Phil Esposito, at left, led the league with 43 goals.

accomplishments were made all the more remarkable by the unfortunate fact that Kenny Wharram, a former member of the Hawks' highly regarded "Skooter Line," suffered a heart attack in training camp and was forced to retire.

The NHL came close to a second on-ice fatality when Boston's Teddy Green and St. Louis' Wayne Maki tangled during a preseason contest in Ottawa. Green, who had been hit over the head by Maki's stick, required emergency surgery to save his life. Further surgery was required to implant a steel plate in Green's head and he did not return to the Bruin lineup that year. For the first time in hockey history, assault charges were laid against both players, but an Ottawa court exonerated them of criminal intent.

Two durable stars doing what they do best: Norm Ullman carrying the puck while being checked by John Ferguson. Toronto and Montreal both missed the playoffs in 1969–70.

In the East Division semi-final, Chicago easily disposed of Detroit in four straight games. In a much closer matchup, Boston needed six games and home-ice advantage to stave off the Rangers in a tense six-game series. Out west, St. Louis continued their domination of the division by taking Minnesota in six games. The Penguins coasted to a four-game sweep of Oakland. The much-ballyhooed East final fell flat, when Boston swept by Chicago in four games. Pittsburgh put up a better showing, falling to St. Louis in six games. Jacques Plante recorded a record 14th playoff shutout in the series.

The biggest excitement of the Stanley Cup final involved Jacques Plante. In the first game of the series, he was felled when a slapshot off the stick of Boston's

Fred Stanfield hit him flush on the mask. Though knocked out, Plante, who perfected the goaltenders' mask, wasn't seriously hurt. The rest of the series was uneventful, though it took some horizontal heroics from Bobby Orr to score the clinching goal in overtime of the fourth game. The photo of Orr flying through the air after netting the winner became a signature for the NHL in the 1970s and symbolized the completed revitalization of the Bruins. Champagne corks popped in a Boston dressing room for the first time since 1941. The team leaders, Orr and Esposito, were largely responsible for the turnaround. Esposito set a playoff record for points with 27 and goals with 13 while Orr shattered the record for goals by a defenseman in the playoffs with 9. Some of the luster was taken off the

## 3. Indoor Ice, Organized Youth Hockey and Hockey Schools

A majority of NHL players in the pre-expansion years learned their love of the game and their basic hockey skills on frozen ponds and creeks during the long winters of their small-town Canadian childhoods. Right into the 1960s, most youth hockey was played on outdoor rinks, giving the advantage in player development to those areas where cold weather allowed for a longer hockey season.

In the 1960s and 1970s, the construction of indoor arenas and artificial ice surfaces increased dramatically throughout North America. Much of this construction was concentrated in urban areas either as part of community centers, private recreation complexes, or high schools and colleges. The best players in every age group, who usually played on teams that were well-organized and located in larger centers, took the greatest advantage of the new indoor facilities, scheduling more games and increasing practice time.

The managers of these new indoor rinks, looking to promote their facilities during the off-season, accelerated the trend to formalized hockey instruction by establishing summer hockey schools and powerskating classes, which have become a primary means of upgrading the skills of young players.

Young hockey players now have access to ice, instruction and game situations twelve months of the year. The urban and suburban areas, with their large populations, combine ample indoor ice time with a high level of youth hockey competition. These areas, in both Canada and the United States, have taken over from small town "pond hockey" as the most fertile territory to develop young players who go on to be professionals. This formalizing of the process of acquiring hockey skills has seen young hockey players from the US become an increasingly important component on NHL rosters. At the time of the 1967–68 expansion, only one American-born player played in the NHL. From 1984 to 1986, 132 American high school hockey players were drafted by NHL teams.

Bruin celebration when Boston coach Harry Sinden retired from hockey to pursue business interests just two days after his biggest victory.

Several scoring milestones were reached during the year. Gordie Howe iced a Red Wing victory in St. Louis with an empty net goal that was his 800th tally including both playoffs and regular-season play. Bobby Hull did not let his early-season contract dispute and the Hawks' new defensive style of play prevent him from becoming the third player in history to reach 500 goals. Hull's milestone goal came on February 21, 1970 in a 4–2 victory over the New York Rangers. The Golden Jet reached the 500 mark in 861 games, two games faster than Maurice ''Rocket'' Richard. On February 16, Alex Delvecchio set up a goal for the Red Wings and became only the third player to score 1,000 points in the NHL.

The Soviet Nationals, winners of the 1970 World Championship, featured a young Vladislav Tretiak in goal and a skilled nucleus of players who would be the mainstays of the club that would play the NHL's best in two years time.

Even more unexpected than Chicago's success was defending Stanley Cup champion Montreal's failure to make the playoffs for the first time in 22 years. The East Division race was so tight that the Rangers and Montreal finished the season with identical 38–22–16 records. In this instance, goals for and against are used to determine which team finishes higher in the standings. The Rangers needed to win their final game and score more than five goals to finish ahead of the Canadiens. In a Sunday afternoon contest carried by CBS, the Rangers peppered 65 shots on the Detroit goal, skating to a 9–3 win. Montreal faced Chicago that evening, with the Hawks needing a win to wrest first place away from the Boston Bruins as both teams had an equal number of points. Montreal needed either a win, a tie or a loss in which they scored five or more goals. Trailing 5–2 in the third period, Montreal coach

Above: Red Berenson of St. Louis remained one of the top scorers in the West Division with 33 goals, second only to Minnesota's Bill Goldsworthy who had 36 in 1969–70. At right: Les Binkley played in 24 games for the Pittsburgh Penguins.

Roger Crozier was in his final season with the Red Wings when Detroit finished third in the East Division with 95 points. Detroit had missed qualifying for post-season play in each of the three previous seasons. Crozier would play in Buffalo the following season.

Claude Ruel pulled netminder Rogie Vachon in favor of a sixth attacker. The move backfired as Chicago scored five empty-net goals to win 10–2.

The Philadelphia Flyers were literally fit to be tied in 1969–70, establishing a league record with 24 ties. They missed the final playoff spot in the West Division because the Oakland Seals had more wins to go with their 58 points. Pittsburgh benefited from the talented coaching of Red Kelly, finishing in second place.

Bobby Orr broke two of his own records for performances by a defenseman. He set the standard for goals by a rearguard with 33, added a record for the most assists with 87 and became only the fourth player to eclipse the 100-point mark by registering 120, the second-highest total accumulated in a single season. Orr swept the post-season awards, winning the Ross, Hart, Norris and Smythe trophies. Orr's performance marked the first time in NHL history that a defenseman was also the league's top point producer.

# YEAR                1969–70

**Stanley Cup Champion:**                Boston Bruins
**Prince of Wales Trophy Winner**    Chicago Blackhawks
**Clarence Campbell Bowl Winner**    St. Louis Blues

**Final Standings**

**East Division**

| Team | GP | W | L | T | GF | GA | PTS |
|------|----|----|----|----|----|----|----|
| Chicago | 76 | 45 | 22 | 9 | 250 | 170 | 99 |
| Boston | 76 | 40 | 17 | 19 | 277 | 216 | 99 |
| Detroit | 76 | 40 | 21 | 15 | 246 | 199 | 95 |
| New York | 76 | 38 | 22 | 16 | 246 | 189 | 92 |
| Montreal | 76 | 38 | 22 | 16 | 244 | 201 | 92 |
| Toronto | 76 | 29 | 34 | 13 | 222 | 242 | 71 |

**West Division**

| Team | GP | W | L | T | GF | GA | PTS |
|------|----|----|----|----|----|----|----|
| St. Louis | 76 | 37 | 27 | 12 | 224 | 179 | 86 |
| Pittsburgh | 76 | 26 | 38 | 12 | 182 | 238 | 64 |
| Minnesota | 76 | 19 | 35 | 22 | 224 | 257 | 60 |
| Oakland | 76 | 22 | 40 | 14 | 169 | 243 | 58 |
| Philadelphia | 76 | 17 | 35 | 24 | 197 | 225 | 58 |
| Los Angeles | 76 | 14 | 52 | 10 | 168 | 290 | 38 |

**Leading Scorers**

| Player | Club | GP | G | A | PTS | PIM |
|--------|------|----|----|----|----|----|
| Orr, Bobby | Boston | 76 | 33 | 87 | 120 | 125 |
| Esposito, Phil | Boston | 76 | 43 | 56 | 99 | 50 |
| Mikita, Stan | Chicago | 76 | 39 | 47 | 86 | 50 |
| Goyette, Phil | St. Louis | 72 | 29 | 49 | 78 | 16 |
| Tkaczuk, Walt | New York | 76 | 27 | 50 | 77 | 38 |
| Ratelle, Jean | New York | 75 | 32 | 42 | 74 | 28 |
| Berenson, Red | St. Louis | 67 | 33 | 39 | 72 | 38 |
| Parise, Jean-Paul | Minnesota | 74 | 24 | 48 | 72 | 72 |
| Howe, Gordie | Detroit | 76 | 31 | 40 | 71 | 58 |
| Mahovlich, Frank | Detroit | 74 | 38 | 32 | 70 | 59 |
| Balon, Dave | New York | 76 | 33 | 37 | 70 | 100 |
| McKenzie, John | Boston | 72 | 29 | 41 | 70 | 114 |

**NHL Award Winners**

| | |
|---|---|
| **Hart (MVP)** | Bobby Orr |
| **Art Ross (Leading Scorer)** | Bobby Orr |
| **Calder (Rookie of the Year)** | Tony Espsoito |
| **Vezina (Lowest Goals-Against)** | Tony Esposito |
| **Lady Byng (Gentlemanly Conduct)** | Phil Goyette |
| **Norris (Top Defenseman)** | Bobby Orr |
| **Conn Smythe (Playoff MVP)** | Bobby Orr |
| **Patrick (Service to US Hockey)** | Eddie Shore, James C.V. Hendy |
| **Masterton (Perseverance)** | Pit Martin |
| **First Overall Draft Selection** | Gilbert Perreault |

| | |
|---|---|
| **World/Olympic Champions** | Soviet Union |
| **AHL Calder Cup Champions** | Buffalo Bisons |
| **Memorial Cup Canadian Jr. Champions** | Montreal Jr. Canadiens |
| **NCAA Champions** | Cornell |
| **Canadian College Champions** | University of Toronto |

The Buffalo Sabres and Vancouver Canucks joined the NHL in 1970–71. Dave Dryden, pictured here, joined Roger Crozier and Joe Daley to make up the goaltending trio for the first-year Sabres.

The Buffalo Sabres were one of two new teams to enter the NHL for the 1970–71 season. The new team was owned by Seymour and Northrop Knox. The Knoxes were prominent Buffalo businessmen and headed a group called the Niagara Frontier Hockey Corporation. Buffalo was a proven hockey town, and home to the Bisons, a successful AHL franchise. Buffalo's close proximity to Toronto concerned the owners of the Maple Leafs. They feared that their lucrative television market in southern Ontario would be eroded by households close to the US border tuning in the Sabres instead of the

Leafs. The Knoxes had sought a franchise in 1967 and when the Buffalo proposal was denied, bought 25 per cent of the financially troubled Oakland Seals in the hope of moving them to Buffalo. The league welcomed the financial aid, but was unwilling to move the Seals. The Knoxes divested themselves of their interest in the Seals and upgraded Buffalo's War Memorial Auditorium to hold 15,000 spectators, waiting for another opportunity to join the NHL. The club also paid a one-million-dollar indemnity to the AHL Bisons, even though none of the Bison players figured in the Sabres plan.

The Sabres' first major announcement

*(continued on page 33)*

## 4. Bobby Orr's Defensive Revolution

It is rare in hockey for one player to be able to revolutionize the way an aspect of the game is played. Rocket Richard, Gordie Howe and Wayne Gretzky are superstar players, but their abilities are so exceptional that they don't lend themselves to easy imitation. Bobby Orr's achievements in the NHL and skills as a player equal those of the game's other great stars, but because he played defense, his success as a puck carrier and scorer defined a new role for defense-

men. It is almost as if he invented a new "offensive defenseman's" position that has, in only twenty years, become an accepted and required component on any good hockey team.

Orr also revolutionized owner-player relations by insisting that his first contract with the Boston Bruins be negotiated by his agent Alan Eagleson. Prior to Orr's arrival in the NHL after a superb career as a junior in Oshawa, Ontario, promising young hockey players signed what was called a "C-form" which committed the player's professional hockey services to one NHL franchise. Without the ability to entertain

offers from other clubs and without union protection, a player who wanted to play hockey was usually forced to take what was offered to him by the club that owned his rights. Orr was so obviously a future star that Boston management accommodated his request and negotiated through Eagleson. Orr received a contract far larger than any other rookie pact signed up to that time. This success added to Eagleson's standing in the hockey community and contributed to the successful organizing of the NHL Players' Association.

On the ice, Orr's great speed and puckhandling skills enabled him to play defense

as it had never been played before. While the league had seen rearguards like Eddie Shore, Red Kelly and Doug Harvey make occasional dashes into the offensive zone, none of them dominated the game like Orr, who continually rushed the puck up ice, defending by attacking the opponent's goal. Orr took the chance of being caught out of position on his end-to-end rushes, but his great speed usually enabled him to recover. In his second season, the NHL expansion year of 1967–68, he emerged as a scorer with 21 goals, bettering a single-season record for NHL defensemen that had stood since Flash Hollet

scored 20 goals for Detroit in 1944–45. This performance was rewarded with the first of eight consecutive Norris Trophies as the league's top defenseman.

Orr accomplished something unheard of for a defenseman in the NHL when he won the scoring title in 1969–70 and 1974–75. In 1970–71 he had 102 assists, which alone would have been enough to win the scoring championship in most seasons. He lifted the goal scoring record for defensemen to 46, where it remained for 11 seasons until Paul Coffey scored 48 goals for Edmonton in 1985–86. He surpassed the 100-point plateau in six consecutive seasons and won the Hart Trophy as the NHL's most valuable player for three straight years.

The emergence of Bobby Orr as a superstar occurred at an opportune time for the NHL, as two of the league's greatest players, Gordie Howe and Jean Beliveau, had just announced their retirements. The NHL lost another top attraction when Bobby Hull left to play in the WHA the following season. Orr, along with Phil Esposito and the early 1970s teams that came to be known as the ''Big Bad Bruins,'' packed arenas around the league. In May of 1970, the Bruins ended a 29–year drought, winning the Stanley Cup for the first time since 1941. While Boston was an easy winner over St. Louis in the 1970 final, Orr's Cup-winning overtime goal in game four has become a vivid image of the arrival of the Bruins as one of the NHL's best teams. Film and photos of this important goal show Orr hurtling horizontally through the air, with an expression of joy on

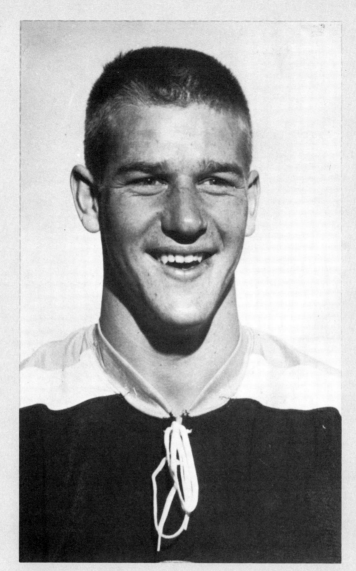

his face. These images were widely used to promote the NHL and the game of hockey in the early 1970s.

Orr and the Bruins became hockey's media darlings, and the best-known NHLers in the United States. Orr's famous number four jersey became the first choice on playground rinks wherever hockey was played.

The Bruins paid a return visit to the Stanley Cup final in 1971–72, as Orr again scored the Cup-winning goal, ending a rugged six-game series with the New York Rangers.

Orr's presence on the ice for the Bruins was so central to their attack that Philadel-phia Flyers' coach Fred Shero devised a special strategy designed to overwork the Bruins star in the 1973–74 final. Rather than follow the conventional wisdom of trying to keep the puck away from Orr, Shero's Flyers were instructed to repeatedly dump the puck into Orr's defensive area, and then skate in to bump and challenge him before he could wheel out and start an offensive rush. This strategy proved effective as the Flyers' heavy checking and Orr's customary 40 minutes of ice time combined to fatigue the Bruins star by the end of the playoffs. In 1973–74 the Flyers became the first expansion team to

capture the Stanley Cup, winning the deciding game 1–0.

Orr's career was interrupted and finally ended by serious knee injuries. After 1975, when he had a fourth operation on his left knee, Orr appeared in only 36 NHL games spread out over four seasons. The Bruins, realizing that it was unlikely that he would be able to play again, allowed him to sign with the Chicago Blackhawks for the 1976–77 season. His last grand performance was during the first Canada Cup international tournament in 1976 when he was named MVP of the tournament, which was won by Team Canada. After fifth and sixth operations, Orr rested for the entire 1977–78 season in the hope that his damaged knee would heal. He returned to play only six games in 1978–79, announcing his retirement in November, 1978. He became the youngest member of the Hockey Hall of Fame when he was inducted in September of the following year.

Defensive play in the NHL was irrevocably changed by Orr. Single-handedly, he made the position a glamorous one; that of the on-ice general or quarterback who dictates the pace and nature of his team's attack. Some of the strongest-skating and most creative young hockey players at the junior, collegiate and youth league levels began to gravitate to defense. Brad Park and Denis Potvin continued the Orr-style game in the NHL, dazzling fans with their skating skills. In more recent seasons, Ray Bourque, Doug Wilson and Paul Coffey have demonstrated that a defenseman playing a vital role in his team's attack is a permanent feature of modern NHL play.

The new NHL Vancouver Canucks were built around veteran players like Orland Kurtenbach, above, who came over from the New York Rangers; Rosaire Paiement, far left, who previously played in Philadelphia and Wayne Maki, left, who played in St. Louis and Chicago. Paiement finished the year with 34 goals; Maki 25 and Kurtenbach, who was only able to play in 52 games, 21.

Rookie left-winger Rejean Houle challenges Philadelphia goaltender Bruce Gamble.

came on January 16, 1970 when they named Punch Imlach as coach and general manager. Buffalo was awarded the first pick in the amateur draft and took Gilbert Perreault, a brilliant young star with the Montreal Junior Canadiens. Imlach's luck held true when he was awarded first choice of the players left unprotected by the established clubs. He took Tom Webster from the Boston organization and traded him to Detroit for Roger Crozier, a goaltender capable of spectacular play. Buffalo also obtained Phil Goyette, Donnie Marshall, Eddie Shack and Reg Fleming.

The Vancouver franchise was awarded to a Minneapolis-based company called Medicor, whose principal shareholder and president was lawyer Thomas Scallen. Medicor already owned the Vancouver Canucks of the Western Hockey League and decided to use the same team name for its new entry in the NHL. Bud Poile, a veteran of the WHL and first general manager of the Philadelphia Flyers, was appointed general manager. Hal Laycoe was named to coach the

team. Unlike the team he assembled in Philadelphia, Poile would not have the luxury of playing in an expansion division. His first pick in the amateur draft was Dale Tallon of the Toronto Marlboros, a defenseman or forward with a penchant for Orr-like offensive rushes. The Canucks took Orland Kurtenbach from the Rangers as their first choice in the expansion draft. They also acquired netminder Charlie Hodge as well as solid veterans like Pat Quinn, Wayne Maki, Andre Boudrias and Rosaire Paiement. Paiement contributed 34 goals in the Canucks' inaugural campaign and, until being injured in December, Kurtenbach was among the league's leading scorers. Neither Buffalo or Vancouver disgraced themselves in their first season. Both clubs finished ahead of Detroit. The Canucks drew near-capacity crowds for every home game, having sold 12,000 season tickets.

Charles O. Finley purchased the Oakland Seals for $4.5 million. Finley was the owner of baseball's Oakland A's, and was always on the lookout for novel promotions. One season he had every member of his baseball club grow a moustache. His hockey innovation was to change the name of the team to the California Golden Seals and have his players wear colored skates. The unique aspect of the Seals' play was the wandering of their netminder Gary Smith. Smith's sojourns up the ice with the puck brought about a rule change that prohibited goalies from crossing the center-ice red line.

The Pittsburgh Penguins had troubles on the ice and at the box office. Michel Briere, one of the club's promising young players, died in a car accident. Club owner Donald Parsons could not sustain continuing financial losses, forcing the league to take over the administration of the franchise.

Many veteran players, reacting to the big contracts given to Gil Perreault and Dale Tallon, "held out" at training camp.

The Rangers were particularly hard hit when Walt Tkaczuk, Jean Ratelle, Vic Hadfield and Brad Park all sat out the pre-season. Other teams were affected as well as Stan Mikita and Derek Sanderson refused to report.

Trades saw a number of established stars change uniforms. Frank Mahovlich and Garry Unger left Detroit to go to Montreal and St Louis, respectively, while Pete Stemkowski and Bruce MacGregor continued the exodus from the Red Wings when they joined the Rangers. Detroit hired Ned Harkness as coach. Sid Abel, who had served the Red Wings as a player, coach and general manager, quit his post, citing irreparable differences with Harkness. Jacques Plante was traded from St. Louis to the Maple Leafs, who needed a veteran goaltender to replace Johnny Bower. Bobby Rousseau and Ted Harris left Montreal to play in Minnesota.

The Stanley Cup champion Bruins continued to set records. In 1970–71 the team shattered 37 records, including wins at home (33) and wins on the road (24). The team scored a record 399 goals and recorded 695 assists. Given ample opportunity to do their jobs, the Boston penalty killers, led by Eddie Westfall and Derek Sanderson, established a record with 25 shorthanded goals. Ten Boston players achieved the 20-goal mark, five reached the 30-goal plateau and three broke the 40-goal barrier. Johnny Bucyk and Phil Esposito became the first players from one team to score 50 goals in the same season. Four Bruins—Esposito, Orr, Bucyk and Ken Hodge—finished as the top four in the scoring race as each had more than 100 points. The line of Esposito, Hodge and Cashman scored 140 goals and 336 points—both new single-season records.

Individually the Bruins were no less dominant. Esposito demolished the single-season league mark for goals with 76 and points with 152. He scored in bunches, recording seven three-goal games and 25 power-play tallies. Both these marks were records. He also set the league standard for game-winning goals with 16. Bobby Orr recorded 102 assists, breaking his own record for points by a defenseman with 139.

Some players other than Bruins scored

Jean Beliveau, Montreal's captain and one of hockey's greatest ambassadors, retired after being part of his tenth Stanley Cup winner.

record-setting goals. On February 11, 1971, Jean Beliveau became the fourth player in NHL history to score 500 career goals. Gilbert Perreault fired his 35th goal of the season against St. Louis to establish a rookie single-season goal-scoring record. Perreault finished the season with 38 goals. Michel Plasse of the Kansas City Blues of the Central League put his name in the record book by becoming the first goaltender in professional hockey to score a goal when he hit the empty net in a contest against the Oklahoma Blazers.

Boston's record-setting regular season didn't put the puck in the net for them in their first-round playoff matchup with the Montreal Canadiens, who benefited from the strong play of Ken Dryden, their 6'4" rookie netminder. Dryden was called up from the minors, and won the last six games of the season for the Habs. Against the Bruins he was brilliant, robbing Orr and Esposito repeatedly. The New York Rangers eliminated Toronto in the other East Division series. Chicago had, as expected, dominated the West Division. They had little difficulty routing the Flyers in four straight in their first playoff matchup. The Minnesota North Stars provided St. Louis with an early exit from the playoffs, winning in

six games. The 1970–71 playoff format saw the league's two semi-finals played between teams from the two divisions for the first time. Montreal struggled to a six-game victory over a surprisingly stubborn Minnesota team and Chicago handled the Rangers in seven free wheeling encounters.

For the first time since expansion, the Stanley Cup final between Montreal and Chicago did not have a heavy favorite. Ken Dryden and Tony Esposito treated hockey fans to brilliant performances. The series went the limit, with Montreal edging Chicago 3–2 in the final game before 20,000 fans in the Chicago Stadium. Henri Richard, who had been openly critical of coach Al MacNeil for benching him earlier in the series, scored the tying and winning goals in game seven. Frank Mahovlich was outstanding for the Canadiens, firing a playoff-record 14 goals. Ken Dryden was the year's playoff hero. Gordie Howe and Jean Beliveau chose the 1970–71 season to bring down the curtain on two of hockey's outstanding careers. Howe, 43, had played 25 seasons for the Detroit Red Wings and was the NHL's all-time leading scorer with 786 goals. Beliveau, 40, played 18 majestic seasons for "Les Canadiens" and rounded out his career with 507 goals.

A mid-season trade which sent Frank Mahovlich to the Montreal Canadiens broke up one of the most potent forward combinations in the NHL. Alex Delvecchio centered Gordie Howe and the Big M. Howe, at left, retired after the 1970–71 campaign — his 25th NHL season. Howe's retirement wouldn't last, and he would be back in the NHL in 1979–80.

# YEAR                                  1970–71

**Stanley Cup Champion**         Montreal Canadiens
**Prince of Wales Trophy Winner**   Boston Bruins
**Clarence Campbell Bowl Winner**   Chicago Blackhawks

**Final Standings**

**East Division**

| Team | GP | W | L | T | GF | GA | PTS |
|------|----|----|----|----|----|----|----|
| Boston | 78 | 57 | 14 | 7 | 399 | 207 | 121 |
| New York | 78 | 49 | 18 | 11 | 259 | 177 | 109 |
| Montreal | 78 | 42 | 23 | 13 | 291 | 216 | 97 |
| Toronto | 78 | 37 | 33 | 8 | 248 | 211 | 82 |
| Buffalo | 78 | 24 | 39 | 15 | 217 | 291 | 63 |
| Vancouver | 78 | 24 | 46 | 8 | 229 | 296 | 56 |
| Detroit | 78 | 22 | 45 | 11 | 209 | 308 | 55 |

**West Division**

| Team | GP | W | L | T | GF | GA | PTS |
|------|----|----|----|----|----|----|----|
| Chicago | 78 | 49 | 20 | 9 | 277 | 184 | 107 |
| St. Louis | 78 | 34 | 25 | 19 | 223 | 208 | 87 |
| Philadelphia | 78 | 28 | 33 | 17 | 207 | 225 | 73 |
| Minnesota | 78 | 28 | 34 | 16 | 191 | 223 | 72 |
| Los Angeles | 78 | 25 | 40 | 13 | 239 | 303 | 63 |
| Pittsburgh | 78 | 21 | 37 | 20 | 221 | 240 | 62 |
| California | 78 | 20 | 53 | 5 | 199 | 320 | 45 |

**Leading Scorers**

| Player | Club | GP | G | A | PTS | PIM |
|--------|------|----|----|----|----|----|
| Esposito, Phil | Boston | 78 | 76 | 76 | 152 | 71 |
| Orr, Bobby | Boston | 78 | 37 | 102 | 139 | 91 |
| Bucyk, John | Boston | 78 | 51 | 65 | 116 | 8 |
| Hodge, Ken | Boston | 78 | 43 | 62 | 105 | 113 |
| Hull, Bobby | Chicago | 78 | 44 | 52 | 96 | 32 |
| Ullman, Norm | Toronto | 73 | 34 | 51 | 85 | 24 |
| Cashman, Wayne | Boston | 77 | 21 | 58 | 79 | 100 |
| McKenzie, John | Boston | 65 | 31 | 46 | 77 | 120 |
| Keon, Dave | Toronto | 76 | 38 | 38 | 76 | 4 |
| Beliveau, Jean | Montreal | 70 | 25 | 51 | 76 | 40 |
| Stanfield, Fred | Boston | 75 | 24 | 52 | 76 | 12 |

**NHL Award Winners**

**Hart (MVP)**                        Bobby Orr
**Art Ross (Leading Scorer)**         Phil Esposito
**Calder (Rookie of the Year)**       Gilbert Perreault
**Vezina (Lowest Goals-Against)**     Ed Giacomin, Gilles Villemure
**Lady Byng (Gentlemanly Conduct)**   John Bucyk
**Norris (Top Defenseman)**           Bobby Orr
**Conn Smythe (Playoff MVP)**         Ken Dryden
**Patrick (Service to US Hockey)**    Willam Jennings, John Sollenberger,
                                      Terry Sawchuk

**Masterton (Perseverance)**          Jean Ratelle
**Pearson (NHLPA MVP)**               Phil Esposito
**First Overall Draft Selection**     Guy Lafleur

**World/Olympic Champions**           Soviet Union

**AHL Calder Cup Champions**          Springfield Indians

**Memorial Cup Canadian Jr. Champions**   Quebec Remparts

**NCAA Champions**                    Boston University

**Canadian College Champions**        University of Toronto

# 1971–1972

The expansion era provided increased opportunities for journeymen, and gave new meaning to the term "suitcase" player. Glen Sather of the New York Rangers played for six teams in 10 NHL seasons, while goaltender Dunc Wilson of the Vancouver Canucks played for five in a ten-year career. Below, Sather eludes Canucks defenceman Dale Tallon.

Immediately following the retirement of two of the game's greatest stars, two young players who would come to be considered among the most thrilling players of all time entered the league. Guy Lafleur, through one of Sam Pollock's complicated deals, was drafted first overall by the Montreal Canadiens after a phenomenal junior career with the Quebec Remparts. Detroit held the second amateur draft choice and claimed Marcel Dionne, a prodigious scorer with the St. Catharines Black Hawks of the Ontario Hockey League.

The NHL's rules committee made changes for the 1971–72 season. The third man entering a fight on the ice would receive an automatic game misconduct penalty. In an attempt to prevent teams from coasting once they had qualified for the playoffs, the old system of the first-place team playing the third and the second-place place playing the fourth was replaced. Instead, the first-place finisher would meet the fourth-place team while the second and third finishers would clash. This provided teams with the incentive to finish as high up in the stand-

## 5. Alan Eagleson and the NHL Players' Association

Prior to the 1967–68 expansion, professional hockey, with its several minor leagues feeding players to the NHL, paid salaries that made it necessary for most NHLers to hold down summer jobs to make ends meet. Until the 1960s, athletes in most professional team sports did not enjoy salaries and benefits comparable to those of other celebrities or popular entertainers. The NHL's team owners had resisted all efforts on the part of their players to unionize. In 1947, a request by the players to have the owners set up a pension fund for them was denied. Instead, the NHL staged an annual all-star game of which two-thirds of the gate receipts were contributed to the players' pension plan. In 1957, Ted Lindsay, a left winger with the Red Wings and one of the NHL's top players, led the formation of a player's union that, although it was never recognized by the league, contributed to improvements in the players' pension fund and share of playoff bonus money as well as the establishment of a base salary of $7,000 per season. Lindsay and several other organizers of the union found themselves traded from contending teams with whom they were popular stars to some of the NHL's least-successful franchises.

In 1966, Alan Eagleson, a Toronto lawyer and financial advisor for several NHL players and a young junior

star named Bobby Orr, was asked to intervene in a dispute between the members of the Springfield Indians hockey club, a farm club of the Boston Bruins, and the club's owner, former NHL all-star Eddie Shore. Shore was one of hockey's great characters, but he had suspended several of his players and earned the enmity of the remaining members of the team. When the players were unable to obtain satisfaction from the executive of the AHL, they considered going on strike. They asked Eagleson to help them state their case. With Eagleson's help, the players didn't go on strike but no longer were subjected to the most objectionable of Shore's autocratic methods. Shore soon retired and sold the Springfield team to the new Los Angeles Kings.

Through Bobby Orr, Eagleson won the right for an agent to negotiate on behalf

of his client with an NHL club. Hap Emms, the general manager of the Bruins, had offered Orr a $5,000 bonus and a rookie contract calling for $8,000 in salary in his first season. This offer was later upped to $10,500. Eagleson, initially excluded from the contract discussions, counseled Orr to hold firm to demands for a much higher salary. Eventually, Eagleson was allowed to negotiate directly, winning a two-year deal for Orr that was said to be worth $75,000.

News of Eagleson's accomplishments with Orr and the Springfield players spread throughout the hockey world. Players wanted better wages and working conditions, and saw in Eagleson an organizer who could stand up to the owners in looking after their interests. During the 1966–67 season, professional hockey players quietly organized into a players' union with Eagleson retained as its director and

Bob Pulford of the Toronto Maple Leafs as its president. At the June, 1967, NHL meetings, the owners of the established NHL teams and the six new clubs that would begin play the following season recognized the NHL Players' Association and Eagleson as its chief negotiator.

Once recognized by the league, the NHLPA's first order of business was an increase in the NHL's minimum salary from $7,500 to $12,000 per year. The players also wanted more freedom to earn additional income through personal endorsements. NHL president Clarence Campbell negotiated a starting salary of $10,000, which was accepted by the players. The NHLPA also obtained changes in the playoff bonus pool with $567,000 split up by playoff performers in 1967–68.

The fall of 1967 saw several important players hold out for better contracts. The following year, Bobby Hull sat out the pre-season before signing the richest contract and first $100,000 deal in the history of the sport.

In the ensuing 20 years, the league and the NHLPA have successfully negotiated several collective bargaining agreements that have improved conditions and remuneration for players while acknowledging the business needs of team owners. Salaries, benefits and conditions of employment for NHL players, coaches and other personnel have steadily improved. Hockey, like other professional sports, now offers its players substantial financial rewards, good working conditions and a collective bargaining process.

During his last season of junior hockey, in 1970–71, Marcel Dionne scored 62 goals in 46 games with the St. Catharines Black Hawks. The following year with the Detroit Red Wings, he scored 28, and would go on to record six 50-goal seasons over the next dozen years.

ings as possible. There was concern in the Buffalo training camp when Gil Perreault arrived weighing 225 pounds. Conservative members of the hockey establishment were shocked when St. Louis's Garry Unger showed up with shoulder-length hair. Several of the NHL's best-known players announced their retirements. St. Louis' Glenn Hall and Toronto's captain George Armstrong, along with John Ferguson, Andy Bathgate, Earl Ingarfield and Leo Boivin, concluded their NHL careers.

Eight coaching changes were made before or during the season. The most significant saw Scotty Bowman leave St.

Louis for Montreal, where he replaced Al MacNeil, the Stanley-Cup-winning coach of the previous year. MacNeil solidified his coaching credentials by leading the Habs' farm club, the Nova Scotia Voyageurs, to first place in the AHL.

On October 16, 1971, Norm Ullman became the fourth player to score 1,000 points. He was followed by Bobby Hull on December 12. Hull became only the second player to reach the 600-goal mark later in a game against Boston. Dean Prentice scored his 350th goal while playing for Minnesota and Phil Esposito became the 16th player to reach 300.

New York fans had plenty to cheer about courtesy of the line of Jean Ratelle, Vic Hadfield and Rod Gilbert, who became known as the Goal-A-Game or GAG Line. The trio became the first line to count 40 or more goals each in a season. Hadfield led the way with 50. In Buffalo, the Sabres made another shrewd draft selection, obtaining Rick Martin. Martin eclipsed teammate Gil Perreault's single-season mark for rookie goal scorers with a 44-goal season. Marcel Dionne was the bright spot for Detroit as his 76 points established a rookie record.

Bobby Orr became hockey's first million-dollar man when he signed a multi-year deal with the Bruins. While most newspaper hockey stories concentrated on contracts and penalty minutes, the *New York Times* ran an article on March 11, 1972 headlined, ''Canadiens Rescue Coach and Guests from Hotel Fire.'' The article detailed the efforts of several Montreal players in the rescue of several people trapped by fire in the Hilton Hotel in St. Louis. Organized by J.C. Tremblay, a volunteer fireman in his hometown of Bagotville, Quebec, the Canadiens players rescued several people trapped on the upper floors by maneuvering ladders up to them. The players rescued coach Scotty Bowman from a fourth-floor ledge. Serge Savard suffered an 18-stitch cut to his ankle when he kicked out a glass panel in an attempt to get to Bowman's room.

The Philadelphia Flyers missed a play-off berth by four seconds. At 19:56 of the third period in the final game of the season, Gerry Meehan's long shot gave Buffalo a 3–2 victory over the Flyers. This allowed the Pittsburgh Penguins,

Fourth-year player Brad Park, above, earned his third consecutive all-star selection in 1971–72 as the Rangers finished with a franchise-high 109 points for the second straight season.

Early Pittsburgh Penguin teams had few sharpshooters. No team member scored more than 26 goals in a season until Jean Pronovost and Greg Polis each hit the 30-goal plateau in 1971–72. At left, Polis throws up a roadblock on an unidentified Montreal Canadien while Bryan Hextall, 7, skates away with the puck.

who finished tied for fourth with the Flyers, to advance to the playoffs by virtue of a better won/lost record. Boston defeated the Toronto Maple Leafs in five games in the opening round of the playoffs. In the other East Division series, Montreal was favored over the New York Rangers. New York's top center, Jean Ratelle, had broken his ankle on March 1, and both Rod Gilbert and Brad Park were hampered by injuries. Once the series with Montreal began, lesser-known players like Pete Stemkowski, Walt Tkaczuk, Bobby Rousseau and Bill Fairbairn led the Rangers to a six-game victory in the series.

In the West Division, Minnesota had been the most improved team in hockey during the regular season. Their respectable 37–28–12 season was sparked by the fine play of goaltender Gump Worsley, who had been talked out of retirement the previous year. The North Stars were eliminated in seven games by the St. Louis Blues when Kevin O'Shea's shot rang off the crossbar, hit Cesare Maniago and dribbled in for an overtime goal. In the other West Division series, the Blackhawks defeated Pittsburgh in four straight games.

In the semi-finals, Boston overpowered St. Louis. Sparked by six goals from

Vic Hadfield, above, enjoyed his most productive NHL season in 1971–72. New York's Goal-A-Game (G-A-G) Line of Jean Ratelle, Hadfield, and Rod Gilbert finished third, fourth and fifth in scoring. Hadfield had 50 goals.

Boston's Gerry Cheevers, at right, shared goaltending chores with Eddie Johnston during 1971–72. Together the pair backstopped the team to its second Stanley Cup in three seasons. The following year Cheevers bolted to the Cleveland Crusaders of the WHA, where he played 191 games before returning to the Bruins part way through the 1975–76 season.

Johnny Bucyk, the Bruins outscored the Blues 28–8 in a four-game sweep. New York also won in four, sweeping Chicago. It would mark the Rangers' first appearance in the Stanley Cup final since the 1949–50 season. Although hobbled by his ailing knee, Bobby Orr dominated the final, leading the Bruins to a six-game triumph and winning the Conn Smythe Trophy as playoff MVP.

As the season ended, a rival professional league, the World Hockey Association (WHA) announced that it was preparing to begin play in the fall of 1972. WHA teams signed US Olympic team goaltender Mike Curran, and raided NHL ros-

ters to sign Wayne Connelly and Larry Pleau. By the time the next NHL season began, the WHA would be actively bidding for the services of top hockey players.

A long-awaited showdown between the NHL's finest and the national team of Soviet Union was set for September. The Soviets were the best amateur team in the world, winning the International Ice Hockey Federation World Championship in nine of the previous ten years. An eight-game series was scheduled, with games to be played in Montreal, Toronto, Winnipeg and Vancouver before the two teams would play four games in Moscow.

# YEAR                    1971–72

**Stanley Cup Champion**            Boston Bruins
**Prince of Wales Trophy Winner**   Boston Bruins
**Clarence Campbell Bowl Winner**   Chicago Blackhawks

**Final Standings**

**East Division**

| Team | GP | W | L | T | GF | GA | PTS |
|------|----|----|----|----|----|----|----|
| Boston | 78 | 54 | 13 | 11 | 330 | 204 | 119 |
| New York | 78 | 48 | 17 | 13 | 317 | 192 | 109 |
| Montreal | 78 | 46 | 16 | 16 | 307 | 205 | 108 |
| Toronto | 78 | 33 | 31 | 14 | 209 | 208 | 80 |
| Detroit | 78 | 33 | 35 | 10 | 261 | 262 | 76 |
| Buffalo | 78 | 16 | 43 | 19 | 203 | 289 | 51 |
| Vancouver | 78 | 20 | 50 | 8 | 203 | 297 | 48 |

**West Division**

| Team | GP | W | L | T | GF | GA | PTS |
|------|----|----|----|----|----|----|----|
| Chicago | 78 | 46 | 17 | 15 | 256 | 166 | 107 |
| Minnesota | 78 | 37 | 29 | 12 | 212 | 191 | 86 |
| St. Louis | 78 | 28 | 39 | 11 | 208 | 247 | 67 |
| Pittsburgh | 78 | 26 | 38 | 14 | 220 | 258 | 66 |
| Philadelphia | 78 | 26 | 38 | 14 | 200 | 236 | 66 |
| California | 78 | 21 | 39 | 18 | 216 | 288 | 60 |
| Los Angeles | 78 | 20 | 49 | 9 | 206 | 305 | 49 |

**Leading Scorers**

| Player | Club | GP | G | A | PTS | PIM |
|--------|------|----|----|----|----|----|
| Esposito, Phil | Boston | 76 | 66 | 67 | 133 | 76 |
| Orr, Bobby | Boston | 76 | 37 | 80 | 117 | 106 |
| Ratelle, Jean | New York | 63 | 46 | 63 | 109 | 4 |
| Hadfield, Vic | New York | 78 | 50 | 56 | 106 | 142 |
| Gilbert, Rod | New York | 73 | 43 | 54 | 97 | 64 |
| Mahovlich, Frank | Montreal | 76 | 43 | 53 | 96 | 36 |
| Hull, Bobby | Chicago | 78 | 50 | 43 | 93 | 24 |
| Cournoyer, Yvan | Montreal | 73 | 47 | 36 | 83 | 15 |
| Bucyk, John | Boston | 78 | 32 | 51 | 83 | 4 |
| Clarke, Bobby | Philadelphia | 78 | 35 | 46 | 81 | 87 |
| Lemaire, Jacques | Montreal | 77 | 32 | 49 | 81 | 26 |

**NHL Award Winners**

| | |
|---|---|
| **Hart (MVP)** | Bobby Orr |
| **Art Ross (Leading Scorer)** | Phil Esposito |
| **Calder (Rookie of the Year)** | Ken Dryden |
| **Vezina (Lowest Goals-Against)** | Tony Esposito, Gary Smith |
| **Lady Byng (Gentlemanly Conduct)** | Jean Ratelle |
| **Norris (Top Defenseman)** | Bobby Orr |
| **Conn Smythe (Playoff MVP)** | Bobby Orr |
| **Patrick (Service to US Hockey)** | Clarence Campbell, John Kelly, Cooney Weiland, James D. Norris |
| **Masterton (Perseverance)** | Bobby Clarke |
| **Pearson (NHLPA MVP)** | Jean Ratelle |
| **First Overall Draft Selection** | Billy Harris |
| **World/Olympic Champions** | Soviet Union (Olympics) Czechoslovakia (World Champions) |
| **AHL Calder Cup Champions** | Nova Scotia Voyageurs |
| **Memorial Cup Canadian Jr. Champions** | Cornwall Royals |
| **NCAA Champions** | Boston University |
| **Canadian College Champions** | University of Toronto |

# 1972–1973

Soviet star Alexander Yakushev (15), below, proved himself the equal of the most skillful NHL players during the Soviet-Canada showdown in 1972.

During 1971–72, defenseman Serge Savard of Montreal came back from serious leg injuries that had sidelined him for the better part of two seasons. At right, Savard applies his ample defensive talents to checking left winger Richard Martin of Buffalo's prolific French Connection line.

972–73 promised to provide at least partial answers to many of the questions surrounding big-time hockey. How would the playing styles of the NHL stars compare to the high-paced training and disciplined team play of the Soviet Nationals? Could the WHA, which had already signed Bobby Hull, one of the NHL's top gate attractions, compete against the NHL for fan support, sponsorship and media attention? Were the Boston Bruins on the verge of establishing a dynasty and could their phenomenal defenseman Bobby Orr come back from off-season knee surgery to remain the top player in the game?

The signing of Bobby Hull to a ten-year $2.75 million contract put the WHA on the hockey map. Once Hull went over, every NHLer had to at least consider offers from new WHA teams. Other NHLers who signed included Johnny McKenzie and Derek Sanderson who left the Stanley Cup champion Bruins to play with the Philadelphia Blazers. The Leafs lost a pair of good young defensemen in Rick Ley and Brad Selwood who joined the New England Whalers.

Harry Sinden returned to hockey as the coach of Team Canada 1972. John Ferguson was named his assistant. Despite public support for his inclusion, Bobby Hull and other WHA defectors were excluded from the team. Bobby Orr was still recuperating from knee surgery and couldn't play. Nonetheless, Team Canada was highly favored. The Soviets were stronger than almost anyone had anticipated, and led the series with two wins and a tie against only one loss at the end of the Canadian portion of the series. After Team Canada played several exhibition games in Sweden and Finland, three players — Vic Hadfield, Richard Martin and Jocelyn Guevremont — quit the team in a dispute over lack of ice time. But spurred on by the inspirational play of Phil Esposito and three game-winning goals by Paul Henderson, Team Canada won the last three games of the series and returned home with a narrow 4–3–1 series victory.

The NHL, now in competition with the WHA for players and markets, expanded into Atlanta and Long Island.

The Atlanta franchise was the brain-

child of real estate developer Tom Cousins. He built an ultra-modern arena called the Omni, which would serve as the hub of a large-scale hotel, shopping, entertainment and office complex. Cousins found backing from other wealthy Southerners and enlisted the services of Bill Putman who had been the the first president of the Philadelphia Flyers. Atlanta could hardly be considered a hockey town: prior to the building of the Omni the city's lone ice rink was just fifty feet long. A name-the-team contest attracted 10,000 entries, from which the name "Flames" was chosen. Putman installed former St. Louis Blues' assistant general manager Cliff Fletcher as the franchise's first general manager and named Bernie "Boom-Boom" Geoffrion as coach. Geoffrion was the "toast of the south" as he tried to affect a southern drawl over his thick French-Canadian accent during speaking engagements. The Flames started the season with a base of more than 7,000 season ticket holders. The club had signed two fine young netminders: Phil Myre from Montreal and Dan Bouchard from Boston. The team's hopes in the amateur draft were pinned on Quebec Rempart junior sensation Jacques Richard.

The New York Islanders became hockey's most expensive franchise when Roy Boe and a group of New York investors purchased the team. Like Atlanta, the Islanders paid a six-million-dollar entry fee to the league, but also had to pay five million dollars in indemnification fees to get permission from the Rangers to locate in the New York market. Boe's knowledge of hockey was limited, but he had experience in professional sports through the American Basketball Association and owned the New York Nets. He hired Bill Torrey as the organization's first general manager.

Torrey excelled in Oakland as part of the club management team that twice coaxed the troubled Seals into the playoffs. Torrey would need similar miracles to make the Islanders competitive, as seven of his twenty draft choices bolted to the WHA. Despite these setbacks, he went to work, drafting a steady goaltender in Gerry Desjardins from Chicago and a proven winner in Eddie Westfall from the Bruins. Phil Goyette was signed to coach. Because of competition from the WHA, Billy Harris, the Islanders' first amateur draft choice, signed a three-year $100,000 per annum contract that was the richest ever offered to a junior player who had never laced up a pair of skates as a pro.

Wren Blair, the general manager of the Minnesota North Stars, offered big money for a proven commodity when he traveled to Winnipeg during the Canada-Russia series to offer the Soviet government one million dollars for the services of Valery Kharlamov. The offer was politely declined. Johnny Bucyk scored his

Montreal's sophomore right winger Guy Lafleur had shown signs of his potential by 1972, but his emergence as the dominant player of the decade was still two seasons away.

# TWENTY TRENDS THAT SHAPED MODERN HOCKEY

## 6. The 1972 Super Series— Team Canada vs. the Soviet Nationals

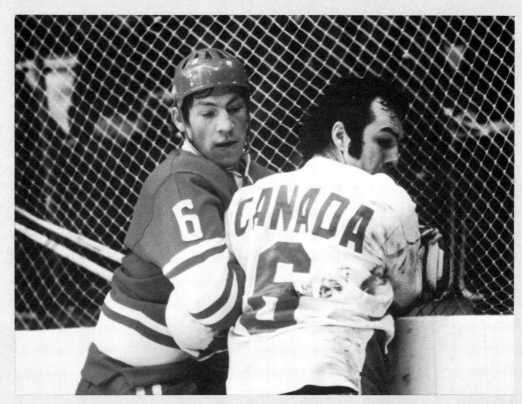

Valery Vasiliev puts an arm-lock on Ron Ellis during the 1972 Soviet-Canada showdown. Ellis played the finest hockey of his career in the eight-game series.

Before the 1972 Super Series between a team of NHL stars and the national team of the Soviet Union, a top NHL squad had never been matched against the perennial winners of Olympic and world championship competitions. The Soviets had become an international hockey power in the mid-1950s, fielding teams that regularly defeated Canada's senior amateur champions and, beginning in 1963, the Canadian national amateur hockey team. As good as the Soviets were, it had always been assumed that they would be unable to establish their deliberate, criss-crossing attacking style against NHL opposition.

Canada had withdrawn from international play in 1969 after the International Ice Hockey Federation (IIHF) had denied Canada the right to use any professional players on its team. The two nations had not met on the ice since that time. The NHL, with most of its franchises in the United States, had little interest in a series that would be promoted as Canada vs. the Soviet Union until it became apparent that the newly established World Hockey Association was prepared to enter into a challenge series with the Soviets. This spurred the NHL into action and a series was arranged for September of 1972.

The complicated negotia-tions involving the NHL Players' Association, the government agency Hockey Canada, the Canadian Amateur Hockey Association, the NHL and the Soviet and International Ice Hockey Federations were orchestrated by Players' Association director Alan Eagleson. The final arrangements called for single games in Montreal, Toronto, and Vancouver, Canada's three NHL cities, one in Winnipeg, the former home of the Canadian national amateur team, and four in Moscow.

Contrary to the predictions of most hockey commentators, the Soviets proved to be more than a match for Team Canada in the first half of the series. After falling behind 2–0 in game one in Montreal, the Soviets came back to win 7–3. In the second game played in Toronto, Team Canada won 4–1. Game three in Winnipeg was tied, 4–4, while game four in Vancouver saw the Soviets win 5–3 and Team Canada booed by its fans. With a 2–1–1 lead in games, the Soviets needed only to split the four games in Moscow.

Game five featured a crushing Soviet comeback. Trailing 4–1 in the third period, the Soviets shifted gears, took control of the play and won 5–4. Team Canada, needing a seemingly impossible three straight wins in Moscow, won the next three games by one-goal margins as Paul Henderson of the Toronto Maple Leafs netted the winning goal each time. Team Canada had won by the narrowest of margins with four wins and a tie

in eight games. It was a victory for heart and spirit, as even the most loyal Team Canada supporter had to concede that the Soviets were in better shape and were better skaters and passers than the NHL's best.

The importance of the 1972 Super Series took time to sink in as the euphoria of Team Canada's marvelous victory swept everything before it. But the Soviet Nationals, when finally compared to an excellent team of NHL stars, showed North American hockey that a game based on speed, conditioning, perpetual motion and short passing was, in many ways, superior to the early-1970s NHL game of dump-and-chase followed up by the booming slapshot.

Bobby Hull's million-dollar signing with the Winnipeg Jets of the WHA in 1972 brought instant recognition not only to the Jets but to the entire WHA. Many observers feel the league could not have survived without him. Within a year or two of his WHA debut, Hull's balding pate disappeared beneath a dense thatching of salon-woven hair, which helped preserve his aura as the Golden Jet.

400th goal and, two weeks later, his 1,000th point in a game against Detroit on November 9, 1972. Alex Delvecchio moved into second place on the all-time scoring list, trailing only his former linemate Gordie Howe. Dave Keon scored his 300th career goal in a game against Vancouver. Frank Mahovlich became only the fifth player to reach the 500 goal plateau when he beat Vancouver's Dunc Wilson in a 3–2 victory for the Habs on March 21, 1973.

NBC became the NHL's new US network and carried Sunday afternoon contests. Bobby Orr's late start enabled him to play in only 63 games, but he scored more than 100 points for the fourth straight year. One of his games against Vancouver featured a record-tying performance by a defenseman when he recorded six assists. Montreal lost only ten games during the season, winning the East Division. In the West, Philadelphia showed great improvement, winning 37 games, the same number as the North Stars. St. Louis finished only two games below .500 as the league gradually moved toward parity. Bobby Clarke of the Flyers became the first expansion club player to reach 100 points, and his teammate Rick MacLeish became the first expansion player to score 50 goals.

The biggest surprise in postseason play was the appearance by the Buffalo Sabres in only their third year in the league. The Sabres featured the spectacular young line of Gilbert Perreault, Rick Martin and Rene Robert. This line was nicknamed the French Connection. The feisty Sabres spotted the Montreal Canadiens three games in the opening round of the playoffs, but bounced back to win games four and five before finally being defeated in game six. A crushing body check by Ranger defenseman Ron Harris helped settle the playoff series with Boston. Harris nailed Phil Esposito in game two of the series at Boston Garden, and the Boston scoring star was through for the series with torn knee ligaments. Boston could not compensate for the loss of their big gunner and was eliminated. The Blackhawks had little trouble sending St. Louis to the sidelines. Hot goaltending from Doug Favell helped Philadelphia overcome Minnesota, who had strong performances from veterans Doug Mohns (34 years old), Ted Harris, (36), Dean Prentice (40) Charlie Burns (37) and Murray Oliver (36). Philadelphia won in six games.

In semi-final action, Montreal spotted the Flyers the first game in the Forum in overtime before reeling off four straight wins for a berth in the Stanley Cup final. In the other series, Tony Esposito was at the top of his game as the Blackhawks skated past New York in five games.

Chicago had reached the Stanley Cup

Billy Harris was the New York Islanders' first-ever draft choice in 1972, and played eight seasons with the Isles before being traded with Dave Lewis to the L.A. Kings for Butch Goring. Below, Bill waits for a Long Island train during his rookie year. The Buffalo Sabres, at right, made the playoffs in their third season, finishing with 88 points in 1972–73. Gilbert Perreault (11, at bottom) won the Lady Byng Trophy and matched his club's output with 88 points of his own.

final without Bobby Hull, but they fared no better than Hull's club (the Winnipeg Jets) did in its trip to the WHA's Avco Cup final against the New England Whalers. It took the Canadiens six games to regain the coveted Stanley Cup. Yvan Cournoyer established a record for goals in the playoffs with 15 and was named the MVP of postseason play. New England won the Avco Cup in five games against the Jets.

After the playoffs, Gordie Howe announced plans to come out of retirement to play with his two sons, Mark and

Marty, with the Houston Aeros of the WHA. Denis Potvin, a high-scoring defenseman from the Ottawa 67s, was chosen first overall by the New York Islanders in the amateur draft. Tom Lysiak of the Medicine Hat Tigers became Atlanta's first pick. In an attempt to slow the increase in players' salaries, an initial attempt was made at an NHL-WHA merger. The NHL Players' Association stated that it would consider launching a suit against the league if there was a merger and the talks between the two leagues never came close to producing an agreement.

# YEAR                                    1972–73

**Stanley Cup Champion**          Montreal Canadiens
**Prince of Wales Trophy Winner**  Montreal Canadiens
**Clarence Campbell Bowl Winner**  Chicago Blackhawks

**Final Standings**

**East Division**

| Team | GP | W | L | T | GF | GA | PTS |
|------|----|----|----|----|----|----|----|
| Montreal | 78 | 52 | 10 | 16 | 329 | 184 | 120 |
| Boston | 78 | 51 | 22 | 5 | 330 | 235 | 107 |
| NY Rangers | 78 | 47 | 23 | 8 | 297 | 208 | 102 |
| Buffalo | 78 | 37 | 27 | 14 | 257 | 219 | 88 |
| Detroit | 78 | 37 | 29 | 12 | 265 | 243 | 86 |
| Toronto | 78 | 27 | 41 | 10 | 247 | 279 | 64 |
| Vancouver | 78 | 22 | 47 | 9 | 233 | 339 | 53 |
| NY Islanders | 78 | 12 | 60 | 6 | 170 | 347 | 30 |

**West Division**

| Team | GP | W | L | T | GF | GA | PTS |
|------|----|----|----|----|----|----|----|
| Chicago | 78 | 42 | 27 | 9 | 284 | 225 | 93 |
| Philadelphia | 78 | 37 | 30 | 11 | 296 | 256 | 85 |
| Minnesota | 78 | 37 | 30 | 11 | 254 | 230 | 85 |
| St. Louis | 78 | 32 | 34 | 12 | 233 | 251 | 76 |
| Pittsburgh | 78 | 32 | 37 | 9 | 257 | 265 | 73 |
| Los Angeles | 78 | 31 | 36 | 11 | 232 | 245 | 73 |
| Atlanta | 78 | 25 | 38 | 15 | 191 | 239 | 65 |
| California | 78 | 16 | 46 | 16 | 213 | 323 | 48 |

**Leading Scorers**

| Player | Club | GP | G | A | PTS | PIM |
|--------|------|----|----|----|----|----|
| Esposito, Phil | Boston | 78 | 55 | 75 | 130 | 87 |
| Clarke, Bobby | Philadelphia | 78 | 37 | 67 | 104 | 80 |
| Orr, Bobby | Boston | 63 | 29 | 72 | 101 | 99 |
| MacLeish, Rick | Philadelphia | 78 | 50 | 50 | 100 | 69 |
| Lemaire, Jacques | Montreal | 77 | 44 | 51 | 95 | 16 |
| Ratelle, Jean | NY Rangers | 78 | 41 | 53 | 94 | 12 |
| Redmond, Mickey | Detroit | 76 | 52 | 41 | 93 | 24 |
| Bucyk, John | Boston | 78 | 40 | 53 | 93 | 12 |
| Mahovlich, Frank | Montreal | 78 | 38 | 55 | 93 | 51 |
| Pappin, Jim | Chicago | 76 | 41 | 51 | 92 | 82 |

**NHL Award Winners**

| | |
|---|---|
| **Hart (MVP)** | Bobby Clarke |
| **Art Ross (Leading Scorer)** | Phil Esposito |
| **Calder (Rookie of the Year)** | Steve Vickers |
| **Vezina (Lowest Goals-Against)** | Ken Dryden |
| **Lady Byng (Gentlemanly Conduct)** | Gilbert Perreault |
| **Norris (Top Defenseman)** | Bobby Orr |
| **Conn Smythe (Playoff MVP)** | Yvan Cournoyer |
| **Patrick (Service to US Hockey)** | Walter L. Bush, Jr. |
| **Masterton (Perseverance)** | Lowell MacDonald |
| **Pearson (NHLPA MVP)** | Phil Esposito |
| **First Overall Draft Selection** | Denis Potvin |
| **World/Olympic Champions** | Soviet Union |
| **WHA Avco Cup Champions** | New England Whalers |
| **AHL Calder Cup Champions** | Cincinnati Swords |
| **Memorial Cup Canadian Jr. Champions** | Toronto Marlboros |
| **NCAA Champions** | Wisconsin |
| **Canadian College Champions** | University of Toronto |

# 1973–1974

Toronto Maple Leafs and Philadelphia Flyers were at the forefront of two new hockey trends. Philadelphia had won its first West Division championship with a small, fast-skating team that was easily handled in the play-offs by the St. Louis Blues. In 1972, Flyer management began to draft big, tough players. The style of play of the revamped Flyers was similar to that of the "Big, Bad Bruins" of the early 1970s. It featured rugged, intimidating players throughout the lineup. The disturbing side effect of the Flyers' style of hockey was that, because of its success in an era when expansion had thinned out the hockey talent pool, other teams felt obliged to get their own big, tough players. Shortly after being pushed around by the Flyers early in the 1973–74 season, the Pittsburgh Penguins combed the league and came up with Bob "Battleship" Kelly and Steve Durbano. Going against this trend of playing a grinding game was the arrival of two Swedish players in the NHL, as Borje Salming and Inge Hammarstrom brought their stylish play to the Toronto Maple Leafs.

The Montreal Canadiens were stunned by the retirement of goaltender Ken Dryden. Dryden, who had graduated from law school, chose to start work with a Toronto law firm. Bernie Parent returned to the Flyers after a year with the Philadelphia Blazers of the WHA. He quickly recorded back-to-back shutouts and shared goaltending's top award, the Vezina Trophy, with the Hawks' Tony Esposito. Derek Sanderson jumped from the WHA's Blazers back to the Bruins, but his return did little to solidify the Boston team. He was suspended after missing a team flight and fighting in the Bruins' dressing room with teammate Terry O'Reilly. Two Bruins returned from injuries: Phil Esposito fired his 400th goal against Vancouver in the season opener and Bobby Orr picked up seven points in a 10–2 November triumph over the Rangers. This set yet another record for

Although the "Big Bad Bruins" finished first overall in 1973–74, it was the bigger and "badder" Philadelphia Flyers who took home the Stanley Cup, knocking off the Bruins in a six-game final. Philadelphia's victory owed a lot to the goaltending of Bernie Parent, seen here robbing Wayne Cashman of a goal during Cup play.

Boston Bruins right winger Ken Hodge sports the fashionably shaggy hair of the early 1970s, but there was nothing shaggy about his 50-goal, 105-point season in 1973–74.

Orr. In an 8–0 win over Detroit, Orr recorded his 453rd assist to break Doug Harvey's mark for career assists by a defenseman. No fewer than three of the league's top centermen attained the 1,000-point plateau. The Blackhawks' Stan Mikita reached the milestone on November 3, while Henri Richard joined the elite circle with an assist on December 20. On his way to his fourth scoring title in five years, Esposito reached the 1,000-point mark on February 15, 1974.

The game lost one of its all-time great defensemen when Tim Horton of the Buffalo Sabres died in a car accident on February 21. Despite the rigors of 22 NHL seasons, Horton was the mainstay of the Sabre defense. Earlier in the year, Gilbert Perreault was lost to the team with a broken leg. The absence of these two players prevented Buffalo from reaching the playoffs.

The Flyers were hockey's Cinderella team, winning the West Division with a surprising 112 points. Bernie Parent's stingy goaltending and the fine defensive play of Joe Watson, Ed Van Impe and Barry Ashbee made the Flyers one of the NHL's best clubs. The offense was sparked by snipers Rick MacLeish and Bill Barber and the dominant presence of captain Bobby Clarke. Clarke, a frail-looking center, played with a white-hot intensity that was an inspiration to his teammates. The Atlanta Flames made the playoffs in only their second year of operation.

In the opening round of the playoffs, the high-powered Boston offense, boasting the NHL's top four scorers, swept the Leafs in four straight games. In the other East Division series, New York and Montreal split their first four games with two wins apiece. The Rangers trailed 2–1 in the dying minutes of game five in the Montreal Forum. New York goaltender Eddie Giacomin was removed for an extra attacker with a minute left to play. Hab netminder Bunny Larocque juggled Brad Park's bullet drive from the point and Bruce MacGregor pounced on the rebound to jam home the equalizer. The Rangers went on to win in overtime, with Ron Harris the unlikely hero. The Rangers won game six and the series with a 5–2 win in Madison Square Garden.

## 7. The Universal Draft

Prior to expansion in 1967–68, talented hockey players were often relegated to long careers in the minor leagues. In the era of the original six, team rosters changed little from season to season. Movement usually came as a result of trades or by unprotected players being selected by other NHL clubs during the intra-league draft. Each of the NHL's six clubs had an established feeder system that included farm teams in the American, Central and/or Western Hockey Leagues, one or more junior clubs and sponsorship agreements with juvenile or community club teams. The six clubs had divided Canada into territories from which each was entitled to pick the best young players. Promising players as young as 13 or 14 years of age were asked to sign a letter of intent known as a "C-form," which tied the aspiring NHLer's professional playing rights to one NHL organization which would assign the player to a club in its feeder system. In many cases, players had to leave high school to report to junior teams far from home in order to progress in their parent clubs' systems.

When expansion doubled the number of players and teams in the NHL, the old system of territorial picks became impractical. It was determined that every player under the age of 20 not already under contract to a sponsored junior club was to be treated as a free agent. The expansion draft of June,

The NHL Entry Draft is held annually in June.

1967 shifted many veteran professional players from the farm clubs of the original six teams to the rosters of the six new NHL organizations and reduced the log-jam of talented hockey players at the top levels of the professional game. This enabled young players graduating into the professional ranks to reach the NHL in fewer seasons, although this change occurred gradually, as the NHL's clubs were still made up of veteran pros in the first post-expansion seasons. For example, the average age of the Pittsburgh Penguins in 1968 was more than 29 and, in 1969, goaltender Marv Edwards and forward Bob Barlow entered the NHL as 34-year-old rookies. By 1974, the average age of players on NHL rosters at the beginning of the season had dropped to just slightly over 26.

Sponsorship of junior hockey clubs had been shifted from NHL organizations to the Canadian Amateur Hockey Association (CAHA). All players at the junior level were required to sign CAHA registration cards. The CAHA collected a development grant from the NHL and fees from NHL clubs drafting junior players, and would in turn distribute these funds to the individual junior clubs, with additional amounts allocated to junior operators who produced players selected in the draft. In the late 1970s, the CAHA's role was assumed by the Canadian Major Junior Hockey League, which was composed of the Ontario, Quebec and western major junior circuits.

By the 1969 amateur draft, almost all of those junior players under contract to NHL organizations had finished

their junior eligibility and most of the top players in junior and college hockey were available to every NHL club in a universal draft. Clubs selected in reverse order of regular-season finish, with the team having the fewest points picking first. Draft positions could be traded or swapped in intra-league deals. Eighty-four players were drafted in 1969. Sam Pollock, general manager of the Canadiens, had obtained the first two selections in the draft, and used them to acquire Rejean Houle and Marc Tardif. Philadelphia took Bobby Clarke with its pick in the second round. In subsequent seasons, it became apparent that most successful teams had been built by drafting their top players rather than by trading to acquire them.

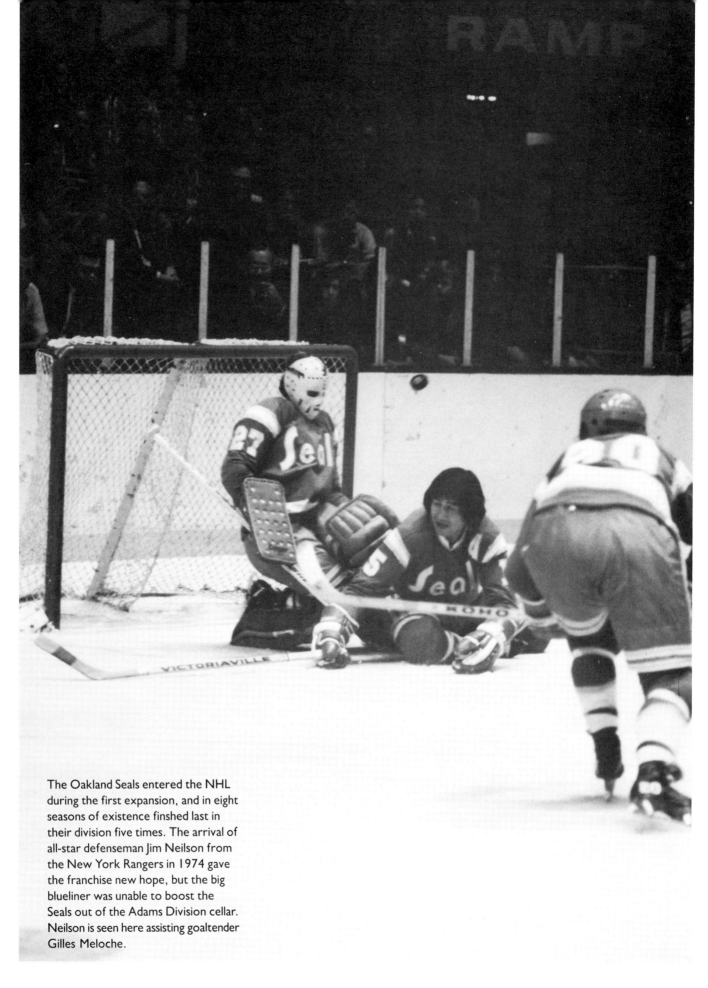

The Oakland Seals entered the NHL during the first expansion, and in eight seasons of existence finshed last in their division five times. The arrival of all-star defenseman Jim Neilson from the New York Rangers in 1974 gave the franchise new hope, but the big blueliner was unable to boost the Seals out of the Adams Division cellar. Neilson is seen here assisting goaltender Gilles Meloche.

Rick Martin's 52-goal output was second only to Phil Esposito's 68 in 1973–74. Martin finished with 86 points, but the Sabres finished fifth in the East Division and out of the playoffs.

Philadelphia continued to win in post-season play, sidelining Atlanta in four straight. The Blackhawks eliminated Los Angeles in five games in a series marked by a lack of offense. The Hawks outscored the Kings 10–7 in the series, winning game three 1–0 despite being outshot 32–10.

The Rangers/Flyers series was a hard-fought seven-game battle. In game four, Flyer defenseman Barry Ashbee was hit in the eye by a Dale Rolfe slapshot. This proved to be a career-ending injury. The deciding game in the Spectrum was a

classic, as the Flyers held on to preserve a 4–3 win that featured fabulous saves by Philadelphia's Bernie Parent in the final period. Boston mastered the Blackhawks' defensive style in their series, winning in six games to advance to the Stanley Cup final.

Bobby Orr was the hero of game one at the Boston Garden as he potted the winner at 19:38 of the third period. The second game saw Philadelphia's Moose Dupont force overtime with a goal in the last minute of regulation time, and Bobby Clarke evened the series with a goal early

Bobby Orr of the Boston Bruins and Yvan Cournoyer of the Montreal Canadiens, at right, were two of the strongest and fastest skaters ever to play in the NHL. Both players' careers were ended in 1978–79 by recurring injuries.

in the overtime session. The Flyers won both games in the Spectrum to take a commanding lead in the series, but the Bruins roared back with a 5–1 victory at home. The sixth game, played in the Spectrum, began with singer Kate Smith's rousing crowd-assisted version of the song "God Bless America." This Flyers' good luck charm appeared to work, as the Flyers made a first period goal by Rick MacLeish stand up and skated off with a 1–0 win and the Stanley Cup. Bernie Parent's outstanding performance in the playoffs earned him the Conn Smythe Trophy.

The Philadelphia victory was important to the NHL. It demonstrated the approaching parity between expansion and established clubs.

In the off-season, the NHL sponsored an international floor hockey tournament held in conjunction with the Canadian Special Olympics for the mentally retarded in Winnipeg from June 13 to 15. Every club in the league sponsored a team in the tournament, with an NHL player serving as coach for each team.

# YEAR                          1973-74

**Stanley Cup Champion**          Philadelphia Flyers
**Prince of Wales Trophy Winner**  Boston Bruins
**Clarence Campbell Bowl Winner**  Philadelphia Flyers

**Final Standings**

**East Division**

| Team | GP | W | L | T | GF | GA | PTS |
|------|----|----|----|----|----|----|----|
| Boston | 78 | 52 | 17 | 9 | 349 | 221 | 113 |
| Montreal | 78 | 45 | 24 | 9 | 293 | 240 | 99 |
| NY Rangers | 78 | 40 | 24 | 14 | 300 | 251 | 94 |
| Toronto | 78 | 35 | 27 | 16 | 274 | 230 | 86 |
| Buffalo | 78 | 32 | 34 | 12 | 242 | 250 | 76 |
| Detroit | 78 | 29 | 39 | 10 | 255 | 319 | 68 |
| Vancouver | 78 | 24 | 43 | 11 | 224 | 296 | 59 |
| NY Islanders | 78 | 19 | 41 | 18 | 182 | 247 | 56 |

**West Division**

| Team | GP | W | L | T | GF | GA | PTS |
|------|----|----|----|----|----|----|----|
| Philadelphia | 78 | 50 | 16 | 12 | 273 | 164 | 112 |
| Chicago | 78 | 41 | 14 | 23 | 272 | 164 | 105 |
| Los Angeles | 78 | 33 | 33 | 12 | 233 | 231 | 78 |
| Atlanta | 78 | 30 | 34 | 14 | 214 | 238 | 74 |
| Pittsburgh | 78 | 28 | 41 | 9 | 242 | 273 | 65 |
| St. Louis | 78 | 26 | 40 | 12 | 206 | 248 | 64 |
| Minnesota | 78 | 23 | 38 | 17 | 235 | 275 | 63 |
| California | 78 | 13 | 55 | 10 | 195 | 342 | 36 |

**Leading Scorers**

| Player | Club | GP | G | A | PTS | PIM |
|--------|------|----|----|----|----|----|
| Esposito, Phil | Boston | 78 | 68 | 77 | 145 | 58 |
| Orr, Bobby | Boston | 74 | 32 | 90 | 122 | 82 |
| Hodge, Ken | Boston | 76 | 50 | 55 | 105 | 43 |
| Cashman, Wayne | Boston | 78 | 30 | 59 | 89 | 111 |
| Clarke, Bobby | Philadelphia | 77 | 35 | 52 | 87 | 113 |
| Martin, Rick | Buffalo | 78 | 52 | 34 | 86 | 38 |
| Apps, Syl | Pittsburgh | 75 | 24 | 61 | 85 | 37 |
| Sittler, Darryl | Toronto | 78 | 38 | 46 | 84 | 55 |
| MacDonald, Lowell | Pittsburgh | 78 | 43 | 39 | 82 | 14 |

**NHL Award Winners**

| | |
|---|---|
| **Hart (MVP)** | Phil Esposito |
| **Art Ross (Leading Scorer)** | Phil Esposito |
| **Calder (Rookie of the Year)** | Denis Potvin |
| **Vezina (Lowest Goals-Against)** | Bernie Parent, Tony Esposito (tie) |
| **Lady Byng (Gentlemanly Conduct)** | John Bucyk |
| **Norris (Top Defenseman)** | Bobby Orr |
| **Conn Smythe (Playoff MVP)** | Bernie Parent |
| **Patrick (Service to US Hockey)** | Alex Delvecchio, Murray Murdoch, Weston Adams, Sr., Charles Crovat |
| **Masterton (Perseverance)** | Henri Richard |
| **Pearson (NHLPA MVP)** | Bobby Clarke |
| **Adams (Coach of the Year)** | Fred Shero |
| **First Overall Draft Selection** | Greg Joly |
| **World/Olympic Champions** | Soviet Union |
| **WHA Avco Cup Champions** | Houston Aeros |
| **AHL Calder Cup Champions** | Hershey Bears |
| **Memorial Cup Canadian Jr. Champions** | Regina Pats |
| **NCAA Champions** | Minnesota |
| **Canadian College Champions** | University of Waterloo |

# 1974–1975

The photographer of the shot below was one of the few people who looked up to the Washington Capitals during their first year in the NHL. The team finished the 1974–75 season with a monumental 446 goals against, a league record. At left, team captain Doug Mohns observes the play of his teammates.

Could the NHL continue to expand? Milt Schmidt, general manager of the new Washington Capitals, and Sid Abel, his counterpart for the new Kansas City Scouts, would put this question to the test. The price tag on an NHL franchise remained at six million dollars. The sixteen existing NHL teams were allowed to protect 15 skaters and two goaltenders in the expansion draft. That left only two players from each team available to the new franchises. With the WHA still offering contracts to players with NHL experience, the talent supply was spread thinly. This filtered down into the minor leagues, as many big-league teams began to share minor-league operations, thereby halving the number of non-NHL professionals they needed under contract.

Abe Pollin, owner of the Capitals, paid $2.5 million to sign his top five amateur draft picks. But the Caps set an NHL record for fewest points in a season, with only eight wins. The team had three coaches—Jim Anderson, George "Red" Sullivan and Schmidt all took a turn behind the bench. Kansas City owner Edwin G. Thompson, a real estate developer, fared little better. A construction strike threatened to prevent completion of the Kemper Arena in time for the club's home opener. It took a three-year, $500,000 contract to prevent their first-round draft choice, Wilf Paiement, from jumping to the WHA. The Scouts received some fine goaltending from Denis Herron and Peter MacDuffe as well as benefiting from a strong effort from their captain Simon Nolet.

With the addition of the Scouts and Capitals, the NHL changed its alignment, adopting a two-conference, four-division setup. One two-division grouping was called the Prince of Wales Conference while the other bore the name of league president Clarence Campbell. The Campbell Conference consisted of the

In 1974–75, Philadelphia goaltender Bernie Parent won both the Vezina and the Conn Smythe trophies, as well as adding his name to the Stanley Cup.

Lester Patrick Division (Atlanta, NY Islanders, NY Rangers and Philadelphia) and the Conn Smythe Division (Chicago, Kansas City, Minnesota, St. Louis and Vancouver). The Prince of Wales Conference encompassed the James Norris Division (Detroit, Los Angeles, Montreal, Pittsburgh and Washington) and the Charles F. Adams Division (Boston, Buffalo, Toronto and California). A new playoff format would entitle 12 teams to play in the postseason. The top team in each division earned a bye from the first round of the playoffs, while the second and the third teams would play in a best-of-three preliminary series. The four second-place and four third-place teams that played in the preliminary round would be ranked by points in the final regular-season standings. The team with the most points would play the team with the least; the team with the second-most would play the team with the second-least, etc.

Injuries beset the New York Rangers when Rod Seiling tore his knee ligaments, Walt Tkaczuk broke his leg, Ron Harris broke his hip, Brad Park strained a knee, and Dale Rolfe suffered a compound ankle fracture that ended his career. The Rangers still managed to finish second to Philadelphia in the Patrick Division. The Flyers went on a late season streak, winning 12 and tying two of their final 14 games. Philadelphia, Montreal and Buffalo all finished with 113 points, but the Flyers were ranked first overall and awarded home-ice advantage in the playoffs by virtue of more wins.

The Bruins' duo of Orr and Esposito finished first and second in the scoring race as big Phil joined the 500-goal club with a marker on December 22, 1974 in a 5–4 win against Detroit. Two other superstars eclipsed club scoring standards when Marcel Dionne broke Gordie Howe's team record for assists (59) and points (103) en route to a 47-goal, 74-assist and 121-point season. And, Guy Lafleur began to fulfill the promise he had shown as a junior, scoring 53 goals to break the single-season Canadiens' team record held by former Hab greats Boom-Boom Geoffrion and Rocket Richard.

The best-of-three elimination series saw major upsets. The Los Angeles Kings posted the finest regular season

*(continued on page 62)*

## 8. The World Hockey Association

Just as the National Football League and the National Basketball Association were challenged by rival leagues in the 1960s, the NHL was confronted by a new league in 1972. The financial success of the NHL's expansion convinced Santa Ana, California, attorney Gary Davidson and promoter Dennis Murphy to launch a new league with the grandiose title of the World Hockey Association. It was Davidson's plan to induce athletes to jump to the new league by operating without a reserve or option clause in players' contracts. The reserve clause in NHL contracts prohibited players from offering their services to other teams by binding them to their original clubs, effectively holding salaries down. Davidson felt that by eliminating the reserve clause, WHA players and owners would share an equal interest in the success of the new league. The WHA filed its articles of incorporation on July 10, 1971 and held a draft of the negotiating rights to NHL and other professional players on February 12, 1972.

Beginning with goaltender Bernie Parent, a number of established NHLers signed contracts with WHA teams. The biggest star to jump to the new league was Bobby Hull, who was coming off a 50-goal season with Chicago. Hull signed a ten-year deal with the Winnipeg Jets that included a one-million-dollar

signing bonus. This bonus was an expense shared by every team in the WHA, as Hull's acquisition was recognized as an important image-builder for the new circuit and a sign to all NHL players that the new league was a genuine alternative.

Almost every NHL club saw players jump to the WHA. The Stanley Cup champion Boston Bruins lost goaltender Gerry Cheevers, defenseman Ted Green and forwards Derek Sanderson and John McKenzie. Defenseman J.C. Tremblay left the Montreal Canadiens. The New York Islanders, whose first NHL season coincided with the start-up of the WHA, were deprived of seven of the 20 players they had chosen in the NHL expansion draft. In order to keep their first draft choice — Billy Harris, a junior star from the Toronto Marlboros — the Islanders signed him to the richest rookie contract in NHL history: a three-year deal worth $100,000 per season. The Toronto Maple Leafs were hit even harder, losing 11 players from their organization. In addition to Bernie Parent, defensemen Rick Ley and Brad Selwood and forwards Guy Trottier and Jim Harrison jumped leagues, and Larry Pleau, a player Toronto had picked up from the Canadiens' organization in the off-season, decided to play for the WHA's New England Whalers. The Leafs' top scorers of 1971–72, Dave Keon, Paul Henderson and Norm Ullman, were all WHAers by 1975.

The NHL filed suit against

THE AVCO WORLD TROPHY

those players who had jumped to the WHA, claiming that the reserve clause in each player's contract bound him to his NHL club. The WHA countered with a $57-million anti-trust suit against the NHL, claiming that the reserve clause represented an unfair monopoly. Many of the WHA's star attractions stayed out of uniform until November, when a ruling from the Federal District Court in Philadelphia allowed them to play in the new league.

The WHA's first season saw 12 teams compete in two divisions. New England defeated Winnipeg four games

to one in the league's first championship series. In the second season, the Houston Aeros convinced Gordie Howe to abandon a two-year retirement from active play to join his sons Mark and Marty on an all-Howe forward line. Frank Mahovlich joined the Toronto Toros and Rejean Houle and Marc Tardif, the two top draft picks of the Montreal Canadiens in 1969, joined the WHA Quebec Nordiques.

As early as April, 1973, secret meetings were held between WHA officials and an NHL contingent led by Bill Jennings of the New York Rangers. Though no deal was immediately forthcoming, an eventual agreement was reached on March 31, 1979, when four WHA franchises — Edmonton, New England (Hartford), Quebec and Winnipeg — became part of the NHL. These four new clubs began play in the NHL in 1979–80.

The seven-year existence of the WHA had lasting effects on North American professional hockey. By creating competition, it forced salaries up in the NHL. Before the new league began play, the average NHL salary was $22,000. After the WHA, this average had jumped to over $100,000. The WHA also introduced many European players to North American hockey audiences. The Swedes, Czechs and Finns who played in the WHA introduced an exotic element to the game in the United States and Canada and proved they could stand up to the rigors of North American hockey.

Veteran left winger Jean-Paul Parise, at right, came to the fledgling New York Islanders from the Minnesota North Stars during the 1974–75 season, and counted 30 points in 41 games.

Buffalo reached the Stanley Cup finals in 1974–75, after a 113-point regular season and a six-game semi-final victory over Montreal. Defenseman Jocelyn Guevremont, below, was acquired in a trade with Vancouver at the beginning of the season and helped make the Sabres one of the NHL's top clubs.

in their history, earning 105 points, but were eliminated in three games by the Leafs. The New York Islanders eliminated their crosstown rivals the Rangers on an overtime marker by J.P. Parise. The Blackhawks were bombed 8–2 in their series opener, but rebounded to send the Bruins to the sidelines. The Penguins made short work of the Blues, winning in two straight games. The Flyers eliminated the Leafs in the quarter-final, requiring the minimum four games. Buffalo skated past the Hawks in a five-game series while Montreal disposed of a feisty Canucks team in five.

Easily the most thrilling series was that between the Penguins and Islanders. It appeared that the Isles would be eliminated when they lost the first three games of the series, but came back, becoming the first club since the 1942 Leafs to erase a three-game deficit. Eddie Westfall scored the only goal in the 1–0 Islander victory in the seventh game.

The semi-final between Montreal and Buffalo demonstrated the value of home-ice advantage. Buffalo opened the series with two victories in the Auditorium and Montreal took both contests in the Forum. The Sabres needed an overtime goal from Rene Robert to win the fifth game. In game six the Sabres built an early 4–1 lead, and hung on to win despite two late Montreal goals.

Centerman Jim Hrycuik, 25, above, wearing the snow-white pants of the early Washington Capitals, topples Ranger goalie Ed Giacomin to record the first goal in Cap history. Hrycuik scored five times in his brief NHL career.

Ron Schock, left, top, led Pittsburgh to that franchise's best-ever record as the club finished with 89 points in 1974–75. The Penguins lost only five of 40 home games and captain Schock recorded 86 points.

With the departure of brother Bobby to the WHA, Dennis Hull, left, bottom, emerged as an NHL star in his own right. His thunderous shot bore the Hull trademark, and in 13 seasons with the Blackhawks he fired nearly 300 goals.

In the other semi-final, the Islanders were working some of their playoff magic against the Flyers. The Flyers encountered little resistance in winning the first three games, when astonishingly, the Islanders fought back to win the next three and send the series to a deciding game. The Flyers, with Kate Smith singing "God Bless America," took the seventh game 4–1.

It had taken eight years for the NHL to produce its first all-expansion Stanley Cup final. It was the Broad Street Bullies trying to stop the French Connection. Again, home ice was an important advantage. The Flyers behind the red-hot goaltending of Bernie Parent won the first two games 4–1 and 2–1 at the Spectrum. Rene Robert provided overtime heroics in game three when his slapshot

found the net late in the first extra stanza. The Sabres were full value for a hard fought 4–2 triumph in game four. The Flyers coasted to a 5–1 home-ice decision the next game. Game six was highlighted by brilliant netminding at both ends of the rink. Roger Crozier replaced Gerry Desjardins between the pipes for Buffalo and matched Parent save for save. In the third period, Bob Kelly bulled his way in from behind the net to jam in the game's first goal. The Flyers checked the Sabres closely as the game wore on before Bill Clement added the Cup-clinching goal late in the game. Philadelphia had answered their critics with a second consecutive Stanley Cup triumph. Bernie Parent became the first player to win the Conn Smythe Trophy in consecutive seasons.

# YEAR                                 1974-75

**Stanley Cup Champion**             Philadelphia Flyers
**Prince of Wales Trophy Winner**    Buffalo Sabres
**Clarence Campbell Bowl Winner**    Philadelphia Flyers

## Final Standings

### PRINCE OF WALES CONFERENCE

#### Norris Division

| Team | GP | W | L | T | GF | GA | PTS |
|------|----|----|----|----|----|----|----|
| Montreal | 80 | 47 | 14 | 19 | 374 | 225 | 113 |
| Los Angeles | 80 | 42 | 17 | 21 | 269 | 185 | 105 |
| Pittsburgh | 80 | 37 | 28 | 15 | 326 | 289 | 89 |
| Detroit | 80 | 23 | 45 | 12 | 259 | 335 | 58 |
| Washington | 80 | 8 | 67 | 5 | 181 | 446 | 21 |

#### Adams Division

| Team | GP | W | L | T | GF | GA | PTS |
|------|----|----|----|----|----|----|----|
| Buffalo | 80 | 49 | 16 | 15 | 354 | 240 | 113 |
| Boston | 80 | 40 | 26 | 14 | 345 | 245 | 94 |
| Toronto | 80 | 31 | 33 | 16 | 280 | 309 | 78 |
| California | 80 | 19 | 48 | 13 | 212 | 316 | 51 |

### CLARENCE CAMPBELL CONFERENCE

#### Patrick Division

| Team | GP | W | L | T | GF | GA | PTS |
|------|----|----|----|----|----|----|----|
| Philadelphia | 80 | 51 | 18 | 11 | 293 | 181 | 113 |
| NY Rangers | 80 | 37 | 29 | 14 | 319 | 276 | 88 |
| NY Islanders | 80 | 33 | 25 | 22 | 264 | 221 | 88 |
| Atlanta | 80 | 34 | 31 | 15 | 243 | 233 | 83 |

#### Smythe Division

| Team | GP | W | L | T | GF | GA | PTS |
|------|----|----|----|----|----|----|----|
| Vancouver | 80 | 38 | 32 | 10 | 271 | 254 | 86 |
| St. Louis | 80 | 35 | 31 | 14 | 269 | 267 | 84 |
| Chicago | 80 | 37 | 35 | 8 | 268 | 241 | 82 |
| Minnesota | 80 | 23 | 50 | 7 | 221 | 341 | 53 |
| Kansas City | 80 | 15 | 54 | 11 | 184 | 328 | 41 |

## Leading Scorers

| Player | Club | GP | G | A | PTS | PIM |
|--------|------|----|----|----|----|----|
| Orr, Bobby | Boston | 80 | 46 | 89 | 135 | 101 |
| Esposito, Phil | Boston | 79 | 61 | 66 | 127 | 62 |
| Dionne, Marcel | Detroit | 80 | 47 | 74 | 121 | 14 |
| Lafleur, Guy | Montreal | 70 | 53 | 66 | 119 | 37 |
| Mahovlich, Pete | Montreal | 80 | 35 | 82 | 117 | 64 |
| Clarke, Bobby | Philadelphia | 80 | 27 | 89 | 116 | 125 |
| Robert, Rene | Buffalo | 74 | 40 | 60 | 100 | 75 |
| Gilbert, Rod | NY Rangers | 76 | 36 | 61 | 97 | 22 |
| Perreault, Gilbert | Buffalo | 68 | 39 | 57 | 96 | 36 |
| Martin, Rick | Buffalo | 68 | 52 | 43 | 95 | 72 |

## NHL Award Winners

| | |
|---|---|
| **Hart (MVP)** | Bobby Clarke |
| **Art Ross (Leading Scorer)** | Bobby Orr |
| **Calder (Rookie of the Year)** | Eric Vail |
| **Vezina (Lowest Goals-Against)** | Bernie Parent |
| **Lady Byng (Gentlemanly Conduct)** | Marcel Dionne |
| **Norris (Top Defenseman)** | Bobby Orr |
| **Conn Smythe (Playoff MVP)** | Bernie Parent |
| **Patrick (Service to US Hockey)** | Donald M. Clark, Bill Chadwick, Tommy Ivan |
| **Masterton (Perseverance)** | Don Luce |
| **Pearson (NHLPA MVP)** | Bobby Orr |
| **Adams (Coach of the Year)** | Bob Pulford |
| **First Overall Draft Selection** | Mel Bridgman |
| **World/Olympic Champions** | Soviet Union |
| **WHA Avco Cup Champions** | Houston Aeros |
| **AHL Calder Cup Champions** | Springfield Indians |
| **Memorial Cup Canadian Jr. Champions** | Toronto Marlboros |
| **NCAA Champions** | Michigan Tech |
| **Canadian College Champions** | University of Alberta |

# 1975–1976

The Philadelphia Flyers were seeking their third straight Stanley Cup championship in 1975–76. Marcel Dionne, unhappy playing in Detroit, was determined to move to another NHL team. New ownership was found for two financially troubled franchises: San Francisco businessman Mel Swig purchased the California Golden Seals, and Wren Blair, Al Savill and Nick Frenzel paid $4.4 million for the bankrupt Pittsburgh Penguins.

The NHL lost NBC as a broadcaster when the Game of the Week telecast was canceled due to poor ratings.

The NHL and the NHL Players' Association signed a five-year collective bargaining agreement. Under this new agreement, a player playing out his option with one club could only be signed by another club after his original team had received compensation. By signing this new collective bargaining agreement, the NHL Players' Association formally acknowledged the owners' right to compensation for players lost to free agency.

The Los Angeles Kings acquired the services of the multi-talented Marcel Dionne. Dionne's former club, Detroit, received Dan Maloney and Terry Harper as compensation. Ron Ellis of Toronto and Henri Richard of Montreal announced their retirements. Goaltender Ken Dryden returned to active duty, after one year out of hockey. Bobby Orr was lost to the Bruins with another knee operation. Emile Francis, general manager of the Rangers, put his entire roster on waivers in an attempt to counteract the indifferent play of his club. When the smoke cleared, Gilles Villemure and Ed Giacomin, New York's two goaltenders, had moved to Detroit and Chicago respectively. In a blockbuster deal on November 7, the Rangers shipped Jean Ratelle, Brad Park and Joe Zanussi to the Bruins for Phil Esposito and Carol Vadnais — the decade's biggest single NHL trade. On October 30, Johnny Bucyk added his name to the short list of 500 goal scorers in a 3–2 victory over St. Louis. Later in the year he passed Alex Delvecchio, moving into second place on the all-time scoring list.

Two Soviet club teams arrived in North American in late December to play an eight-game series with NHL teams. Central Red Army skated to 7–3 triumph over the Rangers before a packed house in Madison Square Garden. The Soviet Wings jumped to a 5–0 lead and held off Pittsburgh to win 7–4. In what many hockey fans consider to be the greatest game of all time, Red Army and the Canadiens skated to a 3–3 tie in the Montreal Forum on New Year's Eve, 1975. Goaltender Vladislav Tretiak played marvelously as the Canadiens held a wide 38–13 margin in shots on goal. The Buffalo Sabres had the old Memorial Auditorium in a happy uproar when they defeated the Soviet Wings 12–6. The Wings rebounded to edge Chicago 4–2, while Red Army defeated the Bruins by a 5–2 count.

The final match of the series featured the Stanley Cup champion Philadelphia

Gilles Gilbert lost only eight of the 51 games in which he played for the Boston Bruins in 1975–76.

Goaltender Tony Esposito, top, and defenseman Keith Magnuson, bottom, played for the Chicago Blackhawks throughout the 1970s. They were products of American college hockey, Esposito coming from the University of Denver. The NHL switched the Hawks from the East to the West Division in 1969–70 and the club responded with four consecutive first place finishes and two berths in the Stanley Cup finals. They finished first in the Smythe Division with 82 points in 1975–76.

After several mediocre seasons with Boston and Oakland, Reggie Leach joined the Philadelphia Flyers in 1974 and scored 106 goals in his first two seasons with the team. Raised on a Manitoba Indian reserve, Reggie played his boyhood hockey in Riverton, Manitoba, where he earned the nickname "the Riverton Rifle." Note the doodle on the heel of his stick.

Flyers against Red Army in the Spectrum on January 11, 1976. In an extremely rugged encounter, the Soviet club retreated to its dressing room for 16 minutes during the first period. The Soviets left the ice after Ed Van Impe had upended and jostled Army and national team star Valery Kharlamov. When the Soviets returned to the ice, they were forechecked to perfection by the Flyers. The Flyers eventually prevailed 4–1.

The season saw some fine individual performances. Despite playing for the lowly Detroit Red Wings, goaltender Jimmy Rutherford recorded three consecutive shutouts. On February 7, the Boston Bruins brought a seven-game winning streak into the Maple Leaf Gardens only to run up against a one-man wrecking crew in Darryl Sittler. Sittler fired in six goals and had four assists in an 11–4 Leafs victory. Pittsburgh's Pierre Larouche became the NHL's youngest 50-goal scorer at just 20 years of age.

Montreal posted the league's best record with 127 points and only 11 losses. Guy Lafleur broke up the monopoly that Orr and Esposito had held on the scoring race by winning the Art Ross Trophy with 125 points. Boston, despite the loss of Bobby Orr, led the Adams Division with 113 points. Orr returned from his fourth knee operation to play in ten games and registered five goals and 13 assists. Unfortunately, Orr's knee locked while he was stepping out of a car. Another operation was required and he was lost to the Boston team for the rest of the season. Philadelphia performed well, despite losing Bernie Parent for most of the season with a neck injury. The Flyers led the Patrick Division with 118 points and received another big year from Bobby Clarke. The Rangers, despite their many deals and the dismissal of Emile Francis, failed to qualify for post-season play. The Islanders, inspired by a 98-point contribution from defenseman Denis Potvin and by the outstanding play of rookie Bryan Trottier, were the NHL's most improved team.

The preliminary series saw the Los Angeles Kings sweep the Atlanta Flames. The New York Islanders also pushed Vancouver to the sidelines in two games. The Leafs, backstopped by the

## 9. The Quest for US Television Revenue

In the days of the six-team NHL, only the two Canadian franchises — Montreal and Toronto — derived significant revenues from national television and/or radio broadcasts on the CBC. The six US cities added in the 1967–68 NHL expansion helped bring the league a new US network television deal. For five years, beginning in 1968, CBS carried a package of late-season and playoff games. NBC took over in 1973.

But hockey turned out to be too regional for the US networks — too rooted in frosty climes to appeal to viewers in sun-belt areas. Stung by low local TV ratings, southern stations exercised their right to decline to carry network hockey. National TV audiences sagged propor-tionately, and after the 1975 playoffs, the networks turn-ed to other attrations they hoped were more universally appealing.

Yet even as the doomsayers were proclaiming the death of hockey as a US sport sim-ply because its pattern of interest did not happen to parallel the distribution requirements of US net-works, NHL teams were experimenting with a new form of television distribution — cable TV — that was to become the league's largest source of broadcast revenue.

In Buffalo and New York City, cable TV operators, rec-ognizing the passionate rela-tionship between the hockey fan and his or her local team, purchased and showed Sabres' and Rangers' home games to help build viewing audiences for their new ser-vices. These experiments were successful, and the alli-ance between NHL teams and cable systems spread to other cities.

Soon the average 20 to 25 over-the-air local telecasts traditionally mounted each season by most US teams had been augmented by cable to the point at which many teams offered more than 60 games on a combination of standard TV and cable TV. As a result, total local broadcasting reve-nues began to surpass what had been received from the networks in the past.

Along with this renaissance of local broadcast activity came a technological advance that opened up new opportu-nities for national distribution of NHL games — the satellite. This now-commonplace de-vice spawned national cable program services such as ESPN, USA Network, Cable News Network and the like. The NHL was a pioneer on national cable, starting ser-vice in 1979 with what is now USA Network.

By the 1980s, the NHL, heartened by the new strength of its local team broadcast packages and im-pressed by the potential of national cable, made a con-scious decision to ignore the US TV networks as a vehicle for broadcast revenue and ex-posure. Instead, each NHL team concentrated on the growth of its local TV/cable package, while the league sought to expand overall ex-posure on national cable.

Key to the development of local TV/cable packages was an NHL policy under which the national cable networks did not pre-empt the local broadcaster in a game aired nationally — a change from the ways of the major US TV networks.

Twenty years after the first NHL expansion, US TV reve-nues are at an all-time high. More than two-thirds of US team games are aired locally, while the NHL's national car-rier, ESPN, showed 33 regular-season games, plus a record 37 playoff games in 1986-87.

Peter Puck was created in 1973 by Hanna-Barbera Productions for NBC hockey telecasts. Peter's mandate was to interpret the intricacies of the game to novice fans, especially in NHL outposts such as Georgia and California.

Relying on masterful playmaking and skating, the Montreal Canadiens defeated the Philadelphia Flyers in four straight games to win the 1975–76 Stanley Cup final. The Montreal victory went a long way to reversing an NHL trend toward unreasonably rough hockey. Above, high-scoring Bill Barber of the Flyers jousts with low-scoring Jimmy Roberts of the Canadiens. Bobby Clarke, at right, and Serge Savard, background, appear to be awaiting the outcome.

quality goaltending of Wayne Thomas, whom the Leafs had obtained from Montreal, edged the Penguins in three games. Buffalo had some unexpected difficulty subduing St. Louis, as the Blues surprised the Sabres with a 5–2 victory in the first game. The Sabres rebounded to advance to the quarter-final with back-to-back overtime victories.

Montreal demolished Chicago with a four-game sweep in one quarter-final series; the Hawks scored only three goals. The Islanders rebounded from a two-game deficit and won four games in a row to capture their series against Buffalo. The Philadelphia/Toronto series featured brawling that caused Ontario Attorney-General Roy McMurtry to press charges against Flyers Joe Watson, Mel Bridgman and Don Saleski. Obscured by this heavy going was a five-goal performance by Darryl Sittler in game six of the se-

ries. The Flyers won the deciding game 7–3 in the Spectrum. The Boston Bruins had their hands full winning a seven-game series with the Kings.

The Boston/Philadelphia semi-final matchup showcased the goal-scoring prowess of Reggie Leach. Leach's career had been salvaged from obscurity when Bobby Clarke asked Philadelphia's management to trade for his old junior linemate—they had played together with the Flin Flon Bombers of the Western Canadian Hockey League. Leach repaid Clarke's confidence in him by scoring an overtime goal in game two to deadlock the series. Back in Philadelphia for game five, he fired five markers in the 6–3 victory that eliminated the Bruins. In the space of a few days Rocket Richard's record for goals in a playoff game had been equaled by Sittler and by Leach.

The New York Islanders' Bill Torrey

Orest Kindrachuk, a feisty centerman, had his best year with the Flyers in 1975–76, finishing with 26 goals and 49 assists for 75 points in the regular season and four goals and seven assists for 11 points in the playoffs.

believed in building his team around draft picks. This strategy was beginning to pay dividends as the Isles became the youngest NHL team ever to surpass 100 points in a season. The Canadiens eliminated the Islanders in a five-game semi-final series in which three of Montreal's wins were by one-goal margins.

The Stanley Cup final of 1976 would sharply contrast two approaches to the game: the Canadiens' skating prowess and the Flyers' tough, territorial game.

Montreal won the series opener in the Forum, 4–3, as Guy Lapointe scored with less than a minute and a half to play. Ken Dryden, who had returned from a year's sabbatical, was sharp in a 2–1 Hab victory in game two. A two-goal performance by Steve Shutt and a rare game-winner by defenseman Pierre Bouchard put the Canadiens in command with 3–2 victory and a 3–0 lead in games. The Habs ended the series on the road, winning 5–3 in the Spectrum with the winning goal coming from Guy LaFleur. Reggie Leach became the third player on a losing squad to be selected MVP of the playoffs. Leach recorded a record-setting 19 goals and a playoff-leading 24 points in 16 postseason games.

# YEAR                                    1975-76

**Stanley Cup Champion**          Montreal Canadiens
**Prince of Wales Trophy Winner**  Montreal Canadiens
**Clarence Campbell Bowl Winner**  Philadelphia Flyers

**Final Standings**

## PRINCE OF WALES CONFERENCE

### Norris Division

| Team | GP | W | L | T | GF | GA | PTS |
|------|----|----|----|----|-----|-----|-----|
| Montreal | 80 | 58 | 11 | 11 | 337 | 174 | 127 |
| Los Angeles | 80 | 38 | 33 | 9 | 263 | 265 | 85 |
| Pittsburgh | 80 | 35 | 33 | 12 | 339 | 303 | 82 |
| Detroit | 80 | 26 | 44 | 10 | 226 | 300 | 62 |
| Washington | 80 | 11 | 59 | 10 | 224 | 394 | 32 |

### Adams Division

| Team | GP | W | L | T | GF | GA | PTS |
|------|----|----|----|----|-----|-----|-----|
| Boston | 80 | 48 | 15 | 17 | 313 | 237 | 113 |
| Buffalo | 80 | 46 | 21 | 13 | 339 | 240 | 105 |
| Toronto | 80 | 34 | 31 | 15 | 294 | 276 | 83 |
| California | 80 | 27 | 42 | 11 | 250 | 278 | 65 |

## CLARENCE CAMPBELL CONFERENCE

### Patrick Division

| Team | GP | W | L | T | GF | GA | PTS |
|------|----|----|----|----|-----|-----|-----|
| Philadelphia | 80 | 51 | 13 | 16 | 348 | 209 | 118 |
| NY Islanders | 80 | 42 | 21 | 17 | 297 | 190 | 101 |
| Atlanta | 80 | 35 | 33 | 12 | 262 | 237 | 82 |
| NY Rangers | 80 | 29 | 42 | 9 | 262 | 333 | 67 |

### Smythe Division

| Team | GP | W | L | T | GF | GA | PTS |
|------|----|----|----|----|-----|-----|-----|
| Chicago | 80 | 32 | 30 | 18 | 254 | 261 | 82 |
| Vancouver | 80 | 33 | 32 | 15 | 271 | 272 | 81 |
| St. Louis | 80 | 29 | 37 | 14 | 249 | 290 | 72 |
| Minnesota | 80 | 20 | 53 | 7 | 195 | 303 | 47 |
| Kansas City | 80 | 12 | 56 | 12 | 190 | 351 | 36 |

**Leading Scorers**

| Player | Club | GP | G | A | PTS | PIM |
|--------|------|----|----|----|-----|-----|
| Lafleur, Guy | Montreal | 80 | 56 | 59 | 125 | 36 |
| Clarke, Bobby | Philadelphia | 76 | 30 | 89 | 119 | 136 |
| Perreault, Gilbert | Buffalo | 80 | 44 | 69 | 113 | 36 |
| Barber, Bill | Philadelphia | 80 | 50 | 62 | 112 | 104 |
| Larouche, Pierre | Pittsburgh | 76 | 53 | 58 | 111 | 33 |
| Ratelle, Jean | Bos., NYR | 80 | 36 | 69 | 105 | 18 |
| Mahovlich, Pete | Montreal | 80 | 34 | 71 | 105 | 76 |
| Pronovost, Jean | Pittsburgh | 80 | 52 | 52 | 104 | 24 |
| Sittler, Darryl | Toronto | 79 | 41 | 59 | 100 | 90 |
| Apps, Syl | Pittsburgh | 80 | 32 | 67 | 99 | 24 |

**NHL Award Winners**

| | |
|---|---|
| **Hart (MVP)** | Bobby Clarke |
| **Art Ross (Leading Scorer)** | Guy Lafleur |
| **Calder (Rookie of the Year)** | Bryan Trottier |
| **Vezina (Lowest Goals-Against)** | Ken Dryden |
| **Lady Byng (Gentlemanly Conduct)** | Jean Ratelle |
| **Norris (Top Defenseman)** | Denis Potvin |
| **Conn Smythe (Playoff MVP)** | Reggie Leach |
| **Patrick (Service to US Hockey)** | Stan Mikita, George A. Leader, Bruce Norris |
| **Masterton (Perseverance)** | Rod Gilbert |
| **Pearson (NHLPA MVP)** | Guy Lafleur |
| **Adams (Coach of the Year)** | Don Cherry |
| **First Overall Draft Selection** | Rick Green |
| **World/Olympic Champions** | Czechoslovakia (Olympics) Soviet Union (World Champions) |
| **WHA Avco Cup Champions** | Winnipeg Jets |
| **AHL Calder Cup Champions** | Nova Scotia Voyageurs |
| **Memorial Cup Canadian Jr. Champions** | Hamilton Fincups |
| **NCAA Champions** | Minnesota |
| **Canadian College Champions** | University of Toronto |

# 1976–1977

It would be a short summer for some of the NHL's stars as preparations began for the first six-nation Canada Cup tournament which was scheduled to begin in early September. Fans in Boston were stunned by the news that Bobby Orr had joined the Chicago Blackhawks.

The Canada Cup tournament commenced play on September 2, with Team Canada playing Finland. The tournament brought together the six major hockey-playing nations: Canada, Czechoslovakia, Finland, the Soviet Union, Sweden and the United States. It was an open competition, so NHL and WHA players were found on the rosters of all but the eastern European teams. Bobby Hull was invited to play for Team Canada and was the lone WHA representative on the team. Team Canada's lineup was a strong unit combining veterans like Hull, Esposito and Orr with rising stars like Lafleur, Dionne and Sittler. Canada won its first three games before dropping a 1–0 decision to Czechoslovakia. The team rebounded, earning a berth in the final with a 3–1 defeat of the Soviet Union. The final was a best-of-three series with the Czechs. Team Canada's offense produced six goals in the first period, while goaltender Rogie Vachon shut out the Czechs en route to a 6–0 victory. The second game was much more evenly matched. It took a goal from Bill Barber to force the contest into overtime, and Darryl Sittler netted the series winner at 11:33 of extra time.

Bobby Orr was named the outstanding Team Canada player in three of the Canadians' games and was later selected as the outstanding player of the tournament. Though hampered by his damaged knee, fans who watched him in the Canada Cup knew that his control of the pace of the game remained intact. If his knee allowed him to play for Chicago at anything approaching his level in the Canada Cup, the Blackhawks were going to be one of the league's strongest clubs. Unfortunately, while the desire burned ever brightly, Orr's knees simply could not withstand the stresses of playing hockey. The most exciting player in the game only appeared in 20 games for the Blackhawks in 1976–77.

Financial problems had become com-

During dramatic quarterfinals between Philadelphia and Toronto in 1976 and 1977, Swedish defenseman Borje Salming of the Maple Leafs matched the toughest Flyer enforcers elbow for elbow, check for check, proving to skeptics that Europeans could compete at the toughest levels of NHL play.

Right winger Al MacAdam was one of few players to distinguish himself during the short unhappy existence of the Cleveland Barons. MacAdam counted 111 points during the team's two-year whistle stop in the NHL.

mon among NHL franchises. The Kansas City Scouts were moved to Denver, where they became the Colorado Rockies. The California Golden Seals were moved to the Richfield Coliseum where they played as the Cleveland Barons. The NHL Players' Association lent the team money to get them through the season. In Atlanta, Flames' players purchased $25,000 worth of tickets to help keep the team afloat. The league stood to lose between 15 and 18 million dollars as 391,477 fewer people went through the turnstiles. The big losers were the Chicago Blackhawks, whose attendance fell off by 112,600.

The year offered some fine individual performances. Maple Leaf defenseman Ian Turnbull established a league mark for rearguards when he potted five goals in a 9–1 thrashing of Detroit on February 2, 1977. The Rangers' Don Murdoch became the first rookie to score five goals in a game since Howie Meeker in 1944. Murdoch accomplished the feat on October 12, 1976, in a 10–4 victory over Minnesota.

Philadelphia's Al Hill wrote his name into the record book with two goals and three assists in his first-ever NHL game, a 6–4 Flyer triumph in St. Louis on February 14, 1977. Former linemates Rod Gilbert and Jean Ratelle both reached the 1,000-point plateau. Gilbert scored a goal

Gilles Gratton is said to have believed that he was a reincarnated jungle cat. According to Winnipeg Jets general manager John Ferguson, Gratton once threw off his mask and gloves during a fight, began to growl, then skated up to an opposition player and pounced on him like a cat on a mouse.

on February 19 to accomplish the feat while Ratelle, who as a Ranger had been responsible for so many of Gilbert's goals, assisted on a goal to reach the mark on April 3 — as a Bruin. Stan Mikita reached the 500-goal mark on February 27 in a 4–3 loss to Vancouver.

The Montreal Canadiens followed their Stanley Cup victory in 1976 with a record-shattering season. The Habs lost only eight times enroute to a record for points with 132. They set all-time single-season records for wins with 60, and wins on the road with 27. The club had two 50-goals scorers: Steve Shutt had 60 goals and Guy Lafleur 56. Lafleur repeated as the Art Ross Trophy winner as the league's leading scorer, setting records for points and assists by a right winger with 136 and 80. He enjoyed a 28–game point-scoring streak. Ken Dryden and Bunny Larocque collected a second consecutive Vezina Trophy.

Philadelphia had another fine year, winning the Patrick Division and the Campbell Conference with 112 points. The youthful Islanders continued to improve with 106 points and 47 wins.

The preliminary rounds of the playoffs saw the Islanders defeat the Hawks and Buffalo beat the North Stars in two straight. Darryl Sittler had a hand in nine of the Leafs 13 goals as they sidelined the Penguins in three games. The Los Angeles Kings rounded out the playoff picture with a three-game decision over Atlanta.

The Canadiens hardly broke a sweat in their quarter-final series with St. Louis in which they were paced by Guy Lafleur's five goals and seven assists. The Islanders followed suit by ushering out the Sabres in the minimum required time behind the fine netminding of Billy Smith. Boston jumped to a three-game lead on the Kings, thanks in large part to Bobby Schmautz's eight goals. The Kings rebounded to take the next two games 7–4 and 3–1. Boston built a three-goal margin in the first eight minutes of game six and held on for a 4–3 victory and a berth in the semi-finals.

The Maple Leafs and Philadelphia took up right where they had left off in the previous year's postseason play. The Leafs produced the unexpected when they won twice in the Spectrum, where

# TWENTY TRENDS THAT SHAPED MODERN HOCKEY

## 10. Combatting Team Intimidation

Beginning in 1970, when the NHL instituted a rule prohibiting and fining players who left their benches to engage in on-ice altercation, the league started prescribing increasingly stiff penalties for actions calculated to provoke and intimidate the opposition. The same season also saw the beginning of more stringent anti-stick measures than had previously been in the rule book, mandating major penalties and even fines for deliberate high-sticking, slashing and spearing.

But despite these rule changes, after expansion, some NHL clubs began to build teams composed of aggressive performers whose puck-handling skills were secondary to their rugged on-ice behavior. The effect of this recruitment was to escalate the contact nature of the sport into physical mayhem. Team intimidation became more calculated, designed to make opponents reluctant to challenge for the puck.

Wild, spontaneous, "pier-six" brawls were occasional features of hockey in the six-team era, but in the years following expansion, it became apparent that existing rules to curtail these incidents did not serve adequately to deter them.

In 1971, the league strengthened the rules against bench-clearing brawls by mandating suspensions. These rules were further strengthened in 1972 by penalizing the first man to leave the bench, and in 1976 by increasing the fines. Also, in 1971, match penalties and league review were instituted for deliberately attempting to injure. Goalkeepers were also prohibited from leaving the crease to enter altercations. The NHL also instituted the "third man in" rule, forbidding a player from intervening in an altercation.

In 1974, major penalties for intentionally spearing, cross-checking and butt-ending were instituted and head-butting became a match penalty.

In 1975, the league acted to protect officials from player abuse, setting stiff penalties for players who abused officials physically or challenged or disputed the officials' calls. These rules, too, have been further strengthened as necessary.

For the first time in 1976, players who initiated fisticuffs were additionally penalized. This ruling, strengthened since its original formulation, is now called the "instigation" rule.

In 1981, players were instructed to move to neutral areas when an altercation between two opponents broke out, in order to decrease the likelihood of escalating incidents.

Hockey players of the 1980s are bigger and more physical than those of the mid-1960s. They skate faster and hit harder. The rules the NHL has enacted and continues to enact are designed to maintain the game's intensity while minimizing the possibility of calculated altercation.

The NHL's more aggressive stance against team intimidation has resulted in on-ice officials calling more major and misconduct penalties for infractions that occur after the whistle.

Rick MacLeish played a team record 287 consecutive games with Philadelphia between 1972 and 1976. The centerman's deft puck handling and hard, accurate shot produced 49 goals during the 1976–77 season.

they had not won since December 1971. Back in Toronto, the Leafs led 3–2 late in the third period of game three. Rick MacLeish, always lethal around playoff time, got the tying goal with 38 seconds to play. In the extra stanza it was MacLeish again scoring the overtime winner. Game four was highlighted by a remarkable Flyer comeback. Trailing 5–2 with less than eight minutes to play, the Flyers were able to tie the game on Bobby Clarke's tally with 16 seconds left. Reggie Leach was the Flyers' hero when he scored at 19:10 of the extra session to win it. The Flyers went on to win in six games.

The tough series with the Leafs must have taken its toll on the club that had been a Stanley Cup finalist the previous three years. The Bruins won back-to-back overtime games in the Spectrum. Back in the Garden, the Bruins allowed the Flyers just one goal in completing a four-game sweep. Gerry Cheevers proved he was still among the NHL's elite goaltenders.

Montreal met with much sterner opposition from the Islanders. The Habs took two victories in the Forum by 4–3 and 3–0 margins, but the Islanders bounced back to outmuscle the Habs 5–3 in the the Nassau Coliseum. Montreal's inspired play in game four produced a 4–0 win, but the Isles returned to the Forum to win the next match 4–3. Hockey's premier defensive forward, Bob Gainey, was the goal-scoring hero of game six as he potted both Hab markers in a 2–1 triumph that eliminated the Islanders.

Montreal won the first two games of the final 7–3 and 3–0. The Bruins fared no better in game three in Boston Garden as Montreal skated off with a 4–2 victory.

Game four provided the best hockey of the series. Bobby Schmautz put the home team in front 1–0. Jacques Lemaire equalized the contest in the second period and the game settled into a see-saw battle for the remainder of regulation time. In overtime, Lafleur feathered a perfect pass to a wide open Lemaire who banged it past Cheevers to win the Stanley Cup. Lafleur paced all playoff scorers with 26 points and was awarded the Conn Smythe Trophy to cap his best season in the NHL.

# YEAR 1976-77

**Stanley Cup Champion** Montreal Canadiens
**Prince of Wales Trophy Winner** Montreal Canadiens
**Clarence Campbell Bowl Winner** Philadelphia Flyers

**Final Standings**

## PRINCE OF WALES CONFERENCE

### Norris Division

| Team | GP | W | L | T | GF | GA | PTS |
|------|----|----|----|----|-----|-----|-----|
| Montreal | 80 | 60 | 8 | 12 | 387 | 171 | 132 |
| Los Angeles | 80 | 34 | 31 | 15 | 271 | 241 | 83 |
| Pittsburgh | 80 | 34 | 33 | 13 | 240 | 252 | 81 |
| Washington | 80 | 24 | 42 | 14 | 221 | 307 | 62 |
| Detroit | 80 | 16 | 55 | 9 | 183 | 309 | 41 |

### Adams Division

| Team | GP | W | L | T | GF | GA | PTS |
|------|----|----|----|----|-----|-----|-----|
| Boston | 80 | 49 | 23 | 8 | 312 | 240 | 106 |
| Buffalo | 80 | 48 | 24 | 8 | 301 | 220 | 104 |
| Toronto | 80 | 33 | 32 | 15 | 301 | 285 | 81 |
| Cleveland | 80 | 25 | 42 | 13 | 240 | 292 | 63 |

## CLARENCE CAMPBELL CONFERENCE

### Patrick Division

| Team | GP | W | L | T | GF | GA | PTS |
|------|----|----|----|----|-----|-----|-----|
| Philadelphia | 80 | 48 | 16 | 16 | 323 | 213 | 112 |
| NY Islanders | 80 | 47 | 21 | 12 | 288 | 193 | 106 |
| Atlanta | 80 | 34 | 34 | 12 | 264 | 265 | 80 |
| NY Rangers | 88 | 29 | 37 | 14 | 272 | 310 | 72 |

### Smythe Division

| Team | GP | W | L | T | GF | GA | PTS |
|------|----|----|----|----|-----|-----|-----|
| St. Louis | 80 | 32 | 39 | 9 | 239 | 276 | 73 |
| Minnesota | 80 | 23 | 39 | 18 | 240 | 310 | 64 |
| Chicago | 80 | 26 | 43 | 11 | 240 | 298 | 63 |
| Vancouver | 80 | 25 | 42 | 13 | 235 | 294 | 63 |
| Colorado | 80 | 20 | 46 | 14 | 226 | 307 | 54 |

### Leading Scorers

| Player | Club | GP | G | A | PTS | PIM |
|--------|------|----|----|----|-----|-----|
| Lafleur, Guy | Montreal | 80 | 56 | 80 | 136 | 20 |
| Dionne, Marcel | Los Angeles | 80 | 53 | 69 | 122 | 12 |
| Shutt, Steve | Montreal | 80 | 60 | 45 | 105 | 28 |
| MacLeish, Rick | Philadelphia | 79 | 49 | 48 | 97 | 42 |
| Perreault, Gilbert | Buffalo | 80 | 39 | 56 | 95 | 30 |
| Young, Tim | Minnesota | 80 | 29 | 66 | 95 | 58 |
| Ratelle, Jean | Boston | 78 | 33 | 61 | 94 | 22 |
| McDonald, Lanny | Toronto | 80 | 46 | 44 | 90 | 77 |
| Sittler, Darryl | Toronto | 73 | 38 | 52 | 90 | 89 |
| Clarke, Bobby | Philadelphia | 80 | 27 | 63 | 90 | 71 |

### NHL Award Winners

| | |
|---|---|
| **Hart (MVP)** | Guy Lafleur |
| **Art Ross (Leading Scorer)** | Guy Lafleur |
| **Calder (Rookie of the Year)** | Willi Plett |
| **Vezina (Lowest Goals-Against)** | Ken Dryden, Michel Larocque |
| **Lady Byng (Gentlemanly Conduct)** | Marcel Dionne |
| **Norris (Top Defenseman)** | Larry Robinson |
| **Conn Smythe (Playoff MVP)** | Guy Lafleur |
| **Patrick (Service to US Hockey)** | John Bucyk, Murray A. Armstrong, John Mariucci |
| **Masterton (Perseverance)** | Eddie Westfall |
| **Pearson (NHLPA MVP)** | Guy Lafleur |
| **Adams (Coach of the Year)** | Scott Bowman |
| **First Overall Draft Selection** | Dale McCourt |
| **World/Olympic Champions** | Czechoslovakia |
| **WHA Avco Cup Champions** | Quebec Nordiques |
| **AHL Calder Cup Champions** | Nova Scotia Voyageurs |
| **Memorial Cup Canadian Jr. Champions** | New Westminster Bruins |
| **NCAA Champions** | Wisconsin |
| **Canadian College Champions** | University of Toronto |

# 1977–1978

John A. Ziegler Jr. took office as the fourth president of the NHL in September, 1977, replacing Clarence Campbell. Ziegler was familiar with the NHL, having served as chairman of the league's board of governors and legal counsel for the Detroit Red Wings.

Heading into the season, the Montreal Canadiens were favored to continue their domination of the NHL with their stiffest competition coming from the New York Islanders, Boston Bruins and Philadelphia Flyers. Vaclav Nedomansky, one of the greatest players in Czechoslovakian hockey, moved from the WHA's Birmingham Bulls to the Detroit Red Wings.

Philadelphia defenseman Tom Bladon departed from the customary defensive style favored by the Flyers when he scored a record four goals and four assists against Cleveland on December 11. Mike Bossy showed his incredible scoring touch: 53 goals as a rookie for the New York Islanders. Bossy had been a high scorer in junior with the Laval Nationals, but to make the jump to the NHL and score more than 50 as a rookie was unprecedented.

In an encouraging development, the Colorado Rockies and Detroit Red Wings qualified for postseason play. The Rockies captured second place in the weak Smythe Division. Wilf Paiement, the franchise's first-ever draft selection, turned in a fine season with 31 goals and 87 points. Rookie defenseman Barry Beck had a 60-point year. Detroit improved its point total, jumping from 41 points in 1976–77 to a creditable second place in the Norris Division and 78 points the following year. Detroit's new coach, Bobby Kromm, brought a winning attitude from his days of coaching the Avco Cup champion Winnipeg Jets in the WHA. The Red Wings also received help in the form of strong rookie seasons from Dale

Of 22 playoff meetings between the Boston Bruins and Montreal Canadiens over the years, the Habs have won 20. In 1977–78, they eliminated the Bruins in the Cup final for the second successive year. Jean Ratelle and goaltender Ken Dryden both want this loose puck.

Barry "Bubba" Beck was chosen second overall by the Colorado Rockies in the 1977 entry draft. During his first year in the NHL the mammoth defenseman scored 22 goals, a mark he never again equaled.

McCourt and Reed Larson. The Toronto Maple Leafs gave up 48 fewer goals using the disciplined system devised by their new coach, Roger Nielson. Darryl Sittler and Lanny McDonald chipped in with 45 and 47 goals.

Once again Montreal had the NHL's best record, losing only 10 games. The Canadiens finished the season with 129 points. Boston had another solid performance from what Don Cherry called his "lunch-bucket" team. The Bruins boasted hockey's second-best record with 113 points. The Islanders continued their steady improvement, beating out the Flyers for the Patrick Division title. The Rangers were back in the playoffs despite a fourth-place finish. New York qualified for postseason play under new rules, which awarded playoff berths to the teams finishing with the most points regardless of their position in the divisional standings.

The preliminary series saw the Flyers

eliminate the Rockies in two straight. The Red Wings continued to improve, sweeping the Atlanta Flames. Buffalo went to three games before sidelining the Rangers, while the Leafs had a hat trick from George Ferguson in the first game and shutout goaltending by Mike Palmateer in the second to sweep Los Angeles.

Boston eliminated the Blackhawks in four straight games in their quarter-final matchup. Montreal skated past the Red Wings in five games and were joined in the semi-final by the Flyers when Buffalo's "French Connection" never got rolling. Bernie Parent revived his playoff magic, having a marvelous series.

The highlight of postseason play was an electrifying seven-game series between the Leafs and the Islanders. The Isles won the first two contests at home, needing an overtime marker·from Mike Bossy to win game two. The Leafs squared the series by taking two at the

## 11. The Snipers: Lafleur and Bossy

The emergence of two players—Guy Lafleur and Mike Bossy—demonstrated that skating and scoring ability could win over intimidation in the NHL.

Lafleur was the first player drafted in 1971. As a junior with the Quebec Remparts, he had scored a phenomenal 307 goals in his final two seasons. He was the top hockey player playing junior in Quebec and, along with Marcel Dionne, was regarded a potential NHL superstar. The Montreal Canadiens, the league's most successful team, had just lost one of hockey finest players and greatest attractions in Jean Beliveau who retired after his tenth Stanley Cup win in 1970–71. Like Lafleur, Beliveau had starred in Quebec City, making comparisons between the two inevitable. Through a complicated series of deals, the Canadiens obtained the first pick in the 1971 draft and took Lafleur. His first three seasons with the club were disappointing, but, in 1974–75, he blossomed into a game-breaking player, with 53 goals and 119 points in 70 games.

Beginning in 1975–76, the Lafleur-led Canadiens won four consecutive Stanley Cups as Lafleur had seasons of 56, 56, 60 and 52 goals. He was the NHL's scoring champion three times and won the Hart Trophy as MVP twice. In 1977, 1978 and 1979 he was the leading goal scorer in the Stanley Cup playoffs.

Beyond impressive statis-

The accuracy and quick release of Mike Bossy's shots are standards among modern sharpshooters.

tics, Lafleur was a magical player who created excitement just by touching the puck. He was a master stick-handler who could beat a defenseman with a stunning repertoire of moves or put the puck past the goaltender with a booming shot.

Guy Lafleur had his sixth consecutive 50-goal season in 1979–80, but injuries hampered his play in 1980–81 and he slipped from the front ranks of NHL scorers. He still had his magic moves and the ability to give and receive perfect passes, but goals no longer came easily to the player fans and teammates called "The Flower." He re-

tired in November of 1984, having scored 518 goals and 1246 points in 14 NHL seasons.

Mike Bossy was drafted 15th overall by the New York Islanders in the first round of the 1977 amateur draft. Like Lafleur, Bossy played in the Quebec Major Junior Hockey League, averaging more than 75 goals a year in four seasons with the Laval Nationals. The Islanders were a team on the verge of great things in the mid-1970s, having built patiently through the amateur draft. Bossy was an immediate sensation with the Islanders, playing on a forward line with the club's top

two draft picks from 1974, Bryan Trottier and Clark Gillies. Bossy established a record for first-year players, scoring 53 times and winning the Calder Trophy as the league's top rookie. He scored 69 goals in his second season, and the year after that helped the Islanders to the first of four consecutive Stanley Cups in 1980. With the exception of the 1986–87 season, when injuries reduced his playing time, Bossy has never scored fewer than 51 goals a season in the NHL, and has earned eight all-star selections in his first nine years in the league. Bossy is the NHL's all-time leading playoff goal scorer: he established a playoff record with 35 points in the 1981 postseason, and led all goal scorers in Stanley Cup play with 17 playoff goals in 1981, 1982 and 1983.

Bossy possesses a fluid skating stride that enables him to dart into openings to pick up passes or loose pucks. He has excellent anticipation of the play and great acceleration that is combined with a highly accurate and quick-release shot. He is the hockey player for whom the term "sniper" was invented, needing little more than a puck-sized opening and an instant of possession to score.

Guy Lafleur and Mike Bossy were inspirational players on clubs that won eight consecutive Stanley Cups. Their successes changed the model that other teams in the league tried to emulate, and reemphasized the electrifying elements of the game of hockey.

After a notable but unheralded 14-year career in the NHL, Philadelphia forward Gary Dornhoefer, above, played his last game in 1977–78. His steady, tough-minded style helped the Flyers win two Stanley Cups.

Gardens, where defenseman Borje Salming was sidelined when he was accidentally hit in the eye by an errant stick. Game five was another overtime session, with Bob Nystrom deciding the issue in the Isles' favor. The sixth game saw some crucial injuries to key Islanders personnel. In this game, Bryan Trottier suffered a fractured jaw in a collision with teammate Billy Harris, and Mike Bossy was carried from the ice with an apparent neck injury after a hard check from the Leafs' Jerry Butler. Bossy and Salming missed the seventh contest, but Trottier played with his swollen jaw protected by a helmet and face mask. Game seven was a hockey gem, punctuated by superb netminding by both Chico Resch and Mike Palmateer. At one point, with the contest tied at one apiece, Palmateer was trapped behind the net as the puck bounced off the boards and in front of the net. As an Islander forward prepared to shoot the puck into the gaping net, the Leaf goalie somehow hurled himself around the goal to block the shot. It was up to Lanny McDonald to break the deadlock in overtime when he corraled a knee-high pass at the Islander blue line and whistled a shot past Resch.

The Leafs were in the semi-finals for

As a big right-winger for the Bruins, below, Terry O'Reilly's 90-point 1977–78 season made him the first player with more than 200 penalty minutes to finish among the top ten scorers in the league.

the first time in eleven years, but their opposition was the powerful Montreal Canadiens, who won the series in four games and advanced to their third consecutive final series appearance. In the other semi-final matchup, the Bruins proved that they could still win in their own rink, parlaying Rick Middleton's overtime goal in the series opener and some poor work by the Flyer defense in the second match into a two-game lead. The Flyers could manage no better than a split in the games at the Spectrum. Hot goaltending from Gerry Cheevers and a five-point night from Peter McNab clinched the series for the Bruins back at the Boston Garden.

The Habs put on a clinic on sound defensive hockey in the first game of the finals, posting a 4–1 victory. The second contest needed extra time before Guy Lafleur scored the winner. Cheevers had been called upon to make 15 saves in overtime before Lafleur scored on a hardshot to the short side to end the game. Boston stopped the Habs' unbeaten string in the finals at ten games with an impressive 4–0 victory at home in game three. Lafleur played a prominent role in the fourth contest when he beat Cheevers with 33 seconds to play and forced overtime. Bobby Schmautz won it for the Bruins in extra time. Larry Robinson took charge of matters in the fifth game

At the height of his career, Guy Lafleur of the Montreal Canadiens played with an almost preternatural combination of skills and spirit. There were nights when his physical and motivational edge made him practically unstoppable.

Toronto's Darryl Sittler, the heart of the Leafs, led his team to a 92-point finish, the club's best since 1950–51. Sittler was the NHL's third-leading scorer with 117 points in the regular season and 11 in the playoffs.

with a spectacular end-to-end rush to open the scoring. The Habs were never headed, skating to a 4–1 victory. Robinson again was the dominant figure on the ice in the sixth and final game. He collected two assists in a 4–1 Canadiens triumph and had a strong game on the point. Robinson ended the postseason tied with Lafleur as the leading point scorer in the playoffs with 21. He was named winner of the Conn Smythe Trophy as playoff MVP.

After the playoffs, Guy Lafleur ''borrowed'' the Stanley Cup and took it to his hometown of Thurso, Quebec. There he put the Cup on dispay on his father's front lawn, where it was admired by almost everyone in town.

Hockey was not immune to the drug problem that had gained widespread notoriety in professional sports. In only his second year in office, league president John Ziegler had to deal with cocaine possession charges against Don Murdoch, the young star of the New York Rangers. This was the first time that a NHL player had been charged with a drug offense. Murdoch was suspended for an entire season, though this was later reduced to 40 games. Ziegler sent out a clear message to all players that drugs would not be tolerated.

# YEAR 1977–78

**Stanley Cup Champion** Montreal Canadiens
**Prince of Wales Trophy Winner** Montreal Canadiens
**Clarence Campbell Bowl Winner** New York Islanders

**Final Standings**

## PRINCE OF WALES CONFERENCE

### Norris Division

| Team | GP | W | L | T | GF | GA | PTS |
|---|---|---|---|---|---|---|---|
| Montreal | 80 | 59 | 10 | 11 | 359 | 183 | 129 |
| Detroit | 80 | 32 | 34 | 14 | 252 | 266 | 78 |
| Los Angeles | 80 | 31 | 34 | 15 | 243 | 245 | 77 |
| Pittsburgh | 80 | 25 | 37 | 18 | 254 | 321 | 68 |
| Washington | 80 | 17 | 49 | 14 | 195 | 321 | 48 |

### Adams Division

| Team | GP | W | L | T | GF | GA | PTS |
|---|---|---|---|---|---|---|---|
| Boston | 80 | 51 | 18 | 11 | 333 | 218 | 113 |
| Buffalo | 80 | 44 | 19 | 17 | 288 | 215 | 105 |
| Toronto | 80 | 41 | 29 | 10 | 271 | 237 | 92 |
| Cleveland | 80 | 22 | 45 | 13 | 230 | 325 | 57 |

## CLARENCE CAMPBELL CONFERENCE

### Patrick Division

| Team | GP | W | L | T | GF | GA | PTS |
|---|---|---|---|---|---|---|---|
| NY Islanders | 80 | 48 | 17 | 15 | 334 | 210 | 111 |
| Philadelphia | 80 | 45 | 20 | 15 | 296 | 200 | 105 |
| Atlanta | 80 | 34 | 27 | 19 | 274 | 252 | 87 |
| NY Rangers | 80 | 30 | 37 | 13 | 279 | 280 | 73 |

### Smythe Division

| Team | GP | W | L | T | GF | GA | PTS |
|---|---|---|---|---|---|---|---|
| Chicago | 80 | 32 | 29 | 19 | 230 | 220 | 83 |
| Colorado | 80 | 19 | 40 | 21 | 257 | 305 | 59 |
| Vancouver | 80 | 20 | 43 | 17 | 239 | 320 | 57 |
| St. Louis | 80 | 20 | 47 | 13 | 195 | 304 | 53 |
| Minnesota | 80 | 18 | 53 | 9 | 218 | 325 | 45 |

### Leading Scorers

| Player | Club | GP | G | A | PTS | PIM |
|---|---|---|---|---|---|---|
| Lafleur, Guy | Montreal | 79 | 60 | 72 | 132 | 26 |
| Trottier, Bryan | NY Islanders | 77 | 46 | 77 | 123 | 46 |
| Sittler, Darryl | Toronto | 80 | 45 | 72 | 117 | 100 |
| Lemaire, Jacques | Montreal | 76 | 36 | 61 | 97 | 14 |
| Potvin, Denis | NY Islanders | 80 | 30 | 64 | 94 | 81 |
| Bossy, Mike | NY Islanders | 73 | 53 | 38 | 91 | 6 |
| O'Reilly, Terry | Boston | 77 | 29 | 61 | 90 | 211 |
| Perreault, Gilbert | Buffalo | 79 | 41 | 48 | 89 | 20 |
| Clarke, Bobby | Philadelphia | 71 | 21 | 68 | 89 | 83 |
| McDonald, Lanny | Toronto | 74 | 47 | 40 | 87 | 54 |
| Paiement, Wilf | Colorado | 80 | 31 | 56 | 87 | 114 |

### NHL Award Winners

| | |
|---|---|
| **Hart (MVP)** | Guy Lafleur |
| **Art Ross (Leading Scorer)** | Guy Lafleur |
| **Calder (Rookie of the Year)** | Mike Bossy |
| **Vezina (Lowest Goals-Against)** | Ken Dryden, Michel Larocque |
| **Lady Byng (Gentlemanly Conduct)** | Butch Goring |
| **Norris (Top Defenseman)** | Denis Potvin |
| **Conn Smythe (Playoff MVP)** | Larry Robinson |
| **Patrick (Service to US Hockey)** | Phil Esposito, Tom Fitzgerald, William T. Tutt, William W. Wirtz |
| **Masterton (Perseverance)** | Butch Goring |
| **Pearson (NHLPA MVP)** | Guy Lafleur |
| **Adams (Coach of the Year)** | Bobby Kromm |
| **Selke (Top Defensive Forward)** | Bob Gainey |
| **First Overall Draft Selection** | Bobby Smith |
| **World/Olympic Champions** | Soviet Union |
| **WHA Avco Cup Champions** | Winnipeg Jets |
| **AHL Calder Cup Champions** | Maine Mariners |
| **Memorial Cup Canadian Jr. Champions** | New Westminster Bruins |
| **NCAA Champions** | Boston University |
| **Canadian College Champions** | University of Alberta |

# 1978–1979

The Rangers were no longer willing to wait for players in their system to mature into winning NHLers. Instead, general manager John Ferguson set out to buy the best hockey talent available. His search took him to Winnipeg, home of the WHA Jets. The Jets were the most European-like hockey team in either the NHL or WHA, being built around a forward line composed of a pair of young Swedes and a rejuvenated Bobby Hull. Dubbed the Luxury Line, this trio was arguably the most exciting line in hockey. Anders Hedberg and Ulf Nilsson had dazzled WHA fans for four glorious seasons, but their goal in leaving Sweden had been to play in the NHL. The Rangers offered them one million dollars each for two years, and the pair jumped to the NHL. The Rangers also struck a deal with the Flyers that saw Cup-winning coach Fred Shero move to New York in exchange for cash and the Rangers' first-round draft selection. Shero became the coach and general manager of the Rangers, while John Ferguson completed the circle by resurfacing in Winnipeg as general manager of the Jets.

The Cleveland Barons and Minnesota North Stars merged as both franchises were in financial difficulty. The merger reduced the NHL to 17 teams. The combined Barons-North Stars franchise would play out of Minnesota, retain the North Stars name and play in the Adams Division. The deal provided the North Stars with an excellent goaltender in Gilles Meloche, a fine defenseman in Greg Smith and a high-scoring forward in Al MacAdam, who played on Minnesota's first line with Steve Payne and Tim Young.

Hockey lost a great player and wonderful ambassador for the game when Bobby Orr announced his retirement on November 9. Orr had sat out the entire 1977–78 season in the hope that his injured knees would heal enough to let him play. He played in six games for Chicago early in the season, but was unable to

Islander goaltender Billy Smith kneels dejected in his crease after a goal by the New York Rangers who eliminated the first-place Islanders from the 1978–79 semifinals. The previous year the Islanders had been eliminated in the quarterfinals by the upstart Toronto Maple Leafs. Not until 1979–80 would the Isles' first Stanley Cup victory expunge their growing reputation as a playoff "choke" team.

Goaltender Ken Dryden strikes the pose for which he became famous in his moments of relaxation during Montreal Canadiens games. In eight seasons with the Habs, Dryden won 258 regular season games, and lost only 57.

perform up to the standard he had set for himself. Rather than play at what he called 35% efficiency, Orr retired.

Denis Potvin took over as the NHL's best defenseman, surpassing 30 goals and 100 points in the regular season. Bryan Trottier broke Lafleur's hold on the scoring title, pacing the Islanders to the NHL's best record with 47 goals and 87 assists. He had a five-goal game on December 23, 1978 in a 9–4 victory over the Rangers. The Rangers had the misfortune of being party to another player's "career" night when Tim Young potted five goals in a 8–1 Minnesota win on January 15, 1979. The league saw the emergence of a pair of scorers south of the Mason-Dixon line when Bob MacMillan set an Atlanta club record for points with 108. His linemate Guy Chouinard became the club's first 50-goal scorer.

Madison Square Garden was the site of some outstanding hockey when the Soviet Union played the NHL All-Stars in a three-game series that replaced the traditional NHL All-Star Game. The NHL stars gave their fans something to cheer about with a 4–2 victory in the first game of the series. In a surge reminiscent of the first game in Moscow in 1972, the Soviets stormed back from a 4–2 deficit in the second period to snatch a 5–4 victory in game two. The deciding game saw the Soviets play their game to perfection, as they showed the NHLers crisp passing, fluid skating and a high-tempo game. Soviet coach Viktor Tikhonov and NHL coach Scotty Bowman both changed goaltenders for the pivotal game. Vladimir Myshkin started instead of Vladislav Tretiak for the Soviets, while Gerry Cheevers replaced Ken Dryden for the NHL All-Stars. After a fast, scoreless first period, the Soviets upped the pace. Myshkin staked them to flawless goaltending in period two, allowing the Soviets to skate away with a 2–0 lead. The Soviets took control in the third period, scoring four times on just seven shots to win the game 6–0.

The Rangers finished the season in third place with 91 points, a distant 25 points behind the Islanders. Still, the club had shown a marked improvement over the previous year. Ulf Nilsson had been the Rangers' best player until he broke his ankle in February. Hedberg led the

(continued on page 89)

Team NHL whipped the Soviets in the first game of the best-of-three 1979 Challenge Cup. But the unflappable Soviets came back to score victories in games two and three. NHL captain Bobby Clarke, right, assisted on a goal just 16 seconds into the first game, but did not register another point in the series.

## 12. International Matches

Team Canada's narrow victory against the Soviet Nationals in their eight-game 1972 series created an enthusiastic audience in North America for more matches between European teams and NHLers. The exotic nature of European opponents, their stylish play and the "us-against-them" patriotism aroused by international games guaranteed their popularity and made further exhibitions and tournaments lucrative opportunities for NHL clubs, the NHL Players' Association, the various European federations and the IIHF.

Within a decade of this historic first series, five types of international hockey event involving the NHL had been staged. In the first, NHL players participated on their respective national teams in a six-country tournament called the Canada Cup. Teams Canada and USA were exclusively NHLers. The Scandinavian teams included some of their countries' best players who already played in the NHL. Team Canada won the Canada Cup in 1976 and 1984, and the Soviets won in 1981.

A second NHL/international format features the NHL All-Stars against the Soviet Nationals. The NHL All-Stars are drawn from across the league, without consideration of national origin. In 1979 and 1987, a series between the NHL All-Stars and the Soviet Nationals replaced the regular NHL All-Star game. In the 1979 match-up, a three-game series called the NHL Chal-

lenge Cup and played in New York City, the Soviets won 2–1, winning game three 6–0. In 1987, the two teams played a two-game set in Quebec City as part of a sports and cultural festival called Rendez-Vous '87. The games were stylish affairs with the NHL All-Stars winning the first match 4–3 and the Soviets coming back with a 5–3 win two nights later.

Perhaps the most interesting games between NHL players and European opponents have been club team exhibition tours. These events have occurred over the Christmas-New Year's period on five occasions and have matched individual NHL clubs against one of the leading clubs from the Soviet Union. The four Soviet clubs

that have appeared against NHL opponents—Central Red Army, Moscow Dynamo, Soviet Wings and Moscow Spartak—have won the majority of their games. A Soviet all-star team played six NHL teams over Christmas and New Year's 1982–83, winning four of its six games.

NHLers also make up the roster of Canada's entry in the World Hockey Championship tournament staged in April of every non-Olympic year. This team is composed of players whose NHL clubs have either failed to qualify for the Stanley Cup playoffs or have been eliminated in the first round of competition. Canada's best finish has been a silver medal in 1985 with a team led by Pittsburgh Penguins' star Mario Lemieux.

Games between NHLers and European opponents have demonstrated the high quality of play practised in Europe. From an overconfident attitude heading into the 1972 Team Canada-Soviet series, today's NHL coaches and players know that they have to play at their highest level both technically and emotionally to win. These exhibition games have accelerated the integration of strategies between the North American and European schools of hockey. The Canada Cup tournaments have shown how well Finns, Czechs and Swedes play against North American professionals on smaller NHL rinks, creating further opportunities for European players to earn spots on NHL rosters.

NHLers played for the North American and Scandinavian teams in the 1976 Canada Cup. Borje Salming wore number five for Sweden's *Tre Kronor*.

Having been fired by the Boston Bruins after a dispiriting loss to the Montreal Canadiens in the 1978–79 semifinals, flamboyant Don Cherry joined the Colorado Rockies and coached them to 19 wins in 1979–80.

team in scoring. The Swedes were effective, but did not dominate play the way they had in the WHA. The Rangers were a surprisingly strong team in the playoffs, eliminating Los Angeles and then upsetting Philadelphia. The postseason surprises did not end there, as the Rangers defeated their closest rivals and the NHL's highest-scoring team, the New York Islanders, despite two heartbreaking losses in overtime.

Montreal continued its winning ways in the playoffs by defeating the Maple Leafs in the quarter-final before renewing acquaintances with the Boston Bruins for a third straight year in postseason play. This marvelous series went the seven-game limit. In the deciding game, it appeared that the Habs' dreams of a

fourth Cup were about to vanish when Rick Middleton scored the go-ahead goal with 3:59 left in the third period. Middleton's tally came in the midst of a Montreal comeback; the defending Stanley Cup champions had been playing catch-up hockey, trailing 3–1 after the second period. By taking the lead again with less than four minutes to play, it seemed that the Bruins were finally going to defeat Montreal in a playoff series. But the Bruins were caught in a poorly timed line change, resulting in a penalty for too many men on the ice. The resulting power-play saw Guy Lafleur score the tying goal with a bullet drive that eluded Gilles Gilbert and sent the game into overtime. In the extra stanza, Montreal outshot the Bruins by a wide margin. At

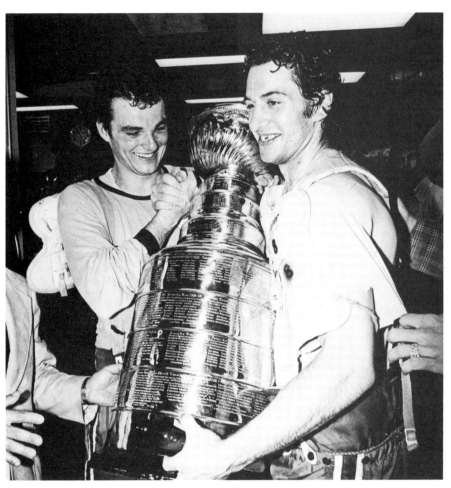

9:33 Doug Risebrough spotted Yvon Lambert in front of the Bruin net, fed him the puck and Montreal was another step closer to a fourth consecutive Stanley Cup.

The fired-up Rangers took the opening game of the final 4–1 in front of the goaltending of John Davidson. The Habs rebounded with a 6–2 decision for a split at the Forum. The Canadiens won twice at Madison Square Garden with a 4–1 victory in game three and a 4–3 win on Serge Savard's overtime goal in game four. The Canadiens clinched the Cup with a 4–1 victory at home. Jacques Lemaire and Guy Lafleur led all scorers in postseason play with 23 points, but Bob Gainey captured the playoff MVP trophy.

Prior to the end of the regular season, the league ratified an agreement to admit four teams from the WHA. Winnipeg, Hartford, Quebec and Edmonton would be part of the NHL for the 1979–80 season. In August, the league ruled that all players signed after June, 1979, would have to wear helmets. All players under contract before 1979 were required to sign a waiver before they would be permitted to play without one.

Mario Tremblay and Doug Risebrough, above, celebrate the Canadiens' 1978–79 Stanley Cup Victory — the team's fourth in a row.

Hall of Fame centerman Dave Keon, at right, spent four seasons in the WHA after a distinguished career with the Toronto Maple Leafs. Keon returned to the NHL with the Hartford Whalers in 1979–80.

# YEAR                                        1978–79

**Stanley Cup Champion**          Montreal Canadiens
**Prince of Wales Trophy Winner**  Montreal Canadiens
**Clarence Campbell Bowl Winner**  New York Islanders

**Final Standings**

## PRINCE OF WALES CONFERENCE

### Norris Division

| Team | GP | W | L | T | GF | GA | PTS |
|------|----|----|----|----|----|----|----|
| Montreal | 80 | 52 | 17 | 11 | 337 | 204 | 115 |
| Pittsburgh | 80 | 36 | 31 | 13 | 281 | 279 | 85 |
| Los Angeles | 80 | 34 | 34 | 12 | 292 | 286 | 80 |
| Washington | 80 | 24 | 41 | 15 | 273 | 338 | 63 |
| Detroit | 80 | 23 | 41 | 16 | 252 | 295 | 62 |

### Adams Division

| Team | GP | W | L | T | GF | GA | PTS |
|------|----|----|----|----|----|----|----|
| Boston | 80 | 43 | 23 | 14 | 316 | 270 | 100 |
| Buffalo | 80 | 36 | 28 | 16 | 280 | 263 | 88 |
| Toronto | 80 | 34 | 33 | 13 | 267 | 252 | 81 |
| Minnesota | 80 | 28 | 40 | 12 | 257 | 289 | 68 |

## CLARENCE CAMPBELL CONFERENCE

### Patrick Division

| Team | GP | W | L | T | GF | GA | PTS |
|------|----|----|----|----|----|----|----|
| NY Islanders | 80 | 51 | 15 | 14 | 358 | 214 | 116 |
| Philadelphia | 80 | 40 | 25 | 15 | 281 | 248 | 95 |
| NY Rangers | 80 | 40 | 29 | 11 | 316 | 292 | 91 |
| Atlanta | 80 | 41 | 31 | 8 | 327 | 280 | 90 |

### Smythe Division

| Team | GP | W | L | T | GF | GA | PTS |
|------|----|----|----|----|----|----|----|
| Chicago | 80 | 29 | 36 | 15 | 244 | 277 | 73 |
| Vancouver | 80 | 25 | 42 | 13 | 217 | 291 | 63 |
| St. Louis | 80 | 18 | 50 | 12 | 249 | 348 | 48 |
| Colorado | 80 | 15 | 53 | 12 | 210 | 331 | 42 |

### Leading Scorers

| Player | Club | GP | G | A | PTS | PIM |
|--------|------|----|----|----|----|----|
| Trottier, Bryan | NY Islanders | 76 | 47 | 87 | 134 | 50 |
| Dionne, Marcel | Los Angeles | 80 | 59 | 71 | 130 | 30 |
| Lafleur, Guy | Montreal | 80 | 52 | 77 | 129 | 28 |
| Bossy, Mike | NY Islanders | 80 | 69 | 57 | 126 | 25 |
| MacMillan, Bob | Atlanta | 79 | 37 | 71 | 108 | 14 |
| Chouinard, Guy | Atlanta | 80 | 50 | 57 | 107 | 14 |
| Potvin, Denis | NY Islanders | 73 | 31 | 70 | 101 | 58 |
| Federko, Bernie | St. Louis | 74 | 31 | 64 | 95 | 14 |
| Taylor, Dave | Los Angeles | 78 | 43 | 48 | 91 | 124 |
| Gillies, Clark | NY Islanders | 75 | 35 | 56 | 91 | 68 |

### NHL Award Winners

| | |
|---|---|
| **Hart (MVP)** | Bryan Trottier |
| **Art Ross (Leading Scorer)** | Bryan Trottier |
| **Calder (Rookie of the Year)** | Bobby Smith |
| **Vezina (Lowest Goals-Against)** | Ken Dryden, Michel Larocque |
| **Lady Byng (Gentlemanly Conduct)** | Bob MacMillan |
| **Norris (Top Defenseman)** | Denis Potvin |
| **Conn Smythe (Playoff MVP)** | Bob Gainey |
| **Patrick (Service to US Hockey)** | Bobby Orr |
| **Masterton (Perseverance)** | Serge Savard |
| **Pearson (NHLPA MVP)** | Marcel Dionne |
| **Adams (Coach of the Year)** | Al Arbour |
| **Selke (Top Defensive Forward)** | Bob Gainey |
| **First Overall Draft Selection** | Rob Ramage |

| | |
|---|---|
| **World/Olympic Champions** | Soviet Union |
| **WHA Avco Cup Champions** | Winnipeg Jets |
| **AHL Calder Cup Champions** | Maine Mariners |
| **Memorial Cup Canadian Jr. Champions** | Peterborough Petes |
| **NCAA Champions** | Minnesota |
| **Canadian College Champions** | University of Alberta |

# 1979–1980

The Montreal Canadiens sought a fifth consecutive Stanley Cup in 1980. Only the Montreal teams of 1956–60 had ever won five straight. This season would also see four former WHA franchises compete in the NHL. Would they be competitive? And would a teenaged center named Wayne Gretzky be able to withstand the rigors of NHL play?

The WHA clubs paid dearly to join the NHL. In addition to their entry fees, the four former WHA clubs were allowed to protect only two of the players on their 1978–79 rosters. The Winnipeg Jets, winners of the WHA's final championship, were the hardest hit, losing classy Swedish forward Kent Nilsson to the Atlanta Flames, two talented hard-working forwards, Terry Ruskowski and Rich Preston, to Chicago and promising defenseman Paul MacKinnon to the Washington Capitals. Winnipeg and Edmonton joined the Smythe Division, while the Quebec Nordiques played in the Adams and the Hartford Whalers in the Norris Divisions. Each of the 21 teams in the NHL played its 20 opponents four times, twice at home and twice on the road.

The Philadelphia Flyers were supposed to be in a rebuilding year after last season's early exit from the playoffs. Coach Pat Quinn was given the task of combining the talents of veteran stars like Rick MacLeish and Bobby Clarke with those of a group of promising youngsters including Ken Linseman, Brian Propp and goaltender Pete Peeters. The club was much changed from the Broad Street Bullies of the mid-1970s, relying on speed and skating ability. The transformation was successful as the Flyers established a league record with a remarkable unbeaten streak of 35 games. They topped the regular-season standings with 116 points.

The Hartford Whalers iced an interesting lineup in their first NHL season. The team made the playoffs with the best record of the four former WHA teams. Late in the season, they acquired Bobby Hull from the Winnipeg Jets. This gave the Whalers three players — Hull (aged 41), Davie Keon (40), and Gordie Howe (52) who had first played together on the 1960–61 NHL all-star team. Howe wrote his name in the record book one more time on February 28, 1980, when he be-

The often fractious Billy Smith was in goal for the New York Islanders as the team won the first of four successive Stanley Cups in 1979–80.

The Greatest and the Great One: Gordie Howe and Wayne Gretzky. 1979–80 marked Howe's final season in professional hockey. It was also the year in which the young Gretzky joined the NHL, finishing in a tie with Marcel Dionne for the NHL scoring championship, with 51 goals and 86 assists.

came the first player in NHL history to score 800 regular-season goals. The club had some fine younger players, as both Mike Rogers and Blaine Stoughton reached the 100-point mark for the season. Stoughton tied with Buffalo's Danny Gare and the Kings' Charlie Simmer for the league lead in goals with 56.

The league's most exciting forward combination played for the Kings in Los Angeles. Marcel Dionne had come to be regarded as one of hockey's superstars while toiling in relative obscurity with Detroit and Los Angeles. In 1979–80, Dionne produced his highest point total (137 points) playing alongside Dave Taylor and Charlie Simmer who scored 90 and 101 points respectively. The "Triple Crown Line" could have produced even greater totals had Taylor not missed 19 games and Simmer not suffered a season-ending broken leg. Simmer es-

tablished a record for the modern era, scoring at least one goal in 13 consecutive games.

Wayne Gretzky was quick to demonstrate his ability to play NHL hockey. On February 15, 1980, he equaled an NHL record for assists in a game with seven in an 8–2 victory over Washington. At the age of 19, he became the youngest player to score 50 goals. Gretzky tied Marcel Dionne for the league scoring lead with 137 points although Dionne was given the Art Ross Trophy by virtue of scoring more goals. In the pressure-packed drive for the playoffs it was Gretzky who spearheaded the Oilers' late charge for a postseason berth.

In February, the US Olympic hockey team played brilliantly to win the gold medal at the Winter Olympics in Lake Placid, New York. A number of the players from this team joined NHL clubs

Perhaps the greatest left winger ever to don a hockey uniform, Bobby Hull suited up with the NHL Hartford Whalers in 1979–80. But by that time the form that had powered Hull through 23 seasons of pro hockey had deserted him, and the perennial all-star called it quits after only nine games with the Whalers.

late in the season. Goaltender Jim Craig was off to Atlanta while defensemen Mike Ramsey and Ken Morrow signed with Buffalo and the Islanders respectively. Dave Christian was an instant success with the Winnipeg Jets, while Steve Christoff joined the Minnesota North Stars for the playoff drive. Mark Johnson joined the Pittsburgh Penguins.

There were a few surprises in the order of finish during a regular season, which saw 21 teams play 840 games to eliminate five clubs from the playoffs. Buffalo, now coached and managed by Scotty Bowman, improved 22 points to lead the Adams Division with 110 points. Philadelphia improved 21 points to lead the Patrick Division, while the Islanders slumped to 91 points, winning 12 fewer games than the previous year. Montreal, led by a record sixth straight 50-goal season from Guy Lafleur, topped the Norris Division.

In the playoffs, the surviving teams were ranked according to points in the final regular-season standings. The club ranked first played the club ranked 16th; second played 15th, etc. Of the former

WHA clubs, Quebec and Winnipeg failed to qualify for postseason play. Philadelphia needed two overtime victories to defeat Edmonton in three straight games in their preliminary series showdown. The previous year's Stanley Cup finalist, the New York Rangers, eliminated Atlanta in four games before losing to the Flyers, who took the best-of-seven quarter-final in five games. Minnesota defeated the Maple Leafs in three straight games to earn a quarter-final berth against defending champion Montreal, which had swept Hartford. In what proved to be the upset of the postseason, Minnesota eliminated the Habs in seven games to advance to the semi-finals against the Flyers and end Montreal's run at a fifth Stanley Cup. The North Stars lost to Philadelphia in five games, sending the Flyers to the Stanley Cup final for the first time in four years.

The New York Islanders found their way into six overtime contests. They needed one overtime victory to subdue the Los Angeles Kings in four games in the preliminary round. Bob Bourne and Clark Gillies provided sudden vic-
*(continued on page 97)*

## 13. College Hockey and American-born Players

In the 1960s, American-born and college-educated hockey players were as scarce as 50-goal scorers. After the US hockey gold medal at the 1960 Winter Olympics, Jack McCartan, the goaltender for the US team, played briefly with the New York Rangers. Tom Williams from Duluth played for the Boston Bruins when that club was the NHL's weakest team. Though the Olympic win promoted the game at the college level, the lack of US-born players in the NHL deprived young American hockey players of local role models who had made it in the big leagues.

Unlike basketball or football, the NHL's traditional system of developing young players took place outside of a college setting. Before expansion, NHL clubs placed promising youngsters on junior clubs sponsored by the parent NHL organization. This system often required young players to leave their home communities without completing their high school education. After expansion, junior hockey clubs were no longer stocked by NHL parent clubs and drew most of their players from close to their home community, allowing more players to stay in school. When US colleges began to offer hockey scholarships, many of the early recipients were young Canadian high school graduates who went to play for schools like Denver, Minnesota and Michigan Tech.

NHL expansion and the success of the Orr-Esposito Boston clubs contributed to increased hockey interest in the US in the early 1970s. Youth and high school hockey programs flourished, allowing colleges to recruit more talented American-born players.

The emergence of the WHA created more opportunities for American hockey players. The New England Whalers had six American-born players on the inaugural Avco Cup-winning team of 1973. Their general manager, Jack Kelly, was from Massachusetts, as were Larry Pleau, Kevin Ahearn, Paul Hurley and John Cunniff. Tom Williams, formerly of the NHL Bruins, and Tim Sheehy were from Minnesota. Pleau, Sheehy, Bobby Sheehan of the New York Raiders and Billy Klatt of the Minnesota Fighting Saints all had thirty-plus goals in the WHA's first season. The following year, Mark and Marty Howe, both American-born and developed in the Detroit amateur hockey system, played for the Houston Aeros.

The NHL saw a major influx of American talent in the 1979–80 season when 66 players made it to the NHL. Eight members of the gold-medal-winning US Olympic team headed directly to the NHL in March, 1980. In 1981, the Washington Capitals, selecting third overall, drafted Rob Carpenter out of St. John's High School in Peabody, Massachusetts. In 1984–85, Carpenter became the first American-born player to register a 50-goal season, scoring 53 times. The Buffalo Sabres drafted Tom Barrasso and Phil Housley out of high school. Barrasso won the Calder and Vezina Trophies in 1984, while Housely scored 31 goals as a defenseman in the same year. Rod Langway of the Washington Capitals won the Norris Trophy as the NHL's best defenseman in 1983–84. The Minnesota North Stars chose Brian Lawton of Mount St. Charles Academy, Rhode Island, as the number one pick in the 1983 entry draft. In 1985–86, the North Stars' Neal Broten became the first American to surpass the 100-point plateau with a 105-point season.

At the start of the 1984–85 season, Americans accounted for 11.4% of the players in the NHL. Including Canadian graduates of American colleges, 17.7% were products of the US collegiate system. Former US Olympic coach Herb Brooks moved up to the NHL, working behind the bench for the New York Rangers. In 1985-86, Bob Johnson, former coach of the University of Wisconsin Badgers and an American, guided the Calgary Flames to the Stanley Cup finals.

In the 1986 NHL Entry Draft, 40 US high school players were selected, along with 22 players from US colleges. The number one draft, Joe Murphy, chosen by Detroit, is a Canadian who played at Michigan State. The second player selected, Jim Carson of the Los Angeles Kings, is an American who played for the Verdun Junior Canadiens of the Quebec Major Junior Hockey League. American players and American collegiate hockey has taken its place as a hockey training ground equal to that of any of the Canadian major junior hockey leagues.

In an attempt to shake up the fortunes of the Toronto Maple Leafs, the club dealt veteran star Lanny McDonald, right, to the Colorado Rockies in the middle of the 1979–80 season.

Swedish import Kent Nilsson, left, nicknamed "the Magic Man" for his mesmerizing puck handling skills, became an Atlanta Flame when his original team, the WHA Winnipeg Jets, joined the NHL in 1979–80. Nilsson, who went on to play in Calgary, Minnesota and Edmonton, gained renown as much for his occasionally lackadaisical attitude as for his clever play.

tory in two wins over Boston in a five-game triumph in the quarter-final. Bob Nystrom won a game for the Isles in the second overtime period as the New Yorkers moved past Buffalo in six games in the semi-final.

All four semi-finalists in 1979–80 — Minnesota, Buffalo, Philadelphia and the Islanders — were expansion clubs.

The Stanley Cup finals opened in the Spectrum and ended in typical Islanders' fashion when Denis Potvin fired the winner in overtime for a 4–3 victory. The Flyers earned a split at home with Paul Holmgren netting a hat trick in an 8–3 victory. The Isles won twice on their home ice, skating off with 6–2 and 5–2 victories. The Flyers stayed in the running with a 6–3 win at home in game five, but Bob Nystrom sent the home crowd into delirium by clinching the Stanley Cup with an overtime tally in game six. The playoff MVP was Bryan Trottier of the Islanders.

Three of the game's greatest players retired at the end of the season: Gordie Howe, Bobby Hull and Stan Mikita. The Atlanta Flames closed down operations in Georgia and moved to Calgary. Until a new facility could be built, the Flames would play in an old, small arena called the Calgary Corral, with a seating capacity of 6,000.

# YEAR

## 1979–80

**Stanley Cup Champion** — New York Islanders
**Prince of Wales Trophy Winner** — Buffalo Sabres
**Clarence Campbell Bowl Winner** — Philadelphia Flyers

### Final Standings

#### PRINCE OF WALES CONFERENCE

**Norris Division**

| Team | GP | W | L | T | GF | GA | PTS |
|------|----|----|----|----|----|----|----|
| Montreal | 80 | 47 | 20 | 13 | 328 | 240 | 107 |
| Los Angeles | 80 | 30 | 36 | 14 | 290 | 313 | 74 |
| Pittsburgh | 80 | 30 | 37 | 13 | 251 | 303 | 73 |
| Hartford | 80 | 27 | 34 | 19 | 303 | 312 | 73 |
| Detroit | 80 | 26 | 43 | 11 | 268 | 306 | 63 |

**Adams Division**

| Team | GP | W | L | T | GF | GA | PTS |
|------|----|----|----|----|----|----|----|
| Buffalo | 80 | 47 | 17 | 16 | 318 | 201 | 110 |
| Boston | 80 | 46 | 21 | 13 | 310 | 234 | 105 |
| Minnesota | 80 | 36 | 28 | 16 | 311 | 253 | 88 |
| Toronto | 80 | 35 | 40 | 5 | 304 | 327 | 75 |
| Quebec | 80 | 25 | 44 | 11 | 248 | 313 | 61 |

#### CLARENCE CAMPBELL CONFERENCE

**Patrick Division**

| Team | GP | W | L | T | GF | GA | PTS |
|------|----|----|----|----|----|----|----|
| Philadelphia | 80 | 48 | 12 | 20 | 327 | 254 | 116 |
| NY Islanders | 80 | 39 | 28 | 13 | 281 | 247 | 91 |
| NY Rangers | 80 | 38 | 32 | 10 | 308 | 284 | 86 |
| Atlanta | 80 | 35 | 32 | 13 | 282 | 269 | 83 |
| Washington | 80 | 27 | 40 | 13 | 261 | 293 | 67 |

**Smythe Division**

| Team | GP | W | L | T | GF | GA | PTS |
|------|----|----|----|----|----|----|----|
| Chicago | 80 | 34 | 27 | 19 | 241 | 250 | 87 |
| St. Louis | 80 | 34 | 34 | 12 | 266 | 278 | 80 |
| Vancouver | 80 | 27 | 37 | 16 | 256 | 281 | 70 |
| Edmonton | 80 | 28 | 39 | 13 | 301 | 322 | 69 |
| Winnipeg | 80 | 20 | 49 | 11 | 214 | 314 | 51 |
| Colorado | 80 | 19 | 48 | 13 | 234 | 308 | 51 |

### Leading Scorers

| Player | Club | GP | G | A | PTS | PIM |
|--------|------|----|----|----|----|----|
| Dionne, Marcel | Los Angeles | 80 | 53 | 84 | 137 | 32 |
| Gretzky, Wayne | Edmonton | 79 | 51 | 86 | 137 | 21 |
| Lafleur, Guy | Montreal | 74 | 50 | 75 | 125 | 12 |
| Perreault, Gilbert | Buffalo | 80 | 40 | 66 | 106 | 57 |
| Rogers, Mike | Hartford | 80 | 44 | 61 | 105 | 10 |
| Trottier, Bryan | NY Islanders | 78 | 42 | 62 | 104 | 68 |
| Simmer, Charlie | Los Angeles | 64 | 56 | 45 | 101 | 65 |
| Stoughton, Blaine | Hartford | 80 | 56 | 44 | 100 | 16 |
| Sittler, Darryl | Toronto | 73 | 40 | 57 | 97 | 62 |
| MacDonald, Blair | Edmonton | 80 | 46 | 48 | 94 | 6 |
| Federko, Bernie | St. Louis | 79 | 38 | 56 | 94 | 24 |

### NHL Award Winners

| | |
|---|---|
| **Hart (MVP)** | Wayne Gretzky |
| **Art Ross (Leading Scorer)** | Marcel Dionne |
| **Calder (Rookie of the Year)** | Ray Bourque |
| **Vezina (Lowest Goals-Against)** | Bob Sauve, Don Edwards |
| **Lady Byng (Gentlemanly Conduct)** | Wayne Gretzky |
| **Norris (Top Defenseman)** | Larry Robinson |
| **Conn Smythe (Playoff MVP)** | Bryan Trottier |
| **Patrick (Service to US Hockey)** | Bobby Clarke, Ed Snider, Fred Shero, 1980 US Olympic Hockey Team |
| **Masterton (Perseverance)** | Al MacAdam |
| **Pearson (NHLPA MVP)** | Marcel Dionne |
| **Adams (Coach of the Year)** | Pat Quinn |
| **Selke (Top Defensive Forward)** | Bob Gainey |
| **First Overall Draft Selection** | Doug Wickenheiser |
| **World/Olympic Champions** | United States |
| **AHL Calder Cup Champions** | Hershey Bears |
| **Memorial Cup Canadian Jr. Champions** | Cornwall Royals |
| **NCAA Champions** | North Dakota |
| **Canadian College Champions** | University of Alberta |

# 1980–1981

The Islanders' 1980 Stanley Cup championship, coming as it did after a 91-point finish in the regular season, demonstrated that the NHL wasn't dominated by any one club. Any of half a dozen teams were capable of winning. The Minnesota North Stars appeared promising after their climb to the semi-final the previous season. The Boston Bruins could only be stronger with the acquisition of netminder Rogie Vachon, another year of maturing for Ray Bourque and a talented first-round pick in Barry Pederson. Hockey fans were curious to see if the Montreal Canadiens, whose winning tradition labeled anything short of capturing the Stanley Cup an "off year," could bounce back after their early departure from the playoffs in 1980.

A great deal of interest was focused on the Quebec Nordiques, where a pair of blue-chip players in international hockey had fled Czechoslovakia to play in *la belle province*. Anton and Peter Stastny had been vital members of the Czech national team, and their defection added scoring punch to the Nordiques' offense. While he could hardly be considered a rookie, Peter Stastny set a record for first-year NHL players with 109 points as the Nordiques improved 17 points in the final standings. No less of a boon to the team, although slightly more surprising, was the emergence of Jacques Richard. Richard had been the first-ever draft selection of the Atlanta Flames and the second man chosen in the amateur draft of 1972. Up to this point his career had been a disappointment but, back in the city where he had seen so much success as a junior, Richard found his scoring touch and recorded 52 goals and 103 points.

The Calgary Flames played an exciting brand of hockey in the cramped quarters of the Calgary Corral. They were led by Kent Nilsson, who dazzled fans with his repertoire of flashy moves. When Daniel Bouchard was traded to Quebec, the goaltending duties were capably filled

*(continued on page 102)*

Powerful Clark Gillies (9) contributed 15 playoff points to the New York Islanders' second Stanley Cup victory in 1980–81. Below, Gillies clotheslines Minnesota's Paul Shmyr in front of goaltender Don Beaupre.

## 14. The European Invasion

Swedish forward Ulf Sterner was the first international player to appear in the NHL, playing four games for the New York Rangers in 1964–65. NHLers resented a "foreigner" playing in their league and subjected Sterner to some particularly heavy hitting. Sterner returned to Sweden where he continued his hockey career. In 1972 prior to the Team Canada-Soviet games in Moscow, the Canadians played an exhibition match against the Swedish Nationals. Tempers grew short in this game and Sterner, perhaps recalling his rough treatment in the NHL, cut Wayne Cashman of the Bruins for 19 stitches.

Juha "Whitey" Widing was Finnish-born and broke in with the Rangers in 1969–70. Having played Canadian junior hockey with the Brandon Wheat Kings, Widing blended into NHL play and lasted eight years in the NHL with New York, Los Angeles and Cleveland.

The first European player to cross the Atlantic and win a steady job in the NHL was Thommie Bergman, a Swedish defenseman who had played strongly in the 1972 Winter Olympics in Sapporo, Japan. The Detroit Red Wings scouted him at the Olympics and purchased his playing rights from the Swedish Ice Hockey Federation. Bergman was a solid performer who played two seasons for Detroit before joining the Winnipeg Jets of the WHA.

The following season, 1973–74, Borje Salming and Inge Hammarstrom joined the Toronto Maple Leafs. Both had fine rookie seasons, with Salming distinguishing himself as the Leafs' best defenseman and Hammarstrom scoring 20 goals. The early 1970s were the years of strategic intimidation in the NHL and both Swedes were repeatedly challenged and fouled.

The "W" in WHA stood for "World" and the new league looked to Europe for some of its star attractions. The Toronto Toros signed Czechoslovakian defectors Richard Farda and Vaclav Nedomansky for 1974–75. "Big Ned" was a superstar in Europe and a top player on the Czech Nationals. He had 56 goals in his second season in the WHA.

The Winnipeg Jets were the most ambitious European recruiters in either league, adding Finns Veli-Pekka Ketola and Heikki Riihiranta along with Swedes Lars-Erik Sjoberg, Ulf Nilsson, Anders Hedberg and Curt Larsson to their 1974–75 roster. Defenseman Sjoberg ran the team's offense while Hedberg and Nilsson combined with Bobby Hull to form a perpetual-motion forward line that many said would have been one of the best in the NHL. Sjoberg was captain of the Jets in their first NHL season. Winnipeg added more Scandinavians in subsequent seasons as Thommie Bergman, Mats Lindh, Willy Lindstrom, Dan Labraaten and Ket Nilsson joined the team.

Hedberg and Ulf Nilsson were recruited by the New York Rangers, joining the NHL in 1978–79. While unable to dominate play as they had in the WHA, both Swedes were among the Rangers' best

Unlike most European imports, Juha Widing played junior hockey in Canada before jumping to the NHL. Widing died suddenly on his farm in the B.C. interior several years after his retirement from pro hockey in 1977–78.

players in a year where the club reached the Stanley Cup final.

Kent Nilsson joined the Flames in Atlanta and Calgary. In 1980–81, he scored 49 goals and had 131 points to finish third in the NHL scoring race and become the first European player to record a 100–point season. In that same year, the Quebec Nordiques signed brothers Anton and Peter Stastny, who had defected from Czechoslovakia. Peter Stastny had 109 points in his first NHL season and has reached the 100-point plateau every year since. He became captain of the Nordiques in 1985–86. Pelle Lindbergh, who was killed in an auto accident in November, 1985, won the Vezina Trophy as the NHL's top goaltender in 1984–85. His fine play led the Philadelphia Flyers to that season's Stanley Cup final. Finnish star Jari Kurri, a linemate of Wayne Gretzky, became one of only three NHL players to score 70 goals in a season, registering 71 while winning the Lady Byng Trophy for gentlemanly play in 1985. Montreal's Mats Naslund had 110 points and was selected to the second all-star team as the Canadiens won the Cup in 1986.

Heading into the 1986–87 season, 25 Swedes, 11 Finns, eight Czechs and West German defenseman Ulli Heimer of the New Jersey Devils hold down spots on NHL rosters. Their crowd-pleasing, high-skill style stresses skating, playmaking and conditioning. European players have improved the caliber of hockey played in the NHL.

Three reasons that the Islanders won four consecutive Stanley Cup championships in the 1980s: Trottier, Potvin and Bossy — the dominant playmaker, defenseman and sniper of the era.

by Pat Riggin and Reggie Lemelin. The St. Louis Blues improved by 27 points over the previous year, due in large part to the outstanding goaltending of Mike Liut. Liut won 33 games as the team compiled 107 points for the second-best record in the NHL. Bernie Federko became the first Blues player to obtain 100 points in a season, and Wayne Babych

became the club's first 50-goal man when he posted 54 tallies.

Two of the NHL's top scorers came close to breaking Rocket Richard's record of 50 goals in 50 games. The Islanders' Mike Bossy scored two goals late in the third period of a game against the Nordiques giving him 50 in 50 and a tie with the Rocket. Charlie Simmer fired

St. Louis Blues goaltender Mike Liut was a first-team all-star in 1980–81. The same year, he was recipient of the NHL Players' Association Lester B. Pearson MVP Award.

three goals in his 50th game, but came up one goal short of the mark now shared by Richard and Bossy. Peter Stastny established a record for points on the road with four goals and four assists in an 11–7 shootout with Washington on February 22, 1981. Islander fans were treated to a five-goal night by John Tonelli in a 6–3 defeat of the Toronto Maple Leafs on January 6. Wayne Gretzky had five goals at the Northlands Coliseum February 18 in a 9–2 triumph over the St. Louis Blues. The 1,000-point fraternity welcomed its first new member in four seasons as Marcel Dionne attained the mark on January 7, 1981, — Guy Lafleur got this 1,000th

on March 4, followed closely by Bobby Clarke on March 19. In January, Phil Esposito announced his retirement as a player to become an assistant coach with the Rangers. He retired having scored 717 goals, second only to Gordie Howe in the all-time scoring race.

Wayne Gretzky became the first player in the modern NHL to average two points a game, handily winning the scoring title with 164 points. The Triple Crown Line had another big year in Los Angeles as all three of its members broke the 100-point barrier. Marcel Dionne had 58 goals while Charlie Simmer and Dave Taylor scored 56 and 47 despite missing

Butch Goring, a quick centerman from Winnipeg, Manitoba, came to the Islanders from the Los Angeles Kings in a trade during 1979–80, and was thought to be the catalyst that initiated the Islanders' four-year reign as Stanley Cup champions.

games due to injury. Dennis Maruk registered the first 50–goal season by a member of the Washington Capitals.

The preliminary round of the playoffs produced an upset when the Edmonton Oilers eliminated the Montreal Canadiens in three straight games. The New York Islanders began the defense of their Stanley Cup championship with a three-game sweep of Toronto. They were extended to six games in subduing the Oilers. Denis Potvin tied a single-game record for power-play goals by a defenseman with three. The team then swept the Rangers in four games to reach the finals for a second straight year.

Minnesota eliminated Boston in three straight games, then forced Buffalo to the sidelines in five. Minnesota next faced Calgary in a semi-final that featured a matchup of former junior teammates. The North Stars' Dino Ciccarelli, on his way to establishing a record for rookie goal scorers in the playoffs, and Calgary netminder Pat Riggin were both graduates of the London Knights of the Ontario Hockey League. The North Stars, paced by the scoring exploits of Ciccarelli, rookie Brad Palmer and Steve Payne, advanced to the finals with a six-game triumph over the Flames.

The Islanders' offense continued to be

Jean Ratelle, left, and Guy Charron, two respected centermen, retired at the end of the 1980–81 season. Ratelle retired as one of the NHL's few 20-year men, and was part of the biggest trade of the 1970s: Ratelle and Brad Park of the Rangers for Phil Esposito and Carol Vadnais of the Bruins. Charron's career spanned twelve seasons with stops in Montreal, Detroit, Kansas City and Washington.

driven by Mike Bossy, Bryan Trottier and Denis Potvin. Butch Goring, known for his hustle and defensive play, took over in an offensive capacity in the final. Despite suffering a 30-stitch gash in his chin in an opening-game 6–3 victory, Goring had a hat trick in a 7–5 decision in game three that left the Isles one victory short of their second Stanley Cup. The North Stars rebounded in game four, winning 4–2 and sending the series back to the Nassau Coliseum. Goring sparked the Islanders again, scoring two goals in a 5–1 victory that captured the Cup. Mike Bossy established a playoff record with 35 points, Bryan Trottier recorded a point in all 18 postseason games, and Denis Potvin set a record for points by a defenseman with 25, but it was Butch

Goring who skated off with the Conn Smythe Trophy.

Jean Ratelle announced his retirement at the end of the season. His career spanned 20 years in the NHL and saw him score 491 goals and 1,267 points.

The league announced that an unbalanced schedule would be adopted for the upcoming season and that teams would advance to the playoffs on the basis of the final standings in each division. The first four teams in each division would advance to postseason play. Many players prepared to shorten their vacations in preparation for the second Canada Cup tournament, scheduled for September, 1981. NHLers were found on the rosters of the American, Canadian, Finnish and Swedish teams.

# YEAR    1980–81

**Stanley Cup Champion** New York Islanders
**Prince of Wales Trophy Winner** Montreal Canadiens
**Clarence Campbell Bowl Winner** New York Islanders

## Final Standings

### PRINCE OF WALES CONFERENCE

#### Norris Division

| Team | GP | W | L | T | GF | GA | PTS |
|------|----|----|----|----|----|----|-----|
| Montreal | 80 | 45 | 22 | 13 | 332 | 232 | 103 |
| Los Angeles | 80 | 43 | 24 | 13 | 337 | 290 | 99 |
| Pittsburgh | 80 | 30 | 37 | 13 | 302 | 345 | 73 |
| Hartford | 80 | 21 | 41 | 18 | 292 | 372 | 60 |
| Detroit | 80 | 19 | 43 | 18 | 252 | 339 | 56 |

#### Adams Division

| Team | GP | W | L | T | GF | GA | PTS |
|------|----|----|----|----|----|----|-----|
| Buffalo | 80 | 39 | 20 | 21 | 327 | 250 | 99 |
| Boston | 80 | 37 | 30 | 13 | 316 | 272 | 87 |
| Minnesota | 80 | 35 | 28 | 17 | 291 | 263 | 87 |
| Quebec | 80 | 30 | 32 | 18 | 314 | 318 | 78 |
| Toronto | 80 | 28 | 37 | 15 | 322 | 367 | 71 |

### CLARENCE CAMPBELL CONFERENCE

#### Patrick Division

| Team | GP | W | L | T | GF | GA | PTS |
|------|----|----|----|----|----|----|-----|
| NY Islanders | 80 | 48 | 18 | 14 | 355 | 260 | 110 |
| Philadelphia | 80 | 41 | 24 | 15 | 313 | 249 | 97 |
| Calgary | 80 | 39 | 27 | 14 | 329 | 298 | 92 |
| NY Rangers | 80 | 30 | 36 | 14 | 312 | 317 | 74 |
| Washington | 80 | 26 | 36 | 18 | 286 | 317 | 70 |

#### Smythe Division

| Team | GP | W | L | T | GF | GA | PTS |
|------|----|----|----|----|----|----|-----|
| St. Louis | 80 | 45 | 18 | 17 | 352 | 281 | 107 |
| Chicago | 80 | 31 | 33 | 16 | 304 | 315 | 78 |
| Vancouver | 80 | 28 | 32 | 20 | 289 | 301 | 76 |
| Edmonton | 80 | 29 | 35 | 16 | 328 | 327 | 74 |
| Colorado | 80 | 22 | 45 | 13 | 258 | 344 | 57 |
| Winnipeg | 80 | 9 | 57 | 14 | 246 | 400 | 32 |

## Leading Scorers

| Player | Club | GP | G | A | PTS | PIM |
|--------|------|----|----|----|-----|-----|
| Gretzky, Wayne | Edmonton | 80 | 55 | 109 | 164 | 28 |
| Dionne, Marcel | Los Angeles | 80 | 58 | 77 | 135 | 70 |
| Nilsson, Kent | Calgary | 80 | 49 | 82 | 131 | 26 |
| Bossy, Mike | NY Islanders | 79 | 68 | 51 | 119 | 32 |
| Taylor, Dave | Los Angeles | 72 | 47 | 65 | 112 | 130 |
| Stastny, Peter | Quebec | 77 | 39 | 70 | 109 | 37 |
| Simmer, Charlie | Los Angeles | 65 | 56 | 49 | 105 | 62 |
| Rodgers, Mike | Hartford | 80 | 40 | 65 | 105 | 32 |
| Federko, Bernie | St. Louis | 78 | 31 | 73 | 104 | 47 |
| Richard, Jacques | Quebec | 79 | 52 | 51 | 103 | 39 |
| Middleton, Rick | Boston | 80 | 44 | 59 | 103 | 16 |
| Trottier, Bryan | NY Islanders | 73 | 31 | 72 | 103 | 74 |

## NHL Award Winners

**Hart (MVP)** Wayne Gretzky
**Art Ross (Leading Scorer)** Wayne Gretzky
**Calder (Rookie of the Year)** Peter Stastny
**Vezina (Lowest Goals-Against)** Richard Sevigny, Denis Herron, Michel Larocque
**Lady Byng (Gentlemanly Conduct)** Rick Kehoe
**Norris (Top Defenseman)** Randy Carlyle
**Conn Smythe (Playoff MVP)** Butch Goring
**Patrick (Service to US Hockey)** Charles M. Schulz
**Masterton (Perseverance)** Blake Dunlop
**Pearson (NHLPA MVP)** Mike Liut
**Adams (Coach of the Year)** Red Berenson
**Selke (Top Defensive Forward)** Bob Gainey
**First Overall Draft Selection** Dale Hawerchuk

**World/Olympic Champions** Soviet Union

**AHL Calder Cup Champions** Adirondack Red Wings

**Memorial Cup Canadian Jr. Champions** Cornwall Royals

**NCAA Champions** Wisconsin

**Canadian College Champions** University of Moncton

# 1981–1982

The 1981 Canada Cup belonged to the Soviet Nationals who defeated Team Canada 8–1 in the championship game. Sergei Shepelev had a hat trick and Igor Larionov two goals in the final match. Gretzky, Bossy and Trottier were the top scorers in the tournament.

The Minnesota North Stars continued to improve as the previous year's rookie sensation in the playoffs, Dino Ciccarelli, scored 55 goals and finished the season with 106 points. Minnesota led the realigned Norris Division. Center Bobby Smith, the number one draft selection in 1978, led the club with 114 points. Another Norris Division club that made great advances in 1981–82 was Winnipeg. The Jets had been the NHL's worst club in 1980–81, winnning only nine games all season. An article in *Sports Illustrated* referred to the club as the "Loser-peg Jets." Coached by Tom Watt, who had won several Canadian collegiate championships at the University of Toronto, the club improved from 32 points to 80 points in one season.

Bobby Carpenter was chosen 3rd overall by the Washington Capitals in the 1981 entry draft, becoming the first American-born player to be picked in the draft's first round. Carpenter made a direct leap from high school hockey in Massachusetts to the NHL, and scored 32 goals during his first pro season.

The Winnipeg Jets made centerman Dale Hawerchuk their top draft choice in 1981, and he rewarded the struggling franchise with 103 points during his first NHL season. Below, Hawerchuk knifes away from the determined checking of Buffalo's Craig Ramsay.

Sparked by the play of first-round draft selection Dale Hawerchuk, who contributed 45 goals and 103 points as a rookie, and a big 43-goal season from Morris Lukowich, the Jets made the playoffs for the first time since joining the NHL. Edmonton was the big story in the Smythe Division as it vaulted to the top of the class with 111 points. Montreal proved it could still win during the regular season, leading the Adams Division with 109 points.

It was the Wayne Gretzky show all year as the "Great One" decimated the record books. He scored 50 goals in only 39 games, knocking 11 games off the fastest-50 record shared by Rocket Richard and Mike Bossy. His record-breaking performance culminated in a five-goal outburst on December 30, 1981, against the Flyers in a 7–5 Oiler victory. Gretzky finished the season with an astonishing 92 goals and 212 points.

Grant Mulvey of the Blackhawks scored five goals in a 9–5 victory over St. Louis on February 3, 1982. Bryan Trot-

Herb Brooks coached the U.S. Olympic team to a stunning upset victory in the Lake Placid Olympics of 1980. Brooks went on to coach the New York Rangers, but in four seasons with the team never gained the success he'd enjoyed at the amateur level.

Richard Brodeur, alias "King Richard," came to the Vancouver Canucks in a trade with the New York Islanders in 1980–81, and the following year led the Canucks to the Stanley Cup final against his former teammates.

tier had a five-goal performance against the Flyers on February 13, and poor Pete Peeters was victimized yet again when Willy Lindstrom scored five times on March 2 in the Jets' 7–6 victory over the Flyers in the Spectrum. Ian Turnbull turned in a big game with the Los Angeles Kings when he fired four goals on December 12 in a 7–5 victory over Vancouver. Gilbert Perreault scored his 1,000th point with an assist on April 3.

The New York Islanders produced the season's best record with 52 victories and 118 points. In a streak beginning January 21 and ending February 20, the Islanders established an NHL record with 15 straight wins. The record-setting win was a 3–2 victory over the Colorado Rockies with ex-Islander Chico Resch in goal.

The new playoff format called for the first four teams in each division to play a five-game divisional semi-final. The two winners in each division advanced to a seven-game divisional final, with the winner advancing to either the Wales or the Campbell conference final.

In the Norris Division, St. Louis had too much playoff experience for the Jets, while the division-leading North Stars were surprised by the Blackhawks. Chicago then eliminated St. Louis in their finest postseason performance in several years. The other Campbell Conference division provided an upset when the Los Angeles Kings controlled Gretzky and the Edmonton Oilers to escape with a five-game victory. In the third game of this series, the Kings fell behind 5–0, caught up and won on an overtime goal by Daryl Evans. Vancouver defeated Calgary in three straight games and eliminated Los Angeles in five to win the Smythe Division championship.

In the Patrick Division, the Islanders needed five games to turn back the Penguins' challenge in the semi-final. The Rangers defeated the Flyers in the other series. In the "Subway Series," the Islanders edged closer to their third Stanley Cup final, beating the Rangers in six games.

The Montreal Canadiens were eliminated by Quebec in five games and the Boston Bruins beat the Buffalo Sabres in four. Quebec and Boston staged the most thrilling matchup of the playoffs, as

# TWENTY TRENDS THAT SHAPED MODERN HOCKEY

## 15. US Olympic Victory, 1980

The last US Olympic team to win the gold medal had been the 1960 squad, which won in Squaw Valley, California. Since that time, the Soviet Union had become the dominant force in international hockey. Team USA had surprised the experts with a silver medal in the 1972 games at Sapporo, Japan, but it appeared that something more than the home ice advantage afforded by the 1980 Olympic site in Lake Placid, New York, was needed to help the team against a very strong international field.

Team USA faced a powerful Swedish team in the opening game. They were badly outplayed in the first period and only the netminding heroics of Jim Craig kept the score from being greater than a 1–0 deficit. The team came out flying to start the second and took momentum away from the Swedes. Bill Baker's 50-foot blast from the point with 27 seconds left in the game earned the Americans a 2–2 tie.

It did not get any easier, as the US squad faced the Czechs with their brilliant star scorers, Ivan Hlinka and Milan Novy, in their second contest. The two teams skated to a 2–2 tie after the opening period. Team USA led 4–2 at the end of the second and most people watching the game felt that the American team would adopt a defensive shell and try to withstand a Czech barrage in the third period. Instead, team USA coach Brooks cast logic

Soviet captain Boris Mikhailov and Team USA defenseman Ken Morrow.

aside and ordered his players to open it up and freewheel with the fluid-skating Czechs. This strategy proved effective as Team USA skated to a 7–3 victory in a major upset.

The team battled off complacency to subdue Norway 5–1, Romania 7–2 and West Germany 4–2. This took them into the medal round and a match with the powerful Soviets. The Russian Nationals had labored in defeating Finland and Canada earlier in the tournament. However, Vladimir Krutov opened the scoring on a deflection, midway through the first period. Mark Pavelich fed Buzz Schneider and his rising slapshot hit the top corner to equal the count, but Sergei Makarov restored the Soviet lead at 17:34. It appeared that the Soviet's would go to the dressing room with a one-goal lead, but with three seconds remaining in the period, Dave Christian uncorked a drive from his side of center. Soviet goaltender Vladislav Tretiak allowed a huge rebound and, with the Soviet defense thinking that the period was over, an alert Mark Johnson barged in to beat everyone to the puck and

stuff it home with one second left in the period.

Vladimir Myshkin replaced Tretiak to start the second period. Team USA appeared to be weak and disorganized as the Russians controlled play and regained a one-goal lead. However, the youthful American contingent refused to wilt and, at 8:39 of the final frame, Johnson again got the tying goal. The rigorous training imposed on the American team by coach Brooks began to pay dividends, as the team seemed to be getting stronger as the game progressed. At the midway point of the period, team captain Mike Eruzione beat Myshkin to give the team its first lead. The Soviets made every effort to get the tying goal, but Jim Craig and the enthusiastic defensive play of all the American skaters kept the puck out of the American net. The Cinderella team of the Winter Olympics retained its composure to win 4–3.

In their final game, Team USA needed a victory over Finland to clinch the gold medal. For the sixth time in seven games, the club found itself trailing 1–0. Steve Christoff tied the game, but

Mikko Leinonen, who later played for the New York Rangers, put the Finns ahead 2–1 after two periods. Phil Verchota converted a pass from Dave Christian to put Team USA back on even terms with two and a half minutes gone in the final period. Four minutes later, Rob McClanahan put them ahead to stay and the Americans did not look back, skating to a 4–2 gold-medal-clinching victory.

Many of Team USA's 1980 players went on to careers in the NHL. Dave Christian, though a defenseman with Team USA, became a high-scoring forward for both the Winnipeg Jets and Washington Capitals. Neal Broten of the Minnesota North Stars was the first American-born player to surpass 100 points. Mike Ramsey is a defenseman with the Buffalo Sabres, while rearguard Ken Morrow went from savoring the Olympic victory to four straight Stanley Cups with the New York Islanders. Mark Pavelich had several good seasons with the New York Rangers, and is now in the Minnesota North Stars' organization. Mark Johnson has played for five NHL clubs, and is now an important part of the New Jersey Devils' improving franchise. Steve Christoff, Dave Silk, Rob McClanahan and Jim Craig all made it to the NHL for varying lengths of time. With the 1980 gold medal, the US Olympic hockey program earned its place as an important proving ground for potential NHLers.

Quebec, now featuring three Stastny brothers (Marian had joined the Nordiques that season) eliminated Boston in seven games.

As the playoffs went on, the Vancouver Canucks found themselves surrounded by a sea of white towels. In the Campbell Conference final, the Canucks had been incensed by what they considered to be a poor call by the referee at Chicago Stadium. Roger Nielson and all the players on the bench waved towels in a derisive gesture of surrender in what they considered to be a poorly officiated game. When the team returned to Van-couver, their fans at the airport waved towels as the players left the aircraft and thousands of towels found their way into Vancouver's Pacific Coliseum for the remainder of the Canucks' playoff matches. Inspired by the play of team leaders Stan Smyl, Harold Snepsts, Dave "Tiger" Williams and goaltender Richard Brodeur, the astonishing Canucks defeated the Hawks in five games to move on to the Stanley Cup final.

Playing with the confidence acquired in two previous Cup wins, the Islanders played strongly in their series with Quebec. Mike Bossy and Bryan Trottier con-

Charlie Simmer's best seasons came in 1979–80 and 1980–81 with the Los Angeles Kings, when he counted a two-season total of 112 goals and 94 assists. He was an NHL all-star both years.

Bob Nystrom of the New York Islanders signals an empty-net goal in the third game of the 1981–82 Stanley Cup final against the Vancouver Canucks. Nystrom had 39 playoff goals during his 13-year career with the Islanders.

tinued to pile up points and Billy Smith, at his best under pressure, handled the goaltending duties. Quebec, feeling the effects of two tough seven-game series in the Adams Division, bowed to the Islanders in four straight.

The Islanders were favored in the Cup final against the Canucks. The five-game division semi-final against Pittsburgh was the closest the Islanders had come to being upset in the postseason. Mike Bossy dismissed any thought of an upset in game one of the final, scoring three times to lift his team to a 6–5 victory. Game two was the Canucks' best effort, but the Islanders' superior fire power gave them a 6–4 win. In game three, Billy Smith shut out the Canucks 3–0. The se-

ries ended with game four, which the Islanders won 3–1. The win allowed the Islanders to join the Leafs and Canadiens as the only NHL teams to win three consecutive Stanley Cups. Mike Bossy was rewarded for his 17-goal postseason with the Conn Smythe Trophy.

In May, Colorado Rockies' owner Peter Gilbert sold the team to a group from New Jersey. John McMullen headed the purchasing group, which included Brendan T. Byrne, a former governor of New Jersey now in private law practice, and John C. Whitehead, a senior partner with an investment firm. The team was to be moved to East Rutherford, New Jersey, where it would play out of the Meadowlands Arena.

# YEAR                                    1981–82

**Stanley Cup Champion**          New York Islanders
**Prince of Wales Trophy Winner**  New York Islanders
**Clarence Campbell Bowl Winner**  Vancouver Canucks

**Final Standings**

## CLARENCE CAMPBELL CONFERENCE

### Norris Division

| Team | GP | W | L | T | GF | GA | PTS |
|------|----|---|---|---|----|----|-----|
| Minnesota | 80 | 37 | 23 | 20 | 346 | 288 | 94 |
| Winnipeg | 80 | 33 | 33 | 14 | 319 | 332 | 80 |
| St. Louis | 80 | 32 | 40 | 8 | 315 | 349 | 72 |
| Chicago | 80 | 30 | 38 | 12 | 332 | 363 | 72 |
| Toronto | 80 | 20 | 44 | 16 | 298 | 380 | 56 |
| Detroit | 80 | 21 | 47 | 12 | 270 | 351 | 54 |

### Smythe Division

| Team | GP | W | L | T | GF | GA | PTS |
|------|----|---|---|---|----|----|-----|
| Edmonton | 80 | 48 | 17 | 15 | 417 | 295 | 111 |
| Vancouver | 80 | 30 | 33 | 17 | 290 | 286 | 77 |
| Calgary | 80 | 29 | 34 | 17 | 334 | 345 | 75 |
| Los Angeles | 80 | 24 | 41 | 15 | 314 | 369 | 63 |
| Colorado | 80 | 18 | 49 | 13 | 241 | 362 | 49 |

## PRINCE OF WALES CONFERENCE

### Adams Division

| Team | GP | W | L | T | GF | GA | PTS |
|------|----|---|---|---|----|----|-----|
| Montreal | 80 | 46 | 17 | 17 | 360 | 223 | 109 |
| Boston | 80 | 43 | 27 | 10 | 323 | 285 | 96 |
| Buffalo | 80 | 39 | 26 | 15 | 307 | 273 | 93 |
| Quebec | 80 | 33 | 31 | 16 | 356 | 345 | 82 |
| Hartford | 80 | 21 | 41 | 18 | 264 | 351 | 60 |

### Patrick Division

| Team | GP | W | L | T | GF | GA | PTS |
|------|----|---|---|---|----|----|-----|
| NY Islanders | 80 | 54 | 16 | 10 | 385 | 250 | 118 |
| NY Rangers | 80 | 39 | 27 | 14 | 316 | 306 | 92 |
| Philadelphia | 80 | 38 | 31 | 11 | 325 | 313 | 87 |
| Pittsburgh | 80 | 31 | 36 | 13 | 310 | 337 | 75 |
| Washington | 80 | 26 | 41 | 13 | 319 | 338 | 65 |

### Leading Scorers

| Player | Club | GP | G | A | PTS | PIM |
|--------|------|----|---|---|-----|-----|
| Gretzky, Wayne | Edmonton | 80 | 92 | 120 | 212 | 26 |
| Bossy, Mike | NY Islanders | 80 | 64 | 83 | 147 | 22 |
| Stastny, Peter | Quebec | 80 | 46 | 93 | 139 | 91 |
| Maruk, Dennis | Washington | 80 | 60 | 76 | 136 | 128 |
| Trottier, Bryan | NY Islanders | 80 | 50 | 79 | 129 | 88 |
| Savard, Denis | Chicago | 80 | 32 | 87 | 119 | 82 |
| Dionne, Marcel | Los Angeles | 78 | 50 | 67 | 117 | 50 |
| Smith, Bobby | Minnesota | 80 | 43 | 71 | 114 | 82 |
| Ciccarelli, Dino | Minnesota | 76 | 55 | 51 | 106 | 138 |
| Taylor, Dave | Los Angeles | 78 | 39 | 67 | 106 | 130 |

### NHL Award Winners

| | |
|---|---|
| **Hart (MVP)** | Wayne Gretzky |
| **Art Ross (Leading Scorer)** | Wayne Gretzky |
| **Calder (Rookie of the Year)** | Dale Hawerchuk |
| **Vezina (Top Goaltender)** | Bill Smith |
| **Lady Byng (Gentlemanly Conduct)** | Rick Middleton |
| **Norris (Top Defenseman)** | Doug Wilson |
| **Conn Smythe (Playoff MVP)** | Mike Bossy |
| **Patrick (Service to US Hockey)** | Emile P. Francis |
| **Masterton (Perseverance)** | Glenn "Chico" Resch |
| **Pearson (NHLPA MVP)** | Wayne Gretzky |
| **Adams (Coach of the Year)** | Tom Watt |
| **Selke (Top Defensive Forward)** | Steve Kasper |
| **Jennings (Lowest Goals-Against)** | Rick Wamsley, Dennis Herron |
| **First Overall Draft Selection** | Gord Kluzak |
| **World/Olympic Champions** | Soviet Union |
| **AHL Calder Cup Champions** | New Brunswick Hawks |
| **Memorial Cup Canadian Jr. Champions** | Kitchener Rangers |
| **NCAA Champions** | North Dakota |
| **Canadian College Champions** | University of Moncton |

# 1982–1983

The trend in the NHL was returning to speed and passing. The recent successes of teams like Montreal, the Islanders and Edmonton reinforced the need for mobile, intelligent players.

The Edmonton Oilers made changes in the offseason. They traded defenseman Risto Siltanen to the Flyers for Ken Linseman. Czech star Jaroslav Pouzar joined the team to play on a line with Gretzky and talented Finn Jari Kurri. Mark Messier was coming off a 50-goal season, indicating no lack of scoring power in Edmonton. Pity the Winnipeg Jets, who had moved out of the Norris and into the high-scoring Smythe Division. New Jersey was placed in the Patrick Division.

Led by Denis Savard and Norris Trophy winner Doug Wilson, the Chicago Blackhawks were the league's most improved team. Savard, a superb skater and playmaker, combined with Al Secord and rookie Steve Larmer to form one of the NHL's best lines. Secord became the first Hawks' player to score 50 goals since Bobby Hull in 1971–72, finishing with 54 while Larmer had 43 tallies. The Hawks led the Norris Division with 104 points.

Edmonton equaled a record set by the 1970–71 Boston Bruins when four of their skaters topped the 100-point barrier. Gretzky led all scorers with 196 points and 71 goals. This, when combined with Mark Messier (48 goals), Glenn Anderson (48), and Jari Kurri (45), allowed the Oilers to set a record for most goals in a season. The team also got a 96-point season from rearguard Paul Coffey and won its division with 106 points. Calgary finished second with 78 points, getting a big season from Lanny McDonald, who scored 66 goals. The Los Angeles Kings missed the playoffs but saw Marcel Dionne score his 500th goal in a 7–2 loss to Washington on December 14, 1982.

The Boston Bruins had the NHL's best record, winning the Adams Division with 110 points despite losing promising 19-

A two-man contest of balance and strength: Montreal defenseman Larry Robinson attempts to reroute Edmonton's Glenn Anderson as he surges toward the net.

*Yeaaaahhh!* Stanley Cup number four for Bryan Trottier and the Islanders.

year-old forward Normand Leveille with a near-fatal brain hemorrhage. Leveille's condition was not hockey-related, but he would never play in the NHL again. Barry Pederson paced the Bruins' attack with 107 points.

Michel Goulet became the Nordiques' first player to reach 50 goals, finishing the season with 57.

Philadelphia had acquired Mark Howe in the three-way trade that sent Risto Siltanen to the Hartford Whalers and Ken Linesman to the Oilers. With Howe on the Flyer defense, the team allowed 73 fewer goals than the previous season. Washington, sparked by a Norris trophy-winning season from defenseman Rod Langway, improved tremendously, climbing to third place with 94 points.

Edmonton defeated the Winnipeg Jets in three straight games in the Smythe Division semi-final, while Calgary needed four games to eliminate Vancouver. The Oilers overpowered the Flames, out-scoring them 35–13 in five games. Chicago defeated St. Louis in four and then met the North Stars, who had eliminated the Leafs in four games. The Hawks won the Norris Division championship by besting the North Stars in five games.

Boston sidelined the Nordiques in four games and was joined in the Adams Division final by Buffalo, who eliminated Montreal in three straight. The Bruins needed all seven games in the final, beating Buffalo in an exciting series. Philadelphia, despite a fine regular season, was upset by the Rangers in three

Brent Sutter, right, is one of six rugged Sutter brothers currently playing in the NHL. Brent joined the Islanders from the Lethbridge Broncos halfway through the 1981–82 season, and during his first five years with the team spent 436 minutes, more than seven hours, in the penalty box.

The Brendan Byrne Meadowlands Arena, home of the New Jersey Devils, hosted its first NHL regular-season game October 5, 1982, as the Penguins and Devils skated to a 3–3 tie.

games. The Islanders made the Washington Capitals' first visit to postseason play a short one, winning in four games. The Isles then moved into the Patrick Division final with a six-game decision over the Rangers.

In the Campbell Conference final, the Oilers defeated the Hawks in the minimum four games. The Bruins were expected to challenge the Islanders as Rick Middleton had established a record for most points in a series other than a final, with five goals and 14 assists in the seven-game series with Buffalo. Barry Pederson was not far behind, with seven goals and nine assists. Goaltender Pete Peeters, newly acquired by Boston, played every game for the Bruins in the playoffs and was performing magic in the Boston net. But Mike Bossy took control of the series for the Islanders, scoring seven goals in lopsided 8–4 and 8–3 victories at the Nassau Coliseum. The Islanders were in the Stanley Cup final for the fourth straight year.

The Islanders-Oilers final matched the two top offensive units in hockey. Mark Messier had already scored three hat tricks in the postseason, equaling Mike Bossy. Gretzky had two three-goal performances and was racking up points at his regular pace: more than two per game. But instead of the high-scoring shootout most fans predicted, the Oilers were completely shut down. Billy Smith shut them out 2–0 in game one before the Islanders' offense took charge with a 6–3 decision in game two. Returning to Long Island, the Islanders displayed tight defense and brilliant goaltending to complete a four-game sweep by scores of 5–1 and 4–2. Billy Smith earned the Conn Smythe Trophy.

At the June NHL meetings, a five-minute overtime period was instituted for regular-season competition. Later in the summer, the St. Louis Blues were purchased from Ralston Purina by Beverly Hills businessman Harry Ornest.

## 16. Speed, Size and Youth

In the years prior to expansion, only the NHL's biggest players were more than six feet tall and over 200 pounds in weight. Today's pro scouts give preference to forwards who are at least 6' 2" and 210 lbs. and defensemen who are six feet and 200 lbs. The prototypical modern NHL player is big enough to stand the heavy going along the boards while still possessing tremendous speed. Size, speed and mobility are sought in every NHL prospect as the 1980s have seen the emergence of the big man in hockey. If the mobility is there, the big man is preferred in almost every game situation. He has a greater reach and is harder to move out from in front of the net. The biggest men in the NHL now reach 6' 5" and 230 lbs.

This trend to speed and size has resulted in younger players and shorter careers. During the 1950s and early 1960s, when rosters changed only gradually, veteran players accumulated their years in the game by playing quite a few seasons after their physical peak. Experience substituted for speed or agility as a coach would assign a veteran player to increasingly less arduous responsibilities as the years went by. Most of the game's 20-year men logged most of their ice time during this era. The pace of today's game, the pressure of big young players fighting for jobs and the rigors of a schedule that, with training camp and playoffs, involves as many as 110 games and runs from September to May makes the prospect of many more 40-year-old skaters and 20-year veterans unlikely.

Better salaries and pension benefits tend to discourage players from playing much past the age of 35. If they have managed their incomes wisely, today's players don't need to hang on. The most recent collective bargaining agreement signed by the NHL Players' Association and the league provides for a lump-sum payment of $250,000 at age 55 to any player who plays 40 NHL games from 1986–87 to 1990–91.

The Stanley Cup winning rosters of 1967 and 1986 offer an interesting comparison. The Maple Leafs, the 1967 winners, were a team of veterans including Allan Stanley (40), Red Kelly (39), Tim Horton, Marcel Pronovost and George Armstrong (all 37). The goaltenders, Johnny Bower and Terry Sawchuk, were 43 and 37. The Canadiens, winners in 1986, had as many as ten rookies in their lineup. Larry Robinson (35), Bob Gainey (32) and Rick Green (30) were the oldest players in the lineup. Playoff scoring star Claude Lemieux and defenseman Petr Svoboda were 20. Goaltender Patrick Roy was 21.

A professional at 17, Edmonton's Mark Messier has all the tools for success in the modern NHL. At six feet and 205 pounds, he's one of the strongest and fastest players in the game. He was an all-star and a 50-goal scorer as a 21-year-old. Dave Maloney of the Rangers is the checker.

Ex–Czech national team star Milan Novy left his homeland and played the 1982–83 season in the uniform of the Washington Capitals. The well-seasoned centerman scored 18 goals and had 30 assists in his only NHL campaign.

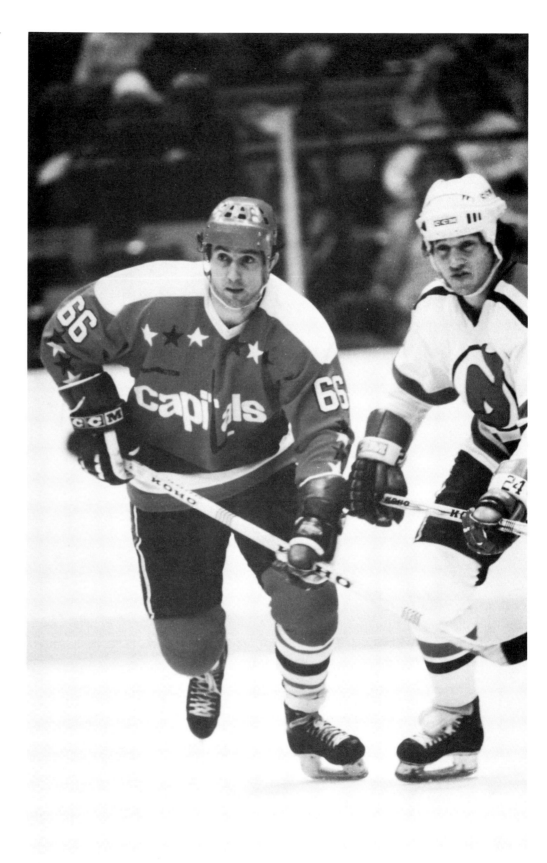

# YEAR                                    1982–83

**Stanley Cup Champion**        New York Islanders
**Prince of Wales Trophy Winner**   New York Islanders
**Clarence Campbell Bowl Winner**   Edmonton Oilers

**Final Standings**

## CLARENCE CAMPBELL CONFERENCE

### Norris Division

| Team | GP | W | L | T | GF | GA | PTS |
|------|----|----|----|----|----|----|----|
| Chicago | 80 | 47 | 23 | 10 | 338 | 268 | 104 |
| Minnesota | 80 | 40 | 24 | 16 | 321 | 290 | 96 |
| Toronto | 80 | 28 | 40 | 12 | 293 | 330 | 68 |
| St. Louis | 80 | 25 | 40 | 15 | 285 | 316 | 65 |
| Detroit | 80 | 21 | 44 | 15 | 263 | 344 | 57 |

### Smythe Division

| Team | GP | W | L | T | GF | GA | PTS |
|------|----|----|----|----|----|----|----|
| Edmonton | 80 | 47 | 21 | 12 | 424 | 315 | 106 |
| Calgary | 80 | 32 | 34 | 14 | 321 | 317 | 78 |
| Vancouver | 80 | 30 | 35 | 15 | 303 | 309 | 75 |
| Winnipeg | 80 | 33 | 39 | 8 | 311 | 333 | 74 |
| Los Angeles | 80 | 27 | 41 | 12 | 308 | 365 | 66 |

## PRINCE OF WALES CONFERENCE

### Adams Division

| Team | GP | W | L | T | GF | GA | PTS |
|------|----|----|----|----|----|----|----|
| Boston | 80 | 50 | 20 | 10 | 327 | 228 | 110 |
| Montreal | 80 | 42 | 24 | 14 | 350 | 286 | 98 |
| Buffalo | 80 | 38 | 29 | 13 | 318 | 285 | 89 |
| Quebec | 80 | 34 | 34 | 12 | 343 | 336 | 80 |
| Hartford | 80 | 19 | 54 | 7 | 261 | 403 | 45 |

### Patrick Division

| Team | GP | W | L | T | GF | GA | PTS |
|------|----|----|----|----|----|----|----|
| Philadelphia | 80 | 49 | 23 | 8 | 326 | 240 | 106 |
| NY Islanders | 80 | 42 | 26 | 12 | 302 | 226 | 96 |
| Washington | 80 | 39 | 25 | 16 | 306 | 283 | 94 |
| NY Rangers | 80 | 35 | 35 | 10 | 306 | 287 | 80 |
| New Jersey | 80 | 17 | 49 | 14 | 230 | 338 | 48 |
| Pittsburgh | 80 | 18 | 53 | 9 | 257 | 394 | 45 |

### Leading Scorers

| Player | Club | GP | G | A | PTS | PIM |
|--------|------|----|----|----|----|----|
| Gretzky, Wayne | Edmonton | 80 | 71 | 125 | 196 | 59 |
| Stastny, Peter | Quebec | 75 | 47 | 77 | 124 | 78 |
| Savard, Denis | Chicago | 78 | 35 | 86 | 121 | 99 |
| Bossy, Mike | NY Islanders | 79 | 60 | 58 | 118 | 20 |
| Dionne, Marcel | Los Angeles | 80 | 56 | 51 | 107 | 22 |
| Pederson, Barry | Boston | 77 | 46 | 61 | 107 | 47 |
| Messier, Mark | Edmonton | 77 | 48 | 58 | 106 | 72 |
| Goulet, Michel | Quebec | 80 | 57 | 48 | 105 | 51 |
| Anderson, Glenn | Edmonton | 72 | 48 | 56 | 104 | 70 |
| Nilsson, Kent | Calgary | 80 | 46 | 58 | 104 | 10 |
| Kurri, Jari | Edmonton | 80 | 45 | 59 | 104 | 22 |

### NHL Award Winners

| | |
|---|---|
| **Hart (MVP)** | Wayne Gretzky |
| **Art Ross (Leading Scorer)** | Wayne Gretzky |
| **Calder (Rookie of the Year)** | Steve Larmer |
| **Vezina (Top Goaltender)** | Pete Peeters |
| **Lady Byng (Gentlemanly Conduct)** | Mike Bossy |
| **Norris (Top Defenseman)** | Rod Langway |
| **Conn Smythe (Playoff MVP)** | Billy Smith |
| **Patrick (Service to US Hockey)** | Bill Torrey |
| **Masterton (Perseverance)** | Lanny McDonald |
| **Pearson (NHLPA MVP)** | Wayne Gretzky |
| **Adams (Coach of the Year)** | Orval Tessier |
| **Selke (Top Defensive Forward)** | Bobby Clarke |
| **Jennings (Lowest Goals-Against)** | Roland Melanson, Billy Smith |
| **Emery Edge (Plus/Minus Leader)** | Charlie Huddy |
| **First Overall Draft Selection** | Brian Lawton |
| **World/Olympic Champions** | Soviet Union |
| **AHL Calder Cup Champions** | Rochester Americans |
| **Memorial Cup Canadian Jr. Champions** | Portland Winter Hawks |
| **NCAA Champions** | Wisconsin |
| **Canadian College Champions** | University of Saskatchewan |

# 1983–1984

The net came off its moorings many times in the rugged 1983–84 playoff edition of the "Battle of New York." Islander goalie Rollie Melanson and Stefan Persson defend against Peter Sundstrom of the Rangers. The Islanders prevailed with an overtime win in game five.

If any club was going to challenge the Islanders for the Stanley Cup, the Edmonton Oilers appeared to be the likely candidate. Only the Montreal Canadiens of the late 1950s had ever won five consecutive championships, and the "drive for five" would sustain the Islanders' intensity during the long season. Some hockey fans wondered if the Oilers could regain their composure after becoming badly flustered in last season's final.

The Washington Capitals promised to be stronger than ever with the acquisition of Dave Christian from Winnipeg. The Buffalo Sabres hoped to move up in the standings with a "youth movement" that included high school draftee Phil Housley, 19 years of age, and Finnish defenseman Hannu Virta, 20. The Sabres dipped into the American high school tal-ent pool again and made 18-year-old goal-tender Tom Barrasso their first-round draft selection.

The NHL took a hard line on the abuse of officials: Chicago Blackhawks' veteran center Tom Lysiak was suspended for twenty games after knocking the skates out from under linesman Ron Foyt. Guy Lafleur recorded his 500th goal on December 20, 1983 in a 5–2 victory over Washington. Wayne Gretzky had his consecutive game point-scoring streak halted at 51 in a 4–2 loss to the the Kings on January 27, 1984. Washinton Capitals Bengt Gustafsson had a five-goal game against the Flyers in a 7–1 win on January 8.

On the way to another record-shatter-ing goal total, the Oilers had five-goal nights from Jari Kurri and utility forward Pat Hughes. It was shades of the old

*(continued on page 124)*

After scoring 17 playoff goals in three successive years, Mike Bossy's production dropped to eight goals during the 1983–84 playoffs. The lapse contributed to the Islanders' failure to win their fifth Stanley Cup in a row.

Rookie goaltender Tom Barrasso joined the Buffalo Sabres directly from Acton-Boxboro high school in Massachusetts for the 1983–84 season. The dauntless rookie proceeded to win the Vezina and Calder trophies, and was named to the league's first all-star team during his first year as a pro. Above, he is beaten for a goal by the Quebec Nordiques.

Pierre Mondou, right, played eight seasons with the Montreal Canadiens, and was at the peak of his career when an eye injury forced his retirement in 1985.

## 17. The Great Gretzky

In 1978 a frail-looking 17-year-old boy left the Sault Ste. Marie Greyhounds of the Ontario Hockey Association to sign a professional contract with the Indianapolis Racers of the WHA. Wayne Gretzky had been named the rookie of the year in the OHA the previous season. The Indianapolis franchise in the WHA was owned by Canadian entrepreneur Nelson Skalbania, who fell upon hard times and folded his team partway into the 1978–79 season. As an underage junior, Gretzky was not eligible to play in the NHL and his rights were purchased eight games into the season by another Canadian entrepreneur, Edmonton Oilers' owner Peter Pocklington. Playing with men as much as twice his age, the kid from Brantford, Ontario, picked up 110 points in his rookie season. Gretzky was the WHA's leading playoff scorer with 10 goals and 20 points as his Edmonton Oilers were defeated four games to two by the Winnipeg Jets in the last Avco Cup final. He was named the WHA rookie of the year and made the WHA's second all-star team.

Gretzky was kept as one of the Oilers' priority selections when the team joined the NHL the following year. There was a widespread feeling that Gretzky's WHA success was merely evidence of the weaker caliber of play in the rival league, and that he would not be able to post nearly as impressive a showing in the tight-checking, hard-hitting competition of the NHL. Many questioned his skating ability and slight physical stature. But while his skating ability may lack the explosive speed of Guy Lafleur or the fluidity of Bobby Orr, it simply does not seem to matter in Gretzky's case.

In his first NHL season he tied Marcel Dionne for the league lead in points with 137. Dionne was awarded the Art Ross Trophy by virtue of scoring more goals, but Gretzky did manage 51 of his own. He also spearheaded

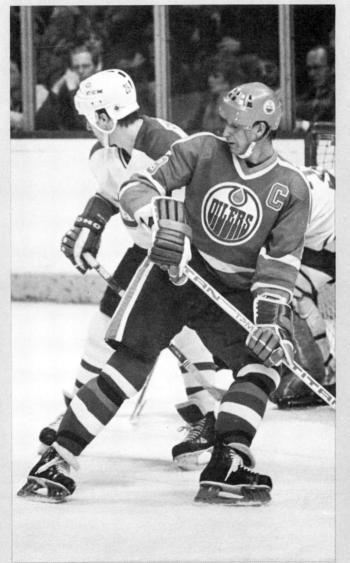

the late-season change that took the Oilers into post-season play. He won the Lady Byng Trophy while being chosen to the second all-star team. Since 1980, Gretzky has put on a mind-boggling display of scoring that has made him the most dominant athlete in professional sports. It often appears that while the game is whirling at top speed around him, his consciousness of what is happening all over the ice surface is so complete that it is as if the play were unfolding in ultra-slow motion visible to Gretzky alone. At six feet tall and 170 lbs., he is often dwarfed in size and strength by his opponents yet, by some sixth sense, is rarely bodychecked.

Gretzky owns every single-season scoring record in the NHL including most goals (92), most assists (163) and total points (215). He has won the Hart Trophy as the league's MVP every year he has played in the NHL. For the past seven years he has earned the Art Ross Trophy as top scorer and been named the center on the first team all-star squad. In the 1981–82 season, he established a new standard for the fastest 50 goals scored from the start of a season with a five-goal outburst on December 30, 1981, against the Philadelphia Flyers in only his 39th game.

On November 2, 1986 Gretzky entered the elite group of 500-goal scorers and accomplished the feat in typical fashion, firing a hat trick in a 5–2 triumph over Vancouver. He attained this plateau — one that virtually guarantees a spot in the Hall of Fame — in only 575 games. (Mike Bossy needed 647 games to score 500. Guy Lafleur 918 games and Phil Esposito 803.) He is the all-time point-scoring leader in Stanley Cup play, eclipsing Jean Beliveau's 176 points in only his eighth year of playoff competition. Wayne Gretzky, like Bobby Orr, possesses that rare gift that allows even casual fans of the game to see artistry and creativity transcend the realm of mere sport.

The Quebec Nordiques and Montreal Canadiens renewed their rivalry in the 1983–84 Adams Division final. Here Guy Carbonneau, in his second year with the Habs, pays special attention to Quebec center Peter Stastny. The Nordiques' Czech star came to North America and the Quebec club with his brother Anton in 1980. A third brother, Marian, followed in 1981. Peter plays with a tough, uncompromising style and has averaged more than 110 points every year he has played in the NHL.

Esposito-and-Orr tandem when Gretzky captured the scoring title with 205 points followed by teammate Paul Coffey. Glenn Anderson scored 54 goals, making the Oilers the first team in NHL history to have four active skaters who had reached the 50-goal mark.

The Islanders were back atop the Patrick Division standings with 104 points. Despite missing 13 games, Mike Bossy became the first NHL player to score 50 or more goals in seven straight seasons. The Islanders' attack became even stronger when Pat LaFontaine joined them after toiling for the 1984 US Olympic team. He was joined by Pat Flatley from the Canadian Olympians. The two were instant starters, and LaFontaine scored 13 goals in only 15 games. Washington continued to be the division's most improved team, finishing in second place with 101 points.

The Boston Bruins parlayed fine seasons from Barry Pederson and Rick Middleton into a first-place finish in the

Adams Division. The Sabres' youth movement paid immediate dividends, as they improved to 103 points. The Montreal Canadiens hired Serge Savard as managing director, hoping that he could revitalize the club, but instead, the team faltered to its worst finish since 1950–51, ending up five games below .500.

Minnesota won the Norris Division and turned back the Blackhawks in five games. St. Louis needed two overtime victories to eliminate the stubborn Detroit Red Wings. Minnesota then won a tough seven-game series over the Blues.

Edmonton disposed of the Jets in three straight, while the Flames were setting up an all-Alberta Smythe Division final by eliminating Vancouver in four. The "natural" rivalry that the NHL had banked upon when the Atlanta franchise was transfered to Calgary was never more vividly displayed than in the thrilling Smythe Division final. The Flames now skated out of Calgary's brand new Olympic Saddledome, and the building had been sold out to season ticket holders before the season started. In an action-packed seven-game series the Oilers moved on to the Campbell Conference final.

Shaking off their poor regular season record, the Montreal Canadiens eliminated the Bruins in three games. The Nordiques made it an all-Quebec Adams Division final by turning aside the Sabres in three straight games. The Canadiens won this bitter rivalry in an exciting six-game series.

It would be hard to imagine more intense rivalries than the ones in Alberta and Quebec, but New York had two teams vying for supremacy in the Patrick Division. The division semi-final matchup between the Islanders and Rangers went to Long Island for the fifth and deciding game. This match was played at a furious pace and went into overtime where Ken Morrow, who had gone from the gold-medal 1980 US Olympic Team to four straight Stanley Cup championships with the Islanders, got the winner for the Isles. The Washington Capitals experienced their first success in postseason play, eliminating the Flyers in the minimum number of games. The

Islanders hit their stride following their close call with the Rangers, defeating the Capitals in five games.

Montreal goaltender Steve Penney continued to be a big story for the Habs as they took the first two games of the Wales Conference final from the Islanders at the Nassau Coliseum. But the Islanders came back to take the next four games and keep the "drive for five" alive. Edmonton had a decidedly easier time, disposing of the North Stars in four straight games.

The matchup that had everyone talking prior to the season had come about. The NHL's two best teams — and last year's finalists — were meeting for the Stanley Cup. The Islanders were a brilliantly coached team made up of players at the peak of their careers. They could play tight defense or fill the net with pucks. The Oilers had the ultimate NHL offense, with what many considered to be the best powerplay in NHL history. Game one was a goaltender's duel, with Grant Fuhr outshining Billy Smith in a 1–0 Oilers' victory. Game two featured a hat trick by Clark Gillies as the Islanders won 6–1, leaving Long Island with a split.

At home in the Northlands Coliseum, the Oilers threw their potent offense into high gear, skating off with a pair of 7–2 decisions. In game five, the Oilers delivered the knockout punch to the Islanders with a 5–2 victory that ended the New Yorkers' dynasty and brought the Cup to Edmonton in the Oilers' fifth NHL season. Wayne Gretzky led all playoff scorers with 35 points and Mark Messier was playoff MVP.

Goaltender Glenn "Chico" Resch is an ardent collector of hockey memorabilia and has donated a number of rare items to the Hockey Hall of Fame. The itinerant goalie played for four minor league teams between 1969 and 1973, and has since worn the pads for four NHL teams, including the New Jersey Devils for whom he played 198 games before joining the Philadelphia Flyers part way through the 1985–86 season.

# YEAR                                    1983–84

**Stanley Cup Champion**            Edmonton Oilers
**Prince of Wales Trophy Winner**   New York Islanders
**Clarence Campbell Bowl Winner**   Edmonton Oilers

**Final Standings**

## CLARENCE CAMPBELL CONFERENCE

### Norris Division

| Team | GP | W | L | T | GF | GA | PTS |
|------|----|----|----|----|----|----|----|
| Minnesota | 80 | 39 | 31 | 10 | 345 | 344 | 88 |
| St. Louis | 80 | 32 | 41 | 7 | 293 | 316 | 71 |
| Detroit | 80 | 31 | 42 | 7 | 298 | 323 | 69 |
| Chicago | 80 | 30 | 42 | 8 | 277 | 311 | 68 |
| Toronto | 80 | 26 | 45 | 9 | 303 | 387 | 61 |

### Smythe Division

| Team | GP | W | L | T | GF | GA | PTS |
|------|----|----|----|----|----|----|----|
| Edmonton | 80 | 57 | 18 | 5 | 446 | 314 | 119 |
| Calgary | 80 | 34 | 32 | 14 | 311 | 314 | 82 |
| Vancouver | 80 | 32 | 39 | 9 | 306 | 328 | 73 |
| Winnipeg | 80 | 31 | 38 | 11 | 340 | 374 | 73 |
| Los Angeles | 80 | 23 | 44 | 13 | 309 | 376 | 59 |

## PRINCE OF WALES CONFERENCE

### Adams Division

| Team | GP | W | L | T | GF | GA | PTS |
|------|----|----|----|----|----|----|----|
| Boston | 80 | 49 | 25 | 6 | 336 | 261 | 104 |
| Buffalo | 80 | 48 | 25 | 7 | 315 | 257 | 103 |
| Quebec | 80 | 42 | 28 | 10 | 360 | 278 | 94 |
| Montreal | 80 | 35 | 40 | 5 | 286 | 295 | 75 |
| Hartford | 80 | 28 | 42 | 10 | 288 | 320 | 66 |

### Patrick Division

| Team | GP | W | L | T | GF | GA | PTS |
|------|----|----|----|----|----|----|----|
| NY Islanders | 80 | 50 | 26 | 4 | 357 | 269 | 104 |
| Washington | 80 | 48 | 27 | 5 | 308 | 226 | 101 |
| Philadelphia | 80 | 44 | 26 | 10 | 350 | 290 | 98 |
| NY Rangers | 80 | 42 | 29 | 9 | 314 | 304 | 93 |
| New Jersey | 80 | 17 | 56 | 7 | 231 | 350 | 41 |
| Pittsburgh | 80 | 16 | 58 | 6 | 254 | 390 | 38 |

**Leading Scorers**

| Player | Club | GP | G | A | PTS | PIM |
|--------|------|----|----|----|----|----|
| Gretzky, Wayne | Edmonton | 74 | 87 | 118 | 205 | 39 |
| Coffey, Paul | Edmonton | 80 | 40 | 86 | 126 | 104 |
| Goulet, Michel | Quebec | 75 | 56 | 65 | 121 | 76 |
| Stastny, Peter | Quebec | 80 | 46 | 73 | 119 | 73 |
| Bossy, Mike | NY Islanders | 67 | 51 | 67 | 118 | 8 |
| Pederson, Barry | Boston | 80 | 39 | 77 | 116 | 64 |
| Kurri, Jari | Edmonton | 64 | 52 | 61 | 113 | 14 |
| Trottier, Bryan | NY Islanders | 68 | 40 | 71 | 111 | 59 |
| Federko, Bernie | St. Louis | 79 | 41 | 66 | 107 | 43 |
| Middleton, Rick | Boston | 80 | 47 | 58 | 105 | 14 |

**NHL Award Winners**

| | |
|---|---|
| **Hart (MVP)** | Wayne Gretzky |
| **Art Ross (Leading Scorer)** | Wayne Gretzky |
| **Calder (Rookie of the Year)** | Tom Barrasso |
| **Vezina (Top Goaltender)** | Tom Barrasso |
| **Lady Byng (Gentlemanly Conduct)** | Mike Bossy |
| **Norris (Top Defenseman)** | Rod Langway |
| **Conn Smythe (Playoff MVP)** | Mark Messier |
| **Patrick (Service to US Hockey)** | John A. Ziegler Jr., Art Ross |
| **Masterton (Perseverance)** | Brad Park |
| **Pearson (NHLPA MVP)** | Wayne Gretzky |
| **Adams (Coach of the Year)** | Bryan Murray |
| **Selke (Top Defensive Forward)** | Doug Jarvis |
| **Jennings (Lowest Goals-Against)** | Al Jensen, Pat Riggin |
| **Emery Edge (Plus/Minus Leader)** | Wayne Gretzky |
| **First Overall Draft Selection** | Mario Lemieux |
| **World/Olympic Champions** | Soviet Union |
| **AHL Calder Cup Champions** | Maine Mariners |
| **Memorial Cup Canadian Jr. Champions** | Ottawa 67s |
| **NCAA Champions** | Bowling Green |
| **Canadian College Champions** | University of Toronto |

# 1984–1985

The third Canada Cup tournament was scheduled for September, 1984. The NHL's top talent would again be matched against the Soviet and Czech national teams in a six-nation tournament.

Canadian hockey fans weren't pleased with the play of Team Canada as the squad of Canadian-born NHL stars played indifferently in the round-robin portion of the Canada Cup. The team opened the tournament with a 4–4 tie against the United States before losing twice, 6–3 to the Soviet Union and 4–2 to Sweden. Their 2–2–1 record was good for fourth place and a berth in the semi-final. Disheartened by the recent performance of NHL players again the Soviets, the fans and media were vocal in their criticism of Team Canada '84. The team felt very much on its own as it prepared for a semifinal showdown against the Soviet Union.

The contest was deadlocked 2–2 after regulation time. In overtime, Paul Coffey made a spectacular play to break up a two-man Soviet break and head-manned the puck up the ice. The puck went into the Soviet end and came back out to Coffey at the point. His shot was deflected in by Mike Bossy. Team Canada then swept the final from the Swedes in two straight games.

Hockey lost one of its most exciting performers when Guy Lafleur retired in November. Lafleur had started slowly in 1984, scoring only two goals in the first five weeks of the season. He wasn't content to remain in the game as just another player and left with 518 goals and 1,246 points.

An all-time coaching record was broken on December 18, 1984, as Scotty Bowman eclipsed the mark for career wins by a coach held by Dick Irvin, Sr.

Canada's Minister for Sport and Recreation, Otto Jelinek, seems every bit as pleased as either Wayne Gretzky or Larry Robinson at Team Canada's victory in the 1984 Canada Cup tournament. Tournament coordinator Alan Eagleson keeps a cautious right hand on the trophy.

The talent-loaded Edmonton Oilers rolled to their second straight Stanley Cup championship in 1984–85. Instrumental in each of the Cup victories were goaltender Grant Fuhr and defenseman Paul Coffey, who counted an impressive 37 points in 18 games during the 1984–85 playoffs.

who had coached from 1940–55. Bowman's 691st victory was a 6–3 decision over the Blackhawks.

The extent of Wayne Gretzky's ability was reinforced on December 19, 1984 when he scored his 1,000th point in a 7–3 victory over the Los Angeles Kings. He accomplished this feat in only 424 games and, as if to underscore his achievement, added five more points in the game. Bryan Trottier, long considered one of the NHL's elite players, reached the 1,000-point mark on January 29, 1985.

Bobby Clarke had taken over the general manager's job in Philadelphia and, together with rookie head coach Mike Keenan, instituted a close-checking, rug-

ged system of hockey that led the Flyers to the best record in the NHL with 113 points. The team sustained the season's longest winning streak (11 games), with a cast of virtual unknowns. Rookies Peter Zezel, Derrick Smith and Rick Tocchet provided the heavy hitting and Tim Kerr and Brian Propp added scoring punch. The defense was anchored by Mark Howe, Brad Marsh and Brad McCrimmon, while Pelle Lindbergh supplied spectacular goaltending, crafting a 40–17–7 record and a 3.02 goals-against average.

Montreal rebounded from an off year the previous season to win the Adams Division. The Nordiques were close behind, led by the sniping of Michel Goulet who surpassed 50 goals for the third straight year.

The St. Louis Blues won the Norris Division under the coaching of Jacques Demers. Bernie Federko helped with a fine 107-point season. Detroit finished third for the second straight year, getting a club record 55 goals from John Ogrodnick.

The Oilers were easy winners in the Smythe Division. Gretzky set a league record with 135 assists and ended the season with 205 points. Jari Kurri finished second in the scoring race with 71 goals and 64 assists for 135 points. The Winnipeg Jets were the season's surprise team, finishing with the fourth-best record and 96 points. Dale Hawerchuk set a club record for goals with 53 and points with 130, and linemate Paul MacLean chipped in with 41 goals and 101 points. Marcel Dionne led the Kings into the postseason for the first time in four years, scoring 46 goals and adding 80 assists to move past Stan Mikita into third place on the all-time points list.

In the Patrick Division semi-finals, Philadelphia got by the Rangers in three games while the Islanders rebounded from two overtime losses to beat the Capitals in five. The Flyers then sidelined the Islanders in five games to advance to the Wales Conference final. In the Adams Division, Montreal and Quebec each needed five games to eliminate Boston and Buffalo. The 1985 edition of the Battle of Quebec went the seven-game limit with Peter Stastny getting the series winner for Quebec in overtime.

*(continued on page 132)*

Mario Lemieux was the NHL's top draft choice in 1984. During his first season with the Pittsburgh Penguins, the towering centerman accumulated an even hundred points and was named NHL Rookie of the Year. Although Mario has been criticized for his sometimes leisurely approach to checking, his fluid skating and his puck handling are a pleasure to watch.

## 18. High-tech Analysis

The advent of the computer age has ushered in a new era in coaching and scouting hockey teams. Many NHL clubs have developed microcomputer programs that compile elaborate statistics on various facets of the game. Teams will assign an assistant coach or other staffer to watch the game from the press box to track shot location and accuracy, ice-time, line combinations and match-ups, turnovers, passing and checking data and face-off information. Helping prepare a squad for an upcoming opponent or even finding a tiny edge that may make a difference at a crucial moment in a big game makes the practice worthwhile.

The Philadelphia Flyers are one team making extensive use of computerized analysis, with assistant coach E. J. McGuire logging ice-time and line combinations for head coach Mike Keenan. McGuire performed this task manually for Keenan when they coached in the minors before their NHL tenure. "I found out I spent most of my time looking down and writing my numbers on a manual form. What computerization does is not only speed up the process, but allows me to just stare at the ice, just as you're able to dial a phone number without looking too closely at the buttons. The information is the same as it was before, but the advantage is we get it quicker and in a more organized fashion. This allows me to give Mike concrete information over the course of a game and enables us to make adjustments if we have to."

Teams also use computerized analysis to assess the relative talents of amateur players they scout prior to drafting. An organization will ask many or all of its scouts to rank players' strengths and weaknesses at different points of the season and then enter the data for analysis. This way they can measure the players' progress and make overall assessments.

Probably the most popular use of new technology in the NHL is the use of video tape to aid scouting and coaching. Pioneered in the 1970s by Roger Neilson, who has coached several NHL teams, the application of video today includes editing or "breaking down" game footage so that separate tapes can be created to show, for example, the systems a team uses to break out of its own end, kill penalties or work a powerplay. Of course, such methods of analysis need not only be a scouting tool. If a team's own powerplay is sputtering, video analysis can help find the flaw.

Since 1985, NHL home teams are required to provide game tapes to the opposition after the game ends. In addition, teams have erected satellite dishes to pull in and tape the signals from games televised in other cities. Some teams have even gone so far as to purchase their own video cameras and equipment so they can customize their video scouting and coaching—such as isolating a particular player—and not have to rely on the television crew's cameras.

Al Arbour's success as coach of the New York Islanders was due in part to his progressive approach to the game. Here, Arbour views a game video in preparation for an upcoming playoff encounter.

In the Smythe Division, Edmonton swept Los Angeles in three games while Winnipeg eliminated Calgary in four, but lost their top scorer, Dale Hawerchuk, with cracked ribs. The Jets were no match for the Oilers, losing in four straight games. In the Norris, Minnesota surprised St.Louis with a three-game victory and Chicago eliminated Detroit. The Blackhawks needed six games to defeat the North Stars.

The Oilers defeated the Blackhawks in the Campbell Conference final, but needed six games to do so as Chicago's Denis Savard attempted to prove that Oiler coach Glen Sather had been mistaken in cutting him from the Team Canada roster the previous September. This series established a record for goals scored as the Oilers and Hawks combined to score 69 times. Jari Kurri's 12 goals in the series set a record, as he scored a hat trick in the fifth game and four goals in the sixth. Gretzky had four goals and a record-tying 18 assists in the series, while Paul Coffey established a playoff record for points in a game by a defenseman with six in the fifth game.

The Flyers/Nordiques Wales Conference final was a tightly played affair, as the netminding of Pelle Lindbergh and Mario Gosselin made for low-scoring games. The Flyers took the series in six games, scoring just 17 goals while limiting Quebec to 12.

The Flyers played their defensive style to perfection in game one of the Cup final, skating off with a 4–1 victory. The Oilers employed their own hard-hitting defensive system in the second game and left the Spectrum with a split thanks to a 3–1 win. Gretzky fired a hat trick in a 4–3 victory for the Oilers in the third game. The Flyers put up a fight in game four, but four unanswered Oiler goals were the difference in a 5–3 Edmonton triumph. Grant Fuhr stopped Ron Sutter on a penalty shot with the Flyers leading 3–1, enabling the Oilers to come back for the victory. Game five was never in doubt as the Oilers routed the Flyers 8–3 to capture their second consecutive Cup. Gretzky established a playoff record for points, breaking his own mark with 47. Paul Coffey established playoff records for goals by a defenseman with 12, assists with 25 and points with 37. Jari Kurri equaled Reg Leach's record for goals in the playoffs with 19 markers. The Conn Smythe Trophy went to Wayne Gretzky, but could have been awarded to any of several Oilers.

During 1984, Bobby Clarke, one of the greatest competitors of the expansion era, moved from the locker room to the general manager's desk in Philadelphia. Clarke recorded a grand total of 1,210 points in 15 years of play, and so far has successfully transferred his zeal as a player to his role as manager of the Flyers.

# YEAR                    1984–85

**Stanley Cup Champion** — Edmonton Oilers
**Prince of Wales Trophy Winner** — Philadelphia Flyers
**Clarence Campbell Bowl Winner** — Edmonton Oilers

**Final Standings**

## CLARENCE CAMPBELL CONFERENCE

### Norris Division

| Team | GP | W | L | T | GF | GA | PTS |
|------|----|----|----|----|----|----|----|
| St. Louis | 80 | 37 | 31 | 12 | 299 | 288 | 86 |
| Chicago | 80 | 38 | 35 | 7 | 309 | 299 | 83 |
| Detroit | 80 | 27 | 41 | 12 | 313 | 357 | 66 |
| Minnesota | 80 | 25 | 43 | 12 | 268 | 321 | 62 |
| Toronto | 80 | 20 | 52 | 8 | 253 | 358 | 48 |

### Smythe Division

| Team | GP | W | L | T | GF | GA | PTS |
|------|----|----|----|----|----|----|----|
| Edmonton | 80 | 49 | 20 | 11 | 401 | 298 | 109 |
| Winnipeg | 80 | 43 | 27 | 10 | 358 | 332 | 96 |
| Calgary | 80 | 41 | 27 | 12 | 363 | 302 | 94 |
| Los Angeles | 80 | 34 | 32 | 14 | 339 | 326 | 82 |
| Vancouver | 80 | 25 | 46 | 9 | 284 | 401 | 59 |

## PRINCE OF WALES CONFERENCE

### Adams Division

| Team | GP | W | L | T | GF | GA | PTS |
|------|----|----|----|----|----|----|----|
| Montreal | 80 | 41 | 27 | 12 | 309 | 262 | 94 |
| Quebec | 80 | 41 | 30 | 9 | 323 | 275 | 91 |
| Buffalo | 80 | 38 | 28 | 14 | 290 | 237 | 90 |
| Boston | 80 | 36 | 34 | 10 | 303 | 287 | 82 |
| Hartford | 80 | 30 | 41 | 9 | 268 | 318 | 69 |

### Patrick Division

| Team | GP | W | L | T | GF | GA | PTS |
|------|----|----|----|----|----|----|----|
| Philadelphia | 80 | 53 | 20 | 7 | 348 | 241 | 113 |
| Washington | 80 | 46 | 25 | 9 | 322 | 240 | 101 |
| NY Islanders | 80 | 40 | 34 | 6 | 345 | 312 | 86 |
| NY Rangers | 80 | 26 | 44 | 10 | 295 | 345 | 62 |
| New Jersey | 80 | 22 | 48 | 10 | 264 | 346 | 54 |
| Pittsburgh | 80 | 24 | 51 | 5 | 276 | 385 | 53 |

## Leading Scorers

| Player | Club | GP | G | A | PTS | PIM |
|--------|------|----|----|----|----|----|
| Gretzky, Wayne | Edmonton | 80 | 73 | 135 | 208 | 52 |
| Kurri, Jari | Edmonton | 73 | 71 | 64 | 135 | 30 |
| Hawerchuk, Dale | Winnipeg | 80 | 53 | 77 | 130 | 74 |
| Dionne, Marcel | Los Angeles | 80 | 46 | 80 | 126 | 46 |
| Coffey, Paul | Edmonton | 80 | 37 | 84 | 121 | 97 |
| Bossy, Mike | NY Islanders | 76 | 58 | 59 | 117 | 38 |
| Ogrodnick, John | Detroit | 79 | 55 | 50 | 105 | 30 |
| Savard, Denis | Chicago | 79 | 38 | 67 | 105 | 56 |
| Federko, Bernie | St. Louis | 76 | 30 | 73 | 103 | 27 |
| Gartner, Mike | Washington | 80 | 50 | 52 | 102 | 71 |

## NHL Award Winners

| | |
|---|---|
| **Hart (MVP)** | Wayne Gretzky |
| **Art Ross (Leading Scorer)** | Wayne Gretzky |
| **Calder (Rookie of the Year)** | Mario Lemieux |
| **Vezina (Top Goaltender)** | Pelle Lindbergh |
| **Lady Byng (Gentlemanly Conduct)** | Jari Kurri |
| **Norris (Top Defenseman)** | Paul Coffey |
| **Conn Smythe (Playoff MVP)** | Wayne Gretzky |
| **Patrick (Service to US Hockey)** | Jack Butterfield, Arthur Wirtz |
| **Masterton (Perseverance)** | Anders Hedberg |
| **Pearson (NHLPA MVP)** | Wayne Gretzky |
| **Adams (Coach of the Year)** | Mike Keenan |
| **Selke (Top Defensive Forward)** | Craig Ramsay |
| **Jennings (Lowest Goals-Against)** | Tom Barrasso, Bob Sauve |
| **Emery Edge (Plus/Minus Leader)** | Wayne Gretzky |
| **First Overall Draft Selection** | Wendel Clark |
| **World/Olympic Champions** | Czechoslovakia |
| **AHL Calder Cup Champions** | Sherbrooke Canadiens |
| **Memorial Cup Canadian Jr. Champions** | Prince Albert Raiders |
| **NCAA Champions** | Rensselaer Polytechnic Institute |
| **Canadian College Champions** | York University |

# 1985–1986

Had it not been for the spectacular goaltending of young Patrick Roy, it is unlikely that the Montreal Canadiens would have captured the 1985–86 Stanley Cup. The rookie goalie won 15 of 20 playoff games for the Habs and was awarded the Conn Smythe Trophy as playoff MVP. Mats Naslund, here dwarfed by big Jim Peplinski of the Calgary Flames, had a standout year for Montreal with 110 points and a second all-star team selection.

The Stanley Cup seemed destined to remain in Edmonton as the Oilers' combination of youth and ability would keep them at the top of the NHL for years to come. Of the other 20 teams in the league, Philadelphia seemed to have the best chance of defeating the Oilers in a playoff matchup. The Detroit Red Wings took steps to improve their club, offering big contracts to American college free agents who had been passed over in the Entry Draft.

Tragedy struck the NHL in November when Pelle Lindbergh, the brilliant Swedish netminder for the Philadelphia Flyers, was killed in a road accident. Although badly shaken by the loss of a friend and teammate, the Flyers rallied together and, backstopped by the goaltending of Bob Froese, won the Patrick Division with 110 points.

Mike Bossy had an exciting year, reaching the 500-goal plateau in only his 647th career game with a goal against the Boston Bruins in a 7–5 Islanders

triumph on January 2, 1986. Nine games later, he became a member of the 1,000-point club. Gilbert Perreault scored his 500th against the New Jersey Devils in a 4–3 Sabres win on March 9, 1986.

Wayne Gretzky's self-imposed scoring ambition for the 1985–86 season was two assists per game or 160 for the year. No other player would have had the temerity to make such a prediction, but when the season ended Gretzky had 163 assists to go with 52 goals for a record 215 points.

Defenseman Paul Coffey had the type of season that most forwards would covet when he established a record for goals by a rearguard with 48. Coffey finished the year with 138 points, one point short of tying Bobby Orr's single-season record. Mike Bossy had a record ninth straight 50-goal season. The Oilers led the Smythe Division and the NHL with 119 points.

Michel Goulet paced the Nordiques,

Bruce Driver, at left, above, a graduate of the Canadian Olympic program, and now a defenseman with the New Jersey Devils, steps into Bob Bourne of the Islanders.

Craig Hartsburg of Minnesota, at left, below, has never been voted an NHL all-star, although he is widely recognized as one of the league's premier defensemen.

Goaltender Mike Liut of the Hartford Whalers is one of hockey's most articulate spokesmen, as well as one of its finest goalies. The graduate of Bowling Green State University has played a large part in the evolution of the Whalers into an NHL contender.

scoring more than 50 goals for a fourth straight season. Peter Stastny contributed 122 points as Quebec led the Adams Division. The Adams was the NHL's closest divisional race, as only twelve points separated the first place team from the last. The Buffalo Sabres missed the playoffs, despite finishing with 80 points. Montreal had a new top scorer with the emergence of Mats Naslund; the one-time Flying Frenchmen were now a team made up of Swedish, American, Czech, English Canadian and Quebecois players.

Detroit failed to get immediate help from their high-priced collegians as both Ray Stazak and Adam Oates spent time in the minors. The Pittsburgh Penguins

had a bonafide blue-chipper in Mario Lemieux, as the sophomore center finished second in the scoring race to Gretzky with 141 points.

The playoffs saw some excellent matchups. In the Adams Division, the Hartford Whalers suprised Quebec in three games. Hartford had made two important trades during the season, acquiring Dave Babych from Winnipeg to shore up their defense and John Anderson from the Quebec. The Whalers were much improved and met Montreal, who had eliminated Boston, in the Adams Division final. This series was dominated by the hot goaltending of rookie Patrick Roy of Montreal and Mike Liut of the Whalers.

The Habs advanced, winning the seventh game 2–1 on rookie Claude Lemieux's overtime marker.

The Rangers were extended to the five-game limit before upsetting the Flyers in the Patrick Division semi-final. Washington provided the Islanders with an early exit, winning in three straight games. The Rangers continued their string of upsets, getting fantastic goaltending from John Vanbiesbrouck in a six-game Patrick Division final series win over Washington.

In the Norris, the Maple Leafs provided an upset of their own, defeating the division-leading Chicago Blackhawks in three games. St. Louis needed five games to eliminate Minnesota. In the Norris Division final between the Leafs and Blues, the series was tied at two games apiece when St. Louis battled back from a 3–0 deficit to tie game five and force overtime. Mark Reeds of the

Blues completed the comeback, firing the game winner at 7:11 of the extra session. The Leafs came back to take the sixth game 5–3 before losing game seven 2–1. St. Louis advanced to the Campbell Conference final.

The Calgary club had also improved, acquiring John Tonelli from the Islanders and Joe Mullen from St. Louis. The Smythe semi-finals saw Calgary and Edmonton eliminate Winnipeg and Vancouver in three-game sweeps to set up another all-Alberta matchup. Against the Oilers, the Flames came through with an upset seven-game victory. The final game was decided by the great goaltending of Mike Vernon and a fluke series-winning goal that Oiler defenseman Steve Smith inadvertently banked off Grant Fuhr into his own net.

Patrick Roy continued to dazzle in the Wales Conference final against the Rangers. Montreal played disciplined

In a playoff year dominated by upsets, none was greater than Calgary's well-earned seven-game victory over Edmonton in the Smythe Division final. Every member of the Flames, including Dan Quinn, 10, below, worked hard for the win.

defensive hockey, getting strong performances from veterans Bob Gainey, Mats Naslund, Larry Robinson and Guy Carbonneau as well as surprising scoring punch from rookies Brian Skrudland and Claude Lemieux. Lemieux picked up another overtime winner in the third game of the final and Montreal allowed only 10 goals-against, winning the series in five games.

The Campbell Conference final seemed destined to be a letdown after the seven-game divisional finals won by St. Louis and Calgary. St. Louis appeared to be eliminated late in game six, but came back to tie the match 5–5, forcing overtime. Doug Wickenheiser forced a seventh game by getting the winner for St. Louis. Game seven was played before a packed house in the Saddledome and the Flames did not disappoint, winning at home 2–1.

There had not been a Stanley Cup final between two Canadian teams since the 1966–67 season. Calgary won the first contest 5–2 at home, but Montreal attained the all-important split on the road with a 3–2 overtime victory on Brian Skrudland's winning goal after only nine seconds of extra time. The Habs played their tight-checking style to perfection at home in games three and four, winning by 5–3 and 1–0 scores. Patrick Roy continued to give the Canadiens excellent goaltending. Up 3–1 in games, the Habs returned to Calgary and won 4–3, to capture their 23rd Stanley Cup. Serge Savard and rookie coach Jean Perron, criticized by media, players and fans during the regular season, savored the vindication of a Cup victory. Like Ken Dryden fifteen years earlier, Patrick Roy had come out of nowhere to star in the postseason. His 1.92 goals-against average over 20 games was rewarded with the Conn Smythe Trophy.

A glowering Wendel Clark watches play from the Toronto Maple Leafs bench. Though just 20 years old, Clark's talent, toughness and vigor have given Leaf fans reason to hope for a resurgence in the fortunes of the team.

# TWENTY TRENDS THAT SHAPED MODERN HOCKEY

## 19. Rule and Equipment Changes to Reduce Injury

Much has been done to reduce the risk of on-ice hockey injury in the 20 years since expansion. Rule changes and improved equipment have made the game safer even though today's players shoot, skate and hit harder than their counterparts of 20 years ago.

In the NHL, helmets were worn by only a handful of players at the time of the 1967 expansion. Today very few NHLers play bare-headed. Previously, players wouldn't consider wearing protective headgear unless recuperating from an existing injury. This attitude began to change with the accidental death of Minnesota's Bill Masterton from a head injury in 1967, the scoring success of helmeted players like Stan Mikita and Red Berenson, and the increasing use of the slapshot in the NHL.

In 1979, the league made the use of helmets mandatory for all players signing their first contracts after June 1, 1979.

In addition to helmets, a growing number of players have also adopted protective face shields to cover their eyes and noses. These transparent plastic visors are a relatively new innovation and while their use is not mandatory, more and more players are either adding them to their equipment or entering the NHL from college or other leagues where the use of the visor is compulsory. As many as one-third of the players in the NHL now wear the shield.

The goal net itself has

An increasing number of NHL players have adopted protective visors. Montreal's Guy Carbonneau was one of the first players to use the device.

been modified for safer play. Following a serious injury to Mark Howe in 1982, the shape of the net was changed, eliminating the pointed center base and upright support. In 1984, magnetic goal posts allowed the net to come off its moorings in the event of a skater's collision with the post.

In the NHL, penalties for high-sticking infractions have been increased. New rules instituted in 1986-87 state that any player carrying his stick above his shoulder may be given a minor or double minor penalty at the discretion of the referee. Any injury to the face or head of an opposing player caused by an intentional or accidental high stick results in an automatic five-minute major penalty. Linesmen as

well as referees can make the call on this infraction and any player who draws two such penalties in a game receives an automatic game misconduct as well.

Equipment design has seen substantial advances since 1967. Padding is now lighter and better fitting, staying in place and providing better protection. Skates and gloves have similarly improved. Goaltenders' mask have evolved into a cage-and-helmet combinations that better protect the face, head and throat.

The pace of the game of hockey has increased as stronger, faster players take advantage of superior protective equipment to play in high gear on every shift. In the NHL, a continuing evolution of the rules aims to provide

on-ice officials with the discretionary powers necessary to discourage dangerous play and reduce injury.

# YEAR

## 1985–86

| | |
|---|---|
| **Stanley Cup Champion** | Montreal Canadiens |
| **Prince of Wales Trophy Winner** | Montreal Canadiens |
| **Clarence Campbell Bowl Winner** | Calgary Flames |
| **President's Trophy Winner** | Edmonton Oilers |

### Final Standings

#### CLARENCE CAMPBELL CONFERENCE

**Norris Division**

| Team | GP | W | L | T | GF | GA | PTS |
|---|---|---|---|---|---|---|---|
| Chicago | 80 | 39 | 33 | 8 | 351 | 349 | 86 |
| Minnesota | 80 | 38 | 33 | 9 | 327 | 305 | 85 |
| St. Louis | 80 | 37 | 34 | 9 | 302 | 291 | 83 |
| Toronto | 80 | 25 | 48 | 7 | 311 | 386 | 57 |
| Detroit | 80 | 17 | 57 | 6 | 266 | 415 | 40 |

**Smythe Division**

| Team | GP | W | L | T | GF | GA | PTS |
|---|---|---|---|---|---|---|---|
| Edmonton | 80 | 56 | 17 | 7 | 426 | 310 | 119 |
| Calgary | 80 | 40 | 31 | 9 | 354 | 315 | 89 |
| Winnipeg | 80 | 26 | 47 | 7 | 295 | 372 | 59 |
| Vancouver | 80 | 23 | 44 | 13 | 282 | 333 | 59 |
| Los Angeles | 80 | 23 | 49 | 8 | 284 | 389 | 54 |

#### PRINCE OF WALES CONFERENCE

**Adams Division**

| Team | GP | W | L | T | GF | GA | PTS |
|---|---|---|---|---|---|---|---|
| Quebec | 80 | 43 | 31 | 6 | 330 | 289 | 92 |
| Montreal | 80 | 40 | 33 | 7 | 330 | 280 | 87 |
| Boston | 80 | 37 | 31 | 12 | 311 | 288 | 86 |
| Hartford | 80 | 40 | 36 | 4 | 332 | 302 | 84 |
| Buffalo | 80 | 37 | 37 | 6 | 296 | 291 | 80 |

**Patrick Division**

| Team | GP | W | L | T | GF | GA | PTS |
|---|---|---|---|---|---|---|---|
| Philadelphia | 80 | 53 | 23 | 4 | 335 | 241 | 110 |
| Washington | 80 | 50 | 23 | 7 | 315 | 272 | 107 |
| NY Islanders | 80 | 39 | 29 | 12 | 327 | 284 | 90 |
| NY Rangers | 80 | 36 | 38 | 6 | 280 | 276 | 78 |
| Pittsburgh | 80 | 34 | 38 | 8 | 313 | 305 | 76 |
| New Jersey | 80 | 28 | 49 | 3 | 300 | 374 | 59 |

### Leading Scorers

| Player | Club | GP | G | A | PTS | PIM |
|---|---|---|---|---|---|---|
| Gretzky, Wayne | Edmonton | 80 | 52 | 163 | 215 | 46 |
| Lemieux, Mario | Pittsburgh | 79 | 48 | 93 | 141 | 43 |
| Coffey, Paul | Edmonton | 79 | 48 | 90 | 138 | 120 |
| Kurri, Jari | Edmonton | 78 | 68 | 63 | 131 | 22 |
| Bossy, Mike | NY Islanders | 80 | 61 | 62 | 123 | 14 |
| Stastny, Peter | Quebec | 76 | 41 | 81 | 122 | 60 |
| Savard, Denis | Chicago | 80 | 47 | 69 | 116 | 111 |
| Naslund, Mats | Montreal | 80 | 43 | 67 | 110 | 16 |
| Hawerchuk, Dale | Winnipeg | 80 | 46 | 59 | 105 | 44 |
| Broten, Neal | Minnesota | 80 | 29 | 76 | 105 | 47 |

### NHL Award Winners

| | |
|---|---|
| **Hart (MVP)** | Wayne Gretzky |
| **Art Ross (Leading Scorer)** | Wayne Gretzky |
| **Calder (Rookie of the Year)** | Gary Suter |
| **Vezina (Top Goaltender)** | John Vanbiesbrouck |
| **Lady Byng (Gentlemanly Conduct)** | Mike Bossy |
| **Norris (Top Defenseman)** | Paul Coffey |
| **Conn Smythe (Playoff MVP)** | Patrick Roy |
| **Patrick (Service to US Hockey)** | John MacInnes, Jack Riley |
| **Masterton (Perseverance)** | Charlie Simmer |
| **Pearson (NHLPA MVP)** | Mario Lemieux |
| **Adams (Coach of the Year)** | Glen Sather |
| **Selke (Top Defensive Forward)** | Troy Murray |
| **Jennings (Lowest Goals-Against)** | Bob Froese, Darren Jensen |
| **Emery Edge (Plus/Minus Leader)** | Mark Howe |
| **First Overall Draft Selection** | Joe Murphy |
| **World/Olympic Champions** | Soviet Union |
| **AHL Calder Cup Champions** | Adirondack Red Wings |
| **Memorial Cup Canadian Jr. Champions** | Guelph Platers |
| **NCAA Champions** | Michigan State |
| **Canadian College Champions** | University of Alberta |

# 1986–1987

Twenty years after the original expansion, the 1986–87 season brought the league closer to parity than ever before. For the first time since the 80-game format was adopted, the team with the best overall record lost more than 20 games. The Edmonton Oilers' league-leading 106 points was the lowest total for a first-place team since the 1969–70 season. The New Jersey Devils and Buffalo Sabres tied for last place overall, each compiling 64 points, more than any previous last-place club.

There were five coaching changes in the course of the season. After a desultory start, the Boston Bruins cashiered rookie coach Butch Goring and hired Boston fan favorite Terry O'Reilly. After a dreadful start, and meagre production from their top draft choices, the Buffalo Sabres' owners removed coach and general manager Scotty Bowman, the NHL coach with the greatest number of wins. Bowman was briefly replaced by long-time Buffalo defensive specialist Craig Ramsay. All was not rosy in the Big Apple, where first-year general manager Phil Esposito responded to player

grumblings about the disciplinarian methods of coach Ted Sator, and fired the second-year coach. But Sator landed on his feet as coach of the Sabres, working with new Buffalo general manager Gerry Meehan, a former Sabre forward. Tommy Webster, hired to replace Sator in New York, lasted only briefly, unable to work full-time because of an inner ear problem. Within days of hiring Webster, Esposito himself stepped behind the bench.

Shortly into the New Year, the NHL ordered an internal investigation when it learned that Pat Quinn had agreed to become the president and general manager of the Vancouver Canucks while still under contract to coach the L.A. Kings. Quinn was relieved of his duties in L.A. and replaced by Mike Murphy. In Minnesota, with only two games left in the season, Glen Sonmor replaced North Stars coach Lorne Henning, marking the fourth time that Sonmor had held the job.

While few major trades took place, there was one bombshell. Hours before the trading deadline, the NHL's third-leading all-time scorer, Marcel Dionne, was acquired from the L.A. Kings by the

The steady play of defenseman Rick Green (5) contributed to Montreal's league-leading defensive record in 1986–87. Wayne Gretzky remained in a class by himself, recording his seventh consecutive scoring championship with 183 points in regular-season play. He added 34 more in 21 playoff games.

New York Rangers for defenseman Tom Laidlaw and forward Bobby Carpenter, who had recently joined the Rangers from Washington. For the first time since Esposito had retired, the Rangers had a superstar.

In Detroit, a series of player moves were made to give new coach Jacques Demers the raw materials he needed for a sound defensive unit. Demers was determined to reduce the Wings' woeful 415 goals–against in 1985–86. The airlift began with the acquisitions of cornermen Tim Higgins, Dave Barr and Mel Bridgeman. Rugged defensemen Lee Norwood and Dave Lewis were brought in to clear the area in front of the net, and veteran goaltender Glen Hanlon was pried out of the Ranger organization to support regular goaltender Greg Stefan. Partway through the season the Wings engineered the season's second most significant trade, sending ex-50-goal man John Ogrodnick, along with Doug Shedden and Basil McRae, to Quebec for Brent Ashton, Gilbert Delorme and Mark Kumpel. The new emphasis on defense and backchecking reduced the team's total goals–against by 141.

The season was a good one for rookies. Christian Ruuttu was a bright spot with the otherwise luckless Buffalo Sabres, acquiring 22 goals and 65 points. Despite the loss of the great Marcel Dionne, the L.A. Kings found something to cheer about in the performances of freshmen Luc Robitaille and Jim Carson. Robitaille counted 45 goals, and Carson chipped in with 37, serving notice of big things to come. Brian Benning, a young defenseman fine-tuned by the Canadian Olympic program, caught on with the St. Louis Blues and contributed 49 points, while nifty Vincent Damphousse put 46 points on the board for the Toronto Maple Leafs. The Winnipeg Jets did the unheard-of, going with two rookie goalies, Eldon "Pokey" Reddick and Daniel Berthiaume, both of whom provided unexpectedly strong performances. In Philadelphia, goaltender Ron Hextall came out of nowhere to stand the league on its ear, logging more ice time than any other goalie, and finishing the season with a superb goals-against-average of 3.00 per game.

It was a season for milestones, as Wayne Gretzky became the league's 13th 500-goal scorer. Later in the season, Gretzky became the fourth player in NHL history to register 1,500 points. On April 4th, Denis Potvin became the 21st player and first defenseman to attain the 1,000-point level. Earlier in the season, Potvin surpassed Brad Park's total of 683 assists to become the all-time assist leader among defensemen. During the last week of the season, two players, Lanny McDonald and Dave Lewis, became the 58th and 59th players to join the 1,000-game club. At one time longevity of this sort would not have been considered significant, but with rosters being filled increasingly by younger players and with careers growing shorter, the two elder statesmen are to be applauded for their durability.

On the negative side, Mike Bossy's attempt to record a 10th consecutive 50-goal season was frustrated, as "the Boss" was hampered by back problems that threatened to end his career. Michel Goulet put forth a gallant effort to reach 50 goals for the fifth straight year, needing a hat trick in the final game of the season against Boston. He managed to net two goals, but was denied his quest when Boston goalie Bill Ranford thwarted him on three furious shots in the last 10 seconds of the game.

Hockey fans were treated to some excellent international hockey when the NHL All-Stars met the Soviet Nationals in February in Quebec City. The All-Stars won the first game of the two-game series 4–3, on a late goal by Flyer forward Dave Poulin, then dropped the second contest by a 5–3 score.

For the seventh consecutive year, the Edmonton Oilers led the Smythe Division, with 106 points. The Oilers' Wayne Gretzky captured the league scoring title with 63 goals and 183 points. Jari Kurri finished second with 54 goals and 108 points, and Mark Messier tied for third spot with 107. The Calgary Flames owned the Oilers in head-to-head combat, winning six regular-season games and tying one in eight contests. The Flames' 95 points was third best in the NHL and the club's highest point total ever. The team got 47 goals from Joey Mullen, and 76 points from Al MacInnis, whose bullet slapshot helped the Flames execute the NHL's most proficient powerplay.

The New York Islanders were crippled by injuries to key players and struggled to a third-place, 82-point finish in the Patrick. Mike Bossy was burdened throughout the season by a bad back, and Denis Potvin missed 22 games with a knee injury. Over at Madison Square Garden, the Rangers finished with 76 points, aided significantly by 40 goals and 87 points, from Walt Poddubny, acquired in the off-season from the Leafs. Ranger general manager Phil Esposito was also delighted by a strong performance from Swedish star Tomas Sandstrom, who had 40 goals in 64 games.

The Pittsburgh Penguins won their first seven games, but in the end failed to make the playoffs. Nonetheless, the Pens drew an average of 14,900 fans per game, thanks in no small part to the presence of Mario Lemieux. The big centerman missed 17 games because of chronic knee pain, but still managed 54 goals and 107 points. The New Jersey Devils improved their record to a franchise-high 64 points, and, with fine young players such as John MacLean, Aaron Broten and Kirk Muller, are looking forward to better things in years to come.

The Adams Division produced a major surprise, as the Hartford Whalers captured first place with 93 points. Whalers goaltender Mike Liut registered a league-leading four shutouts, and the team got big production years from Ron Francis, with 93 points, and Kevin Dineen, who hustled his way to 40 goals. The Montreal Canadiens closed the season with nine straight victories, to finish just a point shy of the Whalers. The Habs' goaltending duo, Patrick Roy and Brian Hayward, won the Jennings Trophy for fewest goals against, averaging 2.97

per game, and Larry Robinson had another fine season with 50 points and a club-leading plus-minus rating of plus–24. The third-place finish of the Boston Bruins was distinguished by little other than the performance of Ray Bourque, who just missed becoming the fourth defenseman in NHL history to record a 100-point season. After missing two games, Bourque could muster only 98 points.

The Quebec Nordiques would have to rate as one of the league's disappointments, compiling only 72 points. Team leader Peter Stastny's production dropped off drastically, largely on account of nagging injuries. The perennial 100-point-plus Czech was limited to 24 goals, and recorded a lackluster plus-minus total of minus–21. Injuries also hit other Nordique regulars, including rugged forward Dale Hunter, who suited up for only 46 games. The Buffalo Sabres began the year with only seven wins in 32 games and appeared to be out of contention by Christmas. However, the team bounced back strongly in the second half, with new coach Ted Sator in the wheelhouse. During the final month of the schedule, the Sabres drew even with Quebec, but faltered in the stretch run to end up in last place with 64 points.

The Winnipeg Jets rebounded from a poor year in 1986 to finish with 88 points, reflecting the disciplined defensive style of their new coach Dan Maloney. The Jets' stylish centerman Dale Hawerchuk was one of only seven players to count more than 100 points, and had his finest season both offensively and defensively. The L.A. Kings returned to post-season play, while the Vancouver Canucks finished out of the running, despite a late-season surge.

Philadelphia goaltender Ron Hextall played in 66 regular-season and 26 playoff games in his rookie NHL season. Hextall's aggressive play protecting his crease did not escape the notice of NHL referees who assessed the Flyers' netminder a total of 147 penalty minutes including playoffs. Here he and defenseman Brad McCrimmon make sure Edmonton's Craig MacTavish doesn't get back into the play in game six of the Stanley Cup finals.

## 20. Improved Training Techniques and Equipment

Prior to expansion, NHL clubs placed little emphasis on off-season conditioning. Training camp was used for players to skate into shape. This prevailing philosophy worked in an era of stable rosters, but as expansion and the startup of the WHA brought more young players into training camps, those players who had allowed themselves to get out of condition in the off-season were placed at a serious disadvantage.

Conditioning has always been an important part of the Soviet hockey system. Coaching seminars and films first seen in North America in the late 1960s revealed a year-round program of dryland training and on-ice drills.

Contemporary NHLers are accustomed to receiving diet counseling and a training regimen for the off-season, and are expected to report in shape and near playing weight. The increased number of indoor arenas allows many players to stay on skates all year. Many talented players work at instructional hockey schools in the summer, staying in condition by working alongside their pupils. The result is faster play in the NHL.

Increased speed places a premium on mobility and flexibility. Powerskating, which teaches fundamental skating skills directly transferrable to hockey, is taught right up to the NHL level. The New York Islanders have used powerskating instruction to smooth the skating stride of several of their players. As well, hockey players now incorporate stretching in their conditioning programs. Conditioning is now seen as an important method of preventing injury and reducing time required for rehabilitation.

The speed of the game has also increased due to innovations in equipment. Padding is lighter, more streamlined and more effective than ever before. Skates afford better foot protection and allow players to turn more sharply. Even skate sharpening has been computerized, guaranteeing an identical edge every time. Superior equipment encourages players to go at full speed even in close quarters.

The Norris Division provided the most hotly-contested divisional race, in spite of the fact that all Norris teams played below .500 hockey. Jacques Martin's debut as head coach of the St. Louis Blues was successful, as the Blues captured first place, but it took an overtime goal by Rob Ramage against Detroit on the final night of the schedule to give the Blues top spot. Detroit dropped back-to-back overtime decisions on the last weekend of the season, and finished one point behind St. Louis. In the Demers mold, the Wings played strong defense, and got a big season from youthful captain Steve Yzerman, who notched 90 points.

There was a furious dog fight for the final two Norris playoff spots, which weren't decided until the season's final game. When the snarling was over, the Blackhawks sat in third place with 72 points, with the Maple Leafs and North Stars tied two points back. The Leafs claimed the playoff position by virtue of a greater number of wins. No one player dominated the Leafs' offense, although Wendel Clark managed 37 goals, and Steve Thomas and Rick Vaive scored 35 and 32, respectively. Denis Savard of the Blackhawks missed 10 games but still managed 40 goals and 90 points, while Dino Ciccarelli of the North Stars saw a 52-goal season go for naught as the Stars took an early vacation.

First spot in the Patrick Division was never in doubt, as the Philadelphia Flyers built a substantial early-season lead and came in with 100 points, for the NHL's second-best record. Tim Kerr paced the Flyers with 58 goals and 95 points. Ron Hextall was a major contributor between the pipes, and Mark Howe owned the league's second best plus-minus rating with a plus-57. The Washington Capitals shook off a poor start to finish the season with a seven-game win streak, to give them 86 points, good enough for second place. Curiously, the Caps' leading scorer was a defenseman, Mike Murphy, who counted 81 points, while fellow rearguard Scott Stephens gathered 61 points, as well as providing much-needed toughness in the rugged Patrick Division.

NHL parity was revealed quickly in postseason play as fourth-place clubs eliminated first place finishers in the Adams and Norris Divisions. In the Adams, the Nordiques lost their first two matches to the Whalers before storming back to win the series in six games. In the Norris, the Maple Leafs received brilliant goaltending from Ken Wregget to upset St. Louis in six.

The other series in these divisions were four-game sweeps as Montreal eliminated Boston, setting up another "Battle of Quebec," and Detroit played airtight defense to sideline Chicago.

In the Smythe Division, the L.A. Kings shocked the Oilers with a 5-2 victory in the opening game. Edmonton won the next four games including a lopsided 13-3 victory in game two. Wayne Gretzky became the NHL's all-time leading playoff scorer in this match and equaled his own single-game playoff record of seven points. In the Winnipeg-Calgary series, the Jets got strong goaltending from young Daniel Berthiaume to win the first two games in the Olympic Saddledome and went on to eliminate the Flames in six. The Jets played their best hockey of the season in a series-clinching 6-1 win at home.

In the Patrick, John Vanbiesbrouck was unbeatable in game one as the Rangers stopped the Flyers 3-0. But Philadelphia's sensational rookie goaltender, Ron Hextall, recorded two shutouts of his own as the Flyers won in six. Washington appeared to be in control with a 3-1 lead in games in its series with the Islanders as the Long Island club was beset by injuries to key players. But "Islander Pride" spurred New York's veterans and rookies to wins in games five and six. In the deciding game, goaltenders Bob Mason of the Caps and Kelly Hrudey of the Isles were spectacular. Overtime was required to determine the series winner. The action raged back and forth through more than three periods of extra time before Pat LaFontaine of the Islanders eliminated the Capitals at 8:47 of the fourth overtime period, ending the longest Stanley Cup playoff game since 1943.

In the Patrick Division final, Philadelphia took a 3-1 lead in games over the Islanders, but again the New York team battled back. Injured Islanders Brent Sutter, Mike Bossy and Denis Potvin all rejoined the lineup and the team was becoming stronger with each game. A 2–1 win in game five and a 4–2 triumph in game six forced a seventh and deciding match. Philadelphia's top scorer, Tim Kerr, injured his shoulder in the sixth game and was finished for the year. But Ilkka Sinisalo and Flyer captain Dave Poulin, fitted with a flak jacket to protect damaged ribs, dressed for game seven. The game turned out to be surprisingly one-sided as Philadelphia penalty killers scored twice while shorthanded. The Flyers led 5–0 until a goal by Denis Potvin in the last minute of play spoiled Ron Hextall's shutout bid.

In the Adams Division, home ice advantage proved to be meaningless as the Nordiques and Canadiens won twice on the road. Brian Hayward replaced Patrick Roy, last year's playoff MVP, in the Canadiens' net after game one. Game five, played in Montreal, was a controversial affair as an offsetting penalty call by referee Kerry Fraser resulted in a goal by Alain Coté being disallowed with just three minutes remaining in a tie game. After the ensuing faceoff, Ryan Walter finished a rink-length rush to score the winner for Montreal. The Nordiques rallied to win game six with three goals in the third period, the last by Normand Rochefort on a fine setup by Peter Statsny. Game seven featured fine goaltending by Brian Hayward and a five-goal explosion by the Canadiens in the second period. Ryan Walter with two, Bobby Smith, Shayne Corson and Mike McPhee gave the Habs a lead that Quebec was unable to overcome.

The Smythe Division final was the most one-sided series of the second round of action as Edmonton eliminated the Winnipeg Jets in a four-game sweep. The Jets, who had never defeated the Oilers in a playoff encounter, came closest in game one which ended with Glenn Anderson's goal in the first minute of overtime. Though the Jets held Edmonton's superstar scorers in check for much of the series, it was the effective work of less celebrated Oilers like Craig MacTavish, Marty McSorley and Dave Hunter that enabled their club to advance to the Campbell Conference championship.

The Norris final saw one of the NHL's classic rivalries renewed as Detroit met Toronto. The Leafs won the first two games in Joe Louis Arena. At the start of the third period of the second game, Red Wings' coach Jacques Demers changed goaltenders, replacing Greg Stefan with Glen Hanlon. Hanlon played superbly in games three and four, but an overtime goal by Mike Allison of the Leafs gave Toronto a commanding 3–1 advantage. The Wings' veteran defense dug in in game five, combining with Hanlon to register a 3–0 shutout. Detroit's disciplined positional play enabled them to tie the series with a 4–2 win in game six and then win it with another shutout victory in game seven. The Red Wings, the NHL's worst team in 1985–86, was one of the last four teams in contention for the Stanley Cup.

Edmonton was highly favored in the Campbell Conference championship series between the Oilers and the Red Wings. But the Red Wings, with Greg Stefan back in the nets, played their checking game to perfection and won game one 3–1. But Detroit's injury list mounted as defenseman Darren Veitch hurt his knee in this game. Mark Messier paced the Oilers to a 4–1 win in game two before the series shifted to Detroit. The third game appeared to be headed to overtime when Edmonton's Marty McSorley capitalized on a defensive miscue to score in the last minute of the third period. Mike Krushelnyski broke a 2–2 tie with a third period goal in game four and late-season recruit Kent Nilsson scored twice into an empty net to eliminate the valiant Red Wings in game five.

The Wales Conference championship featured the NHL's two best defensive clubs — Philadelphia and Montreal. The Flyers, playing without Tim Kerr and, for much of the series, Dave Poulin, relied on goaltender Ron Hextall to make important saves in every game. The Flyers were at their opportunistic best, grabbing an overtime win in game one and playing better than the Canadiens in the third period of every match. The sixth game in Montreal was marred by a brawl that erupted during the teams' pre-game warm-up. Substantial fines were later levied by the league. Once the game was underway, the Flyers again demonstrated their third period superiority, fighting back from a 3–1 deficit to win the game 4–3. The NHL was guaranteed a new Stanley Cup champion for 1987.

The Stanley Cup finals between the Edmonton Oilers and the Philadelphia Flyers brought together the top two finishers in regular-season play. The Oilers won the first two games of the series on home ice and split the next two in Philadelphia. Though the Flyers were receiving fine goaltending and inspired play from young players like Rick Tocchet, Derrick Smith and Scott Mellanby, it appeared that the Oilers were simply too strong and that the Cup final series was destined to end quickly. But the Flyers played brilliantly in games five and six, defeating the Oilers by one-goal margins in regulation time. J.-J. Daigneault's third period blast from the point lifted the Flyers to a comeback win at home in game six and sent the series back to Edmonton for a seventh and deciding contest. The NHL's final series had not gone the limit since Montreal defeated Chicago in 1971.

In the deciding game, the Oilers played high-speed hockey throughout. They set a blistering pace and despite a first-period powerplay goal by Philadelphia, controlled play, finally taking the lead in the second period on a sharp-angle shot just inside the post by Jari Kurri. The Flyers responded with a poised defensive effort and were still looking for the tying goal when a long shot by Glenn Anderson eluded Ron Hextall and put the Oilers in front 3–1 with just three minutes to play. The Oilers were Stanley Cup champions for the third time in their eight years in the NHL. Team captain and leading playoff scorer Wayne Gretzky accepted the Cup from NHL president John Ziegler and after hoisting it aloft, handed the trophy to Steve Smith, the young Edmonton defenseman whose errant clearing pass deflected into his own net for Calgary's winning goal when the Oilers were eliminated in 1986. By coming back to win in 1987, the Oilers had taken their place as a hockey dynasty.

Philadelphia goaltender Ron Hextall was awarded the Conn Smythe Trophy as playoff MVP. The last player to win the award as a member of the losing team in the final was also a Flyer, Reggie Leach, who won in 1976.

# YEAR 1986–87

**Stanley Cup Champion** — Edmonton Oilers
**Prince of Wales Trophy Winner** — Philadelphia Flyers
**Clarence Campbell Bowl Winner** — Edmonton Oilers
**President's Trophy Winner** — Edmonton Oilers

## Final Standings

### CLARENCE CAMPBELL CONFERENCE

#### Norris Division

| Team | GP | W | L | T | GF | GA | PTS |
|------|----|----|----|----|----|----|-----|
| St. Louis | 80 | 32 | 33 | 15 | 281 | 293 | 79 |
| Detroit | 80 | 34 | 36 | 10 | 260 | 274 | 78 |
| Chicago | 80 | 29 | 37 | 14 | 290 | 310 | 72 |
| Toronto | 80 | 32 | 42 | 6 | 286 | 319 | 70 |
| Minnesota | 80 | 30 | 40 | 10 | 296 | 314 | 70 |

#### Smythe Division

| Team | GP | W | L | T | GF | GA | PTS |
|------|----|----|----|----|----|----|-----|
| Edmonton | 80 | 50 | 24 | 6 | 372 | 284 | 106 |
| Calgary | 80 | 46 | 31 | 3 | 318 | 289 | 95 |
| Winnipeg | 80 | 40 | 32 | 8 | 279 | 271 | 88 |
| Los Angeles | 80 | 31 | 41 | 8 | 318 | 341 | 70 |
| Vancouver | 80 | 29 | 43 | 8 | 282 | 314 | 66 |

### PRINCE OF WALES CONFERENCE

#### Adams Division

| Team | GP | W | L | T | GF | GA | PTS |
|------|----|----|----|----|----|----|-----|
| Hartford | 80 | 43 | 30 | 7 | 287 | 270 | 93 |
| Montreal | 80 | 41 | 29 | 10 | 277 | 241 | 92 |
| Boston | 80 | 39 | 34 | 7 | 301 | 276 | 85 |
| Quebec | 80 | 31 | 39 | 10 | 267 | 276 | 72 |
| Buffalo | 80 | 28 | 44 | 8 | 280 | 308 | 64 |

#### Patrick Division

| Team | GP | W | L | T | GF | GA | PTS |
|------|----|----|----|----|----|----|-----|
| Philadelphia | 80 | 46 | 26 | 8 | 310 | 245 | 100 |
| Washington | 80 | 38 | 32 | 10 | 285 | 278 | 86 |
| NY Islanders | 80 | 35 | 33 | 12 | 279 | 281 | 82 |
| NY Rangers | 80 | 34 | 38 | 8 | 307 | 323 | 76 |
| Pittsburgh | 80 | 30 | 38 | 12 | 297 | 290 | 72 |
| New Jersey | 80 | 29 | 45 | 6 | 293 | 368 | 64 |

## Leading Scorers

| Player | Club | GP | G | A | PTS | PIM |
|--------|------|----|----|----|-----|-----|
| Wayne Gretzky | Edmonton | 79 | 62 | 121 | 183 | 28 |
| Jari Kurri | Edmonton | 79 | 54 | 54 | 108 | 41 |
| Mario Lemieux | Pittsburgh | 63 | 54 | 53 | 107 | 57 |
| Mark Messier | Edmonton | 77 | 37 | 70 | 107 | 73 |
| Doug Gilmour | St. Louis | 80 | 42 | 63 | 105 | 58 |
| Dino Ciccarelli | Minnesota | 80 | 52 | 51 | 103 | 92 |
| Dale Hawerchuk | Winnipeg | 80 | 47 | 53 | 100 | 54 |
| Michel Goulet | Quebec | 75 | 49 | 47 | 96 | 61 |
| Tim Kerr | Philadelphia | 75 | 58 | 37 | 95 | 57 |
| Ray Bourque | Boston | 78 | 23 | 72 | 95 | 36 |

## NHL Award Winners

**Hart (MVP)** — Wayne Gretzky
**Art Ross (Leading Scorer)** — Wayne Gretzky
**Calder (Rookie of the Year)** — Luc Robitaille
**Vezina (Top Goaltender)** — Ron Hextall
**Lady Byng (Gentlemanly Conduct)** — Joey Mullen
**Norris (Top Defenseman)** — Ray Bourque
**Conn Smythe (Playoff MVP)** — Ron Hextall
**Patrick (Service to US Hockey)** — Hobey Baker, Frank Mathers
**Masterton (Perseverance)** — Doug Jarvis
**Pearson (NHLPA MVP)** — Wayne Gretzky
**Adams (Coach of the Year)** — Jacques Demers
**Selke (Top Defensive Forward)** — Dave Poulin
**Jennings (Lowest Goals-Against)** — Brian Hayward
**Emery Edge (plus/Minus Leader)** — Wayne Gretzky
**First Overall Draft Selection** — Pierre Turgeon

**World/Olympic Champions** — Sweden

**AHL Calder Cup Champions** — Rochester Americans

**Memorial Cup Canadian Jr. Champions** — Medicine Hat Tigers

**NCAA Champions** — University of North Dakota

**Canadian College Champions** — Trois-Rivières

# ALL-STAR TEAMS 1967–1987

| Position | First Team | Second Team |
|---|---|---|
| **Left Wing** | Valery Kharlamov<br>Alexander Yakushev<br>Bobby Hull<br>Mark Messier | Frank Mahovlich<br>Vladimir Krutov<br>Bill Barber<br>Michel Goulet |
| **Center** | Wayne Gretzky<br>Phil Esposito<br>Marcel Dionne<br>Bryan Trottier | Bobby Clarke<br>Peter Stastny<br>Denis Savard<br>Mario Lemieux |
| **Right Wing** | Guy Lafleur<br>Sergei Makarov<br>Mike Bossy<br>Jari Kurri | Lanny McDonald<br>Rick Middleton<br>Yvan Cournoyer<br>Gordie Howe |
| **Defense** | Bobby Orr<br>Denis Potvin<br>Larry Robinson<br>Vyatcheslav Fetisov<br>Brad Park<br>Mark Howe | Paul Coffey<br>Rod Langway<br>Ray Bourque<br>Borje Salming<br>Serge Savard<br>Doug Wilson |
| **Goaltender** | Vladislav Tretiak<br>Ken Dryden | Bernie Parent<br>Tony Esposito |
| **Defensive Specialists** | Bob Gainey<br>Doug Jarvis<br>Butch Goring<br>Guy Carbonneau<br>Jim Schoenfeld | Craig Ramsey<br>Don Luce<br>Ed Westfall<br>Joe Watson<br>Lee Fogolin |
| **Coach** | Al Arbour | Scotty Bowman |
| **General Manager** | Sam Pollack | Bill Torrey |

## Wayne Gretzky

(center, 1979 to date) is the most dominant performer in sports. He has been selected the most valuable player in the NHL every year he has been in the league and has won the NHL's scoring championship for seven straight years from 1981 to 1987. He holds 41 NHL scoring records, including single-season marks for most goals (92), most assists (162), and most points (215).

## Rick Middleton

(right wing, 1974 to date)
played his first two seasons
with the New York Rangers
before being traded to
Boston. Beginning in
1979–80, Middleton, one of
the least-penalized players in
the NHL, enjoyed five consecutive years with more than
40 goals and 90 points. He
had 51 goals in 1981–82,
winning a second team all-
star selection and the Lady
Byng Trophy as the NHL's
most gentlemanly player that
same year. ▼

## Mario Lemieux

(center, 1984 to date)
was an instant star in the
NHL, finishing his rookie season with 100 points and the
Calder Trophy. His stylish
puck-handling skills and scoring touch have rekindled
hockey excitement in Pittsburgh. He had 141 points in
his second season, and though
sidelined by a knee injury for
several weeks in 1986–87,
was one of the NHL's top
scorers in that season too.

## Lanny McDonald

(right wing, 1973 to date)
is one of the NHL's most
recognizable figures, sporting red hair and a big handle-
bar moustache. McDonald is
one of the NHL's strongest
corner men and possesses a
blazing slapshot. He had three
40-goal seasons in Toronto,
and, after parts of three seasons in Colorado, joined the
Calgary Flames where he has
been a important team leader.
He had 66 goals in 1982–83
and was a vital contributor to
Calgary's Campbell Conference championship in 1986.

## Jari Kurri

(right wing, 1980 to date)

has played the right side on a line with Wayne Gretzky for almost all of his NHL career. He scored 14 playoff goals in the Oilers' 1984 Stanley Cup win and, the following year, became only the third player in NHL history to score more than 70 goals in a season. He had 19 goals in the 1985 playoffs, and was selected a first all-star and winner of the Lady Byng Trophy that same year.

## Peter Stastny

(center, 1980 to date)

was already a proven international star with the Czech Nationals when he and his brother Anton joined the Quebec Nordiques. He won the Calder Trophy as NHL rookie of the year, setting records for points and assists by a first-year player in 1980–81. His physical style has enabled him to adapt to the hitting game played in the NHL.

## Michel Goulet

(left wing, 1978 to date)

is a pure goal scorer who recorded four consecutive 50-goal seasons for the Quebec Nordiques from 1983 to 1986. His hard, accurate slapshot and skating ability enabled him to score 121 points in 1983–84, a record for left wingers. He is a three-time NHL all-star and got his start in professional hockey as an 18-year-old playing for the Birmingham Bulls in the WHA.

## Marcel Dionne

(center, 1971 to date)

has spent his remarkable NHL career with teams that have had little success in the playoffs. He is the NHL's second-leading all-time scorer, trailing only Gordie Howe. His career with Detroit, (1971–75), Los Angeles (1975–87) and the New York Rangers (1987 on) has been a model of consistency. He has topped 40 goals ten times and 50 goals on six occasions. He has had eight 100-point years. He is a four-time all-star, two-time winner of the Lady Byng Trophy and winner of the Art Ross Trophy as the NHL's leading scorer in 1980.

## Denis Savard
(center, 1980 to date)
was Chicago's first choice in the 1980 Entry Draft. He is a fast skater and excellent stickhandler, with a large array of dekes and feints designed to baffle opposing defensemen. He holds the Chicago Blackhawks' club records for assists with 87 in 1981–82, and points with 121 in 1982–83. Savard had 29 points in 15 games in the 1985 playoffs and was brilliant in Chicago's six-game loss to Edmonton in the Campbell Conference final.

## Bryan Trottier
(center, 1975 to date)
was NHL rookie of the year in 1975–76 and won the Hart and Ross trophies as MVP and top scorer in 1978–79. He won the Conn Smythe Trophy as playoff MVP in 1980, leading the Islanders to the first of four consecutive Stanley Cups. Trottier plays a rugged style at center and is a top two-way player. He has more than 1,100 points in regular-season play.

## Mike Bossy

(right wing, 1977 to date)
is the NHL's number-one
sniper. He scored more than
50 goals every year he played
in the NHL until 1986–87. In
his ninth season, he became
the 11th player in league
history to score 500 regular-
season goals and has scored
60 or more goals on five
occasions. In three of the
four Stanley Cup wins by the
New York Islanders, Bossy
was the NHL's leading playoff
goal scorer. He has been
selected to NHL all-star teams
eight times and is a three-
time winner of the Lady Byng
Trophy for gentlemanly play.

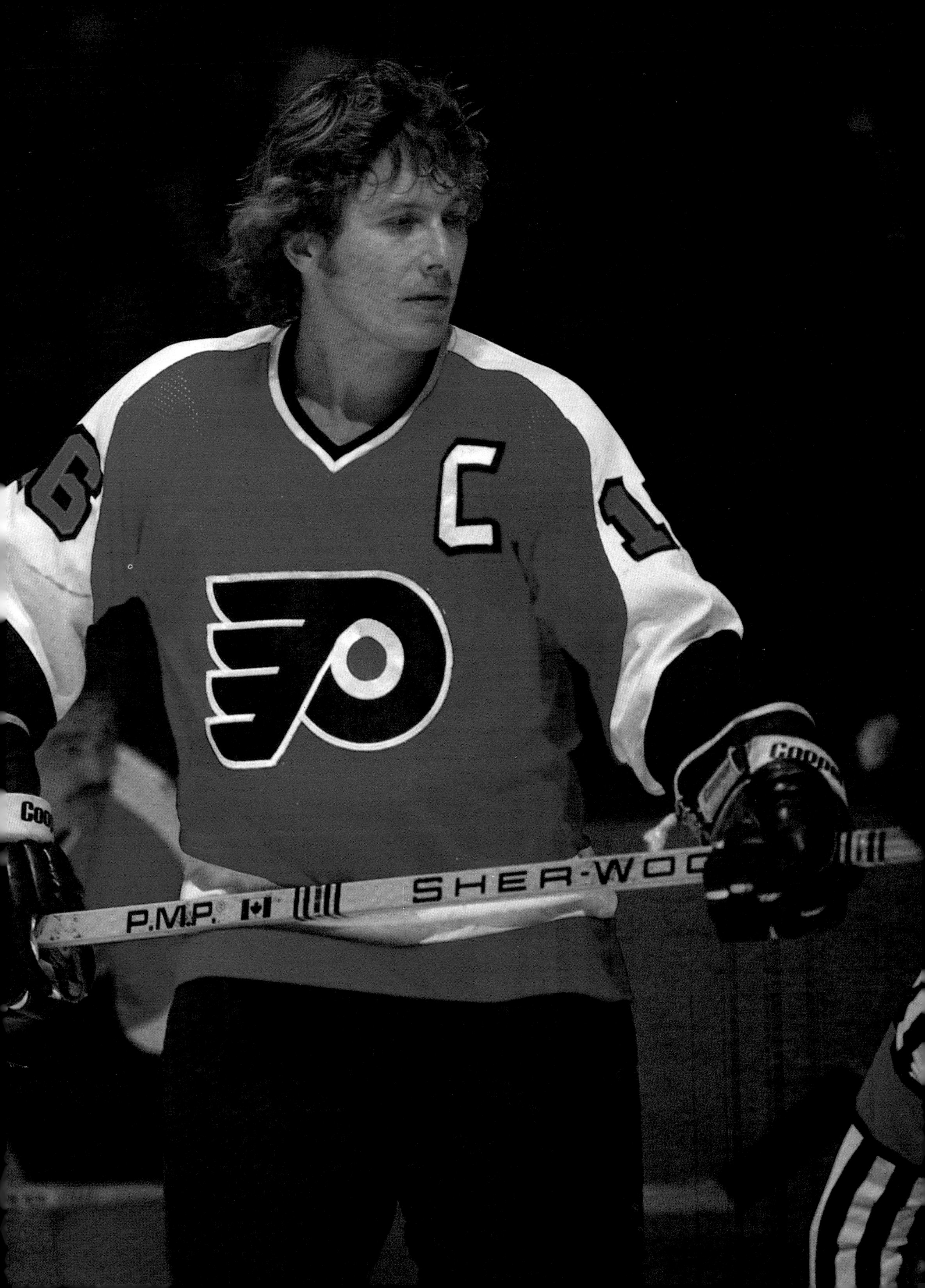
P.M.P.
SHER-WOO

## ◀ Bobby Clarke

(center, 1969–1984)

has put his personal stamp on hockey in Philadelphia first as a player and now as the team's general manager. On the ice, Clarke personified the Flyers' style, playing an intense whatever-it-takes-to-win game that led his club to the Stanley Cup in 1974 and 1975. He won the Hart Trophy as MVP three times and, in 1973, became the first player from an expansion franchise to score more than 100 points in a season. His versatility is demonstrated by the fact that during his career he has been both the league's assist leader and the winner of the Selke Trophy as top defensive forward.

## Phil Esposito

(center, 1963–1981)

was the NHL's scoring machine through the first eight years of expansion, capturing the Art Ross Trophy five times. He was traded from Chicago to Boston in 1967 and went on to become the first NHL player to score more than 100 points in a season, recording 126 in 1968–69. Along with Bobby Orr, Esposito made the "Big, Bad Bruins" the top offensive club in the league and Stanley Cup winners in 1970 and 1972. In 1971, he had 76 goals, surpassing the single-season goal-scoring mark by 18 goals.

## Guy Lafleur ▶

(right wing, 1971–1985)

was hockey's most exciting player from 1974 to 1980. The Montreal star had complete hockey skills, possessing breakaway speed, stickhandling ability and a devastating shot. He had six consecutive 50-goal seasons and first all-star selections. He was the NHL's leading scorer three times, was selected MVP in both the regular-season and the play-offs in 1977 and was part of five Stanley Cup winners. He retired with 518 regular-season goals.

## Frank Mahovlich

**(left wing, 1957–1978)**

was NHL rookie of the year
and part of four Cup winners
with the Toronto Maple Leafs
prior to expansion. In 1968,
he was traded to Detroit and
had seasons of 49 and 38
goals on a line with Gordie
Howe. He was traded again
in 1971, joining Montreal in
time to set a playoff scoring
record with 14 goals and 13
assists in 20 games, as the
Canadiens won the Cup. He
had 96 and 93 points in the
following two regular-season
campaigns with the Cana-
diens. He finished his career
with four seasons in Toronto
and Birmingham of the WHA.

## Bobby Hull
(left wing, 1957–1980)

was the NHL's superstar scorer of the 1960s, and hockey's most successful proponent of the slapshot. He became the first player in the NHL to break the 50-goal plateau with 54 in 1966. He was the league's top goal-scorer in the first two seasons after expansion, setting a single-season record with 58 goals in 1968–69. He jumped to the Winnipeg Jets of the WHA in 1972 and had four 50-goal seasons, including a record 77 goals in 78 games in 1974–75. Combining NHL and WHA play, Hull scored 913 regular-season goals in 23 seasons.

## Yvan Cournoyer
(right wing, 1963–1979)

was one of the game's fastest skaters and top stickhandlers. Despite being small by NHL standards, Cournoyer was a high-scorer, with 25 or more goals in 12 consecutive seasons. "The Roadrunner" scored 428 regular-season goals and was part of ten Cup winners with the Canadiens. He was an all-star four times and won the Conn Smythe Trophy as playoff MVP in 1973.

## Valery Kharlamov

(left wing, 1967 to 1981)

was the high-scoring left winger on the Central Red Army and Soviet National team's number-one forward line, playing alongside Vladimir Petrov and Boris Mikhailov for most of the 1970s. Kharlamov, who was killed in an automobile accident, was a great individual star playing within the Soviet system. His success was built upon his marvelous skating ability and his endless array of improvisational moves with the puck. In Soviet hockey circles, his hockey is considered ballet on ice. He is the third-leading all-time scorer with the Soviet Nationals, scoring 197 goals in 287 games.

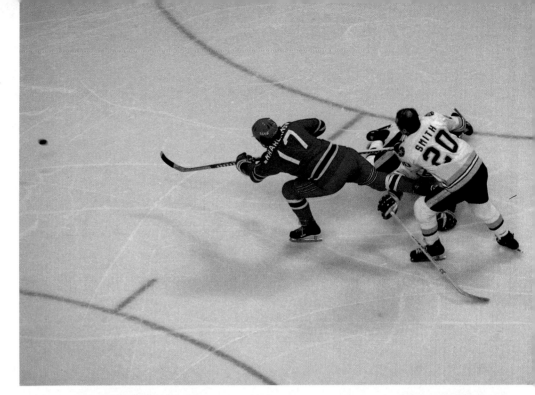

## Gordie Howe

(right wing, 1946–1980)

was already a veteran of 21 NHL seasons at the time of expansion. He was selected to the first all-star team in each of the first three seasons after the league increased in size. In 1969 he had his most productive NHL season, joining Phil Esposito and Bobby Hull as the only players to score 100 points in a single campaign. After a two-year retirement, he joined the Houston Aeros of the WHA where he had four more productive seasons playing with his two sons. He finished his 32-year career in the NHL with Hartford in 1980, having scored 801 NHL regular-season goals.

## Bill Barber

(left wing, 1972–1984)
joined the Philadelphia Flyers
after only 11 games in the
minors. He was a steady
scorer and adept at playing
both in the corners and in the
slot in front of his opponents'
net. He had 50 goals and 112
points in 1975–76, a year in
which he was a first all-star
selection. He had 40 goals on
four other occasions, finishing his career with 883 points
in 903 games.

## Sergei Makarov

(right wing, 1978 to date)
has been the Soviet Union's
leading scorer for six of the
past seven seasons. He is
endowed with tremendous
speed and balance, making
him difficult to check. Through
the 1985–86 season, he had
257 goals and 535 points in
384 games for Central Red
Army in the Soviet National
League. He has 139 goals in
215 games with the Soviet
National team and has twice
been selected European
Player of the Year.

## Mark Messier

(left wing/center,
1978 to date)

began his professional career
as a 17-year-old with Indianapolis and Cincinnati of the
WHA. He joined Edmonton
when that club became part
of the NHL and blossomed
into a 50-goal scorer and
first all-star in 1981–82. He
had 106 points the following
season and won the Conn
Smythe Trophy as playoff MVP
during the Oilers' Stanley
Cup victory of 1984. He is
one of the fastest and strongest players in the NHL.

## Alexander Yakushev

(left wing, 1966 to 1980)

was another astonishingly talented player on the 1972
Soviet National team that
played a team of Canadian
NHL stars. "The Yak" played
for Moscow Spartak in the
Soviet National League and,
along with linemates Viktor
Shalimov and Vladimir
Shadrin, led his team to a
rare league championship in
an era when Soviet league
play was dominated by Red
Army. As a national team-
player, Yakushev scored 141
goals.

## Vladimir Krutov

**(left wing, 1977 to date)**
plays on a line with Sergei
Makarov and center Igor
Larionov that has been the
top scoring unit in Soviet
league play every season
since 1980–81. He was the
top Soviet scorer in the 1984
Canada Cup and has scored
more than 100 goals as a
member of the Soviet National
team. His 31 goals in 40
games led all Soviet league
scorers in 1985–86.

# DEFENSEMEN

## Doug Wilson

(defense, 1977 to date) has one of the hardest shots in the NHL. He scored 39 goals in 1981–82, the third-highest single-season total ever recorded by a defenseman. He received the Norris Trophy as the NHL's top defenseman that season and was named to the first all-star team. He logs a tremendous amount of ice time for the Chicago Blackhawks, playing the point on power-plays.

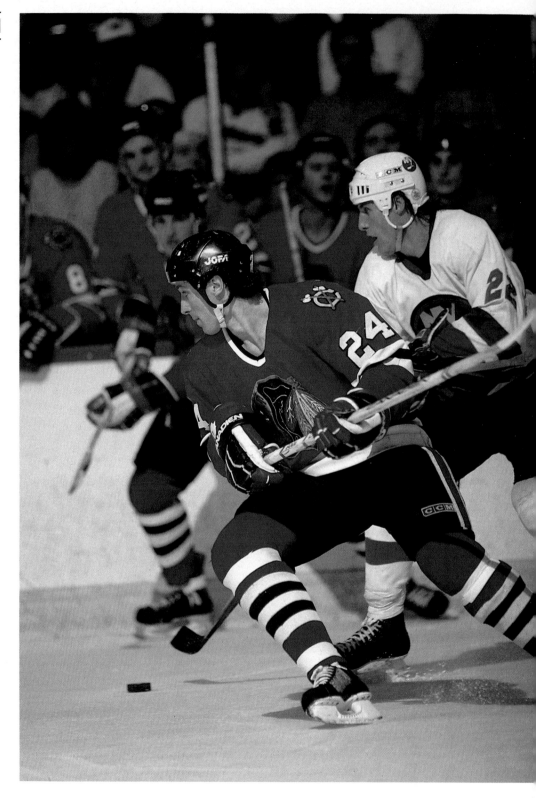

## Vyatcheslav Fetisov

(defense, 1974 to date)

is a star player with Central Red Army and the Soviet National team. Hailed by some as the best player in the world, Fetisov is a creative, rushing defenseman in the Bobby Orr mold. He has been selected Soviet player of the year on two occasions, the most recent being 1985–86, and was named to the tournament all-star team at the 1986 World Championships.

## Ray Bourque

(defense, 1979 to date)

was an instant success as an NHLer, electrifying fans with his spectacular rushes. He was rookie of the year in 1980 and won a first all-star selection in that year. He has been named to either the first or second all-star team every year he has been in the league. His point-a-game scoring pace and durability could allow him to become one of the highest-scoring defensemen in NHL history.

## Paul Coffey

(defense, 1980 to date)

is a gifted skater with a scoring touch who reaps the benefits of playing with the Edmonton Oilers, the most productive offensive team in the history of the NHL. His 48 goals in 1985–86 are the most scored by a defenseman in a single season. He has won five consecutive all-star team berths and was awarded the Norris Trophy in 1985 and 1986.

## Mark Howe

**(defense, 1973 to date)**

begin his professional career as a 17-year-old forward, playing alongside his father, Gordie, and brother, Marty, with the WHA's Houston Aeros. He was with Hartford when that team joined the NHL and was traded to Philadelphia in 1982 where he blossomed into one of the most effective defensemen in the league. In addition to two first all-star selections, he has won the Emery Edge Award as the leading plus/minus player in the league.

## Rod Langway

**(defense, 1978 to date)**

clears the front of the net and takes charge of play in his own end as well as any defenseman in the NHL. He is a throw-back to the old-style defensive rearguard and, as captain of the Washington Capitals, has led his team to one of the best defensive records in today's NHL. He is a three-time all-star and two-time Norris Trophy winner.

### Denis Potvin

(defense, 1973 to date)

was the New York Islanders' first draft choice in 1973. He was NHL rookie of the year in 1974 and has been a vital part of the Islanders ascent from expansion team to four-time Stanley Cup champion. He holds every career scoring mark for defensemen, including most goals, assists and points and is the only defenseman to score more than 1,000 points in regular-season play. He had 101 points in 1978–79, and has scored more than 150 points in play-off competition.

### Borje Salming

(defense, 1973 to date)

is the first European to establish himself as an NHL star. A superb skater, Salming has come back from two serious eye injuries to lead the Toronto Maple Leafs' defense. He has been selected to the NHL all-star team six times and, with 702 points at the start of the 1986–87 season, is the fifth-leading scorer among defensemen.

## Larry Robinson

**(defense, 1973 to date)**
is capable of out-muscling or
out-finessing his opponents.
His great size and mobility
made him almost impossible
to beat at the blueline and,
when added to his effective
low shot from the point, enabled him to win six all-star
selections and the Norris
Trophy in 1977 and 1980. He
has played on six Cup winners in Montreal, winning
the Conn Smythe Trophy in
1978 when he tied for the
playoff scoring lead with teammate Guy Lafleur.

## Serge Savard
### (defense, 1967–1983)

was a part of seven Stanley Cup winners as a player for Montreal. In 1969, he won the Conn Smythe Trophy as playoff MVP. He was one of the game's great rushing defensemen until a badly broken leg threatened his career and contributed to his adopting a more conservative style. Along with teammates Guy Lapointe and Larry Robinson, Savard gave the Canadiens of the late 1970s the finest defense in the NHL.

## Brad Park
### (defense, 1968–1985)

never failed to appear in postseason competition during his 17 years in the NHL. His skills in the offensive zone rivaled those of Bobby Orr, as his hard, accurate shot from the point and knowledge of the game made him the on-ice general in power-play situations. His 683 regular-season assists and 213 goals make him the third-leading scorer among NHL defensemen.

## Bobby Orr
### (defense, 1966–1979)

evokes images of thrilling end-to-end rushes just by mention of his name. He was the prototype for today's puck-carrying defensemen, having redefined the way the position is played. Orr won the Calder Trophy as top rookie in 1967, the last year of the six-team league, and then reeled off eight successive Norris Trophies as top defenseman. He was league MVP in 1970, 1971 and 1972, playoff MVP in 1970 and 1972 and — unprecedented for defensemen — NHL scoring leader in 1970 and 1975.

### Tony Esposito
(goaltender, 1968–1984)
won both the Vezina and Calder Trophies with Chicago in 1969–70 when he recorded 15 shutouts, the most in a single season since 1928. His butterfly style and quickness enabled him to share in two more Vezina wins in the 1970s. In 16 NHL seasons, he recorded 76 shutouts with a goals-against average of 2.92.

## Ken Dryden

**(goaltender, 1971–1979)**

was an overnight sensation in the NHL, appearing at the end of the regular season in 1971 to lead the Montreal Canadiens to an upset Stanley Cup victory. His characteristic pose — standing with his arms crossed on the top on his stick — became one of the most recognizable images in hockey in the 1970s. He backstopped the Habs to another Cup win in 1973 and, after taking a year off in 1974, returned to Montreal to be part of four straight Stanley Cups from 1976 to 1979.

## Bernie Parent

**(goaltender, 1966–1979)**

played 13 seasons with Boston, Philadelphia in both the NHL and WHA, and Toronto. His finest years were with the Flyers in the mid-1970s, when, in 1973–74 and 1974–75, he won consecutive Vezina and Conn Smythe Trophies as the Flyers won the Stanley Cup both years. During these years, Parent's goals-against average hovered around 2.00 in both regular-season and playoff competition.

## Vladislav Tretiak

(goaltender, 1968–1984)
is the most celebrated goaltender ever to play international hockey. Tretiak played
on a record 13 World Championship teams and three Olympic gold medallists with the
Soviet Nationals. He was sensational in the 1972 Team
Canada-Soviet series and
brought a technically correct
and athletic approach to the
position that enabled him to
remain at the top of his game
for 14 seasons.

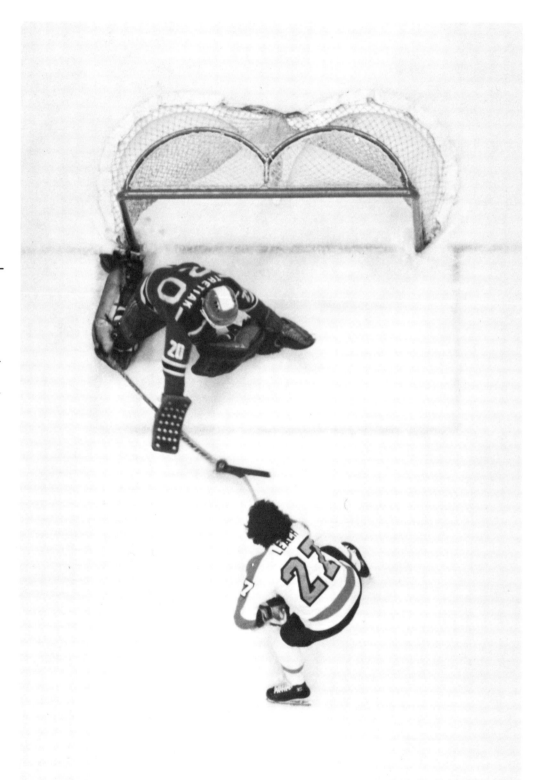

Don Luce, 1969–1982

# DEFENSIVE SPECIALISTS

Goals and assists are the easiest statistics to tabulate in hockey, but any hockey team needs players with skills that don't show up in scoring summaries. These players are checkers, faceoff men, defensive forwards, shot-blockers and penalty killers. They are as important to winning regular-season games, Stanley Cups and gold medals as 50-goal scorers.

**Craig Ramsay and Don Luce** gave the Buffalo Sabres one of the NHL's top penalty-killing tandems throughout the 1970s. Their success was due in equal part to checking and tireless skating. Ramsay won the Selke Trophy as the NHL top defensive forward in 1985; Luce the Masterton Trophy for perseverance and dedication in 1975.

Craig Ramsay, 1971–1985

**Doug Jarvis** became the NHL's iron man in 1986, breaking Garry Unger's long-standing mark of 914 consecutive games played. Jarvis has played for Montreal, Washington and Hartford, taking important faceoffs and making each team better. He won the Selke Trophy with Washington in 1984. In Montreal he killed penalties with **Bob Gainey** who was the top defensive forward in the NHL in the late 1970s and early 1980s, winning the Selke Trophy the first four years it was awarded. Another Montreal penalty killer, **Guy Carbonneau**, played a vital role in the Canadiens' 1986 Stanley Cup victory, scoring seven goals including two short-handed markers. Carbonneau skates like a flashy scorer, but concentrates on checking duties and blocking shots from the point.

Bob Gainey, 1973 to date

Doug Jarvis, 1975 to date

Guy Carbonneau, 1981 to date

Butch Goring, 1969–1985

Ed Westfall, 1961–1979

**Butch Goring** was a two-way player and one of the NHL's top faceoff men. Despite 375 goals and 888 points, he is remembered for his hustle and tough, clean play. He won the Lady Byng and Masterton Trophies with Los Angeles in 1978 and the Conn Smythe Trophy as playoff MVP with the Islanders in 1981. **Ed Westfall** played 18 seasons in the NHL with Boston and the New York Islanders. In Boston he combined with Derek Sanderson on a penalty-killing unit that was a constant threat to score shorthanded. He was the New York Islanders' first captain and on-ice leader. In nine playoff years, he scored eight shorthanded goals.

**Lee Fogolin** is one of the NHL's most effective shot-blocking defensemen. He broke into the NHL with Buffalo in 1974–75 and went to Edmonton where he was captain of the Oilers from 1980–83. He was an important contributor to Edmonton's Cup wins in 1984 and 1985. **Joe Watson,** who typified the hard-working Flyers, was another great shot-blocker who had plenty of chances to kill penalties with the rugged Philadelphia teams of the mid-1970s. **Jim Schoenfeld**, whose Buffalo Sabres played the Flyers in the 1975 Cup final, used his great size to challenge opposing shooters, blocking shots like a second goaltender.

Lee Fogolin, 1974 to date

Joe Watson, 1964–1979

Jim Schoenfeld, 1972–1985

## Al Arbour

(coach, 1970–1986)

was a steady defenseman who played on four Stanley Cup champions in the 1950s and 1960s. He played on winners in Detroit (1953–54), Chicago (1960–61) and Toronto (1961–62 and 1963–64). He coached parts of three seasons in St. Louis before taking over as head coach of the New York Islanders in 1973–74, the franchise's second year in the NHL. Arbour was a player's coach who demanded and got best efforts from his entire roster. He coached the Islanders to four consecutive Cup wins from 1980 to 1983.

## Scotty Bowman

(coach, 1967–1986)

began his professional coaching career in the Montreal system, but went to the St. Louis Blues for his first NHL coaching job. With St. Louis, he guided the club to the Stanley Cup finals in each of its first three seasons. Bowman took over coaching responsibilities in Montreal beginning with the 1971–72 season, winning the Stanley Cup in 1973 and in four consecutive years from 1976 to 1979. Bowman took on the dual job of coach and general manager of the Buffalo Sabres in the fall of 1979, finally leaving Buffalo in 1986. In that time he had become the NHL coach with the greatest number of career victories.

# GENERAL MANAGER

## Sam Pollock

(general manager,
1963–1978)

took over from Frank Selke, Sr. as general manager of the Canadiens in 1963–64. After expansion, Pollock shrewdly acquired draft choices in exchange for talented journeyman players who were sent to expansion teams looking for immediate help. Wise use of these draft choices and Pollock's patience in allowing young talent to develop within the Montreal farm system made the Canadiens the NHL's most successful club with ten Cup wins from 1965 to 1980.

## Bill Torrey

(general manager,
1972 to date)

built the New York Islanders into a 100-point team after only four seasons in the NHL. Torrey drafted wisely, selecting Denis Potvin in 1973, Clark Gillies and Bryan Trottier in 1974 and Mike Bossy and John Tonelli in 1977. When his team seemed on the verge of a Cup win, Torrey traded for center Butch Goring who added the toughness and experience that was necessary to put the Islanders over the top, with four championships and five final series appearances from 1980 to 1984.

# TWENTY BIG GAMES

May 7, 1968
Game Two          Stanley Cup Final
Montreal 1              St. Louis 0

Above: Glenn Hall appears pinned in his net in the first post-expansion Stanley Cup final. Noel Picard (4) and Bob Plager (5) defend for St. Louis as John Ferguson (22) and Ralph Backstrom (6) look for the loose puck.

The question on the minds of hockey fans during the first Stanley Cup final after expansion was not who would win but, rather, how badly would the Montreal Canadiens outclass the St. Louis Blues. After all, Montreal had led the East Division during the regular season with 94 points. St. Louis had finished third in the newly established West Division with 70 points and a below-.500 record. As well, the Canadiens were playing well; they had crushed the NHL's highest scoring team, the Boston Bruins, in four straight games and then shut down the league's leading point getter, Stan Mikita, and the game's top marksman, Bobby Hull, in five games to reach the finals.

St. Louis has struggled to defeat the Philadelphia Flyers in seven games. They needed three overtime victories to subdue the Minnesota North Stars, squeaking by with a 2–1 overtime victory in the

seventh game. The Blues' leading scorer in the playoffs was Dickie Moore, a player who had retired from the Canadiens at the end of the 1962–63 season. The Blues had former Montreal penalty killer Jim Roberts and two players from the Montreal organization, Noel Picard and Red Berenson, who could not make the big club. The defensive pairing of Al Arbour, who had come out of retirement, and Jean-Guy Talbot had played on several Cup winners. Arbour's experience dated back to the 1953–54 Red Wings, while Talbot was on the Canadiens dynasty teams that owned the Stanley Cup from 1956–60. While the team was laden with veterans with a winning tradition, it was widely held that the "Flying Frenchmen" would simply skate away from them, making a mockery of hockey's most prestigious award. The Blues certainly had no talented rookies like Serge Savard or Jacques Lemaire. What they had was a ton of heart, a clever coach in Scotty Bowman and one of the greatest goaltenders of all time in Glenn Hall.

Hall won the Vezina Trophy with Denis DeJordy playing for Chicago in 1967, but quit the Blackhawks after that season. He had performed brilliantly for twelve season in Detroit and Chicago, but the trauma of goaltending caused him to be physically ill before and, often, during every game.

Hall had been coaxed out of retirement and gave the Blues a fine season with five shutouts and a 2.48 goals-against average. He had been simply spectacular in the playoffs, starting all 14 games with relief from Seth Martin in two encounters. He had shut out Philadelphia 1–0 in the first game of the West Division semifinals. Hall robbed Minnesota's leading scorer, Wayne Connelly, on a breakaway in the first overtime period of the seventh game of the West Division final, enabling the Blues to reach the Stanley Cup.

Though the Blues were already a veteran team, they shored up their defensive corps just prior to the playoffs by bringing up 43-year-old Doug Harvey, who was the playing coach of their farm team in Kansas City. Between 1955 and 1962 Harvey had won the Norris Trophy seven times, six with the Habs and one with the New York Rangers, where he was playing coach in 1962.

The Blues surprised everyone with a superlative effort in the first game, losing 3–2 in overtime. St. Louis held a 2–1 lead late in the second period when Larry Keenan's shot eluded Gump Worsley only to hit the goalpost. The Habs skated right back down the ice and scored when Yvan Cournoyer took a pass from John Ferguson and beat Glenn Hall with a blast over his shoulder. The period ended deadlocked at 2–2, despite the Blues' 18–13 edge in shots. The two veteran goaltenders were outstanidng in the final stanza, forcing the contest into overtime. Jacques Lemaire settled the encounter with a hard slapshot from just inside the blueline at 1:41 of the extra frame.

The strong performance in game one brought out a record crowd of 16,177 for the second matchup. The Blues were confident that they could compete with the Habs on an equal footing. St. Louis held Montreal in check with their pesky forechecking and hustle in the opening period. Glenn Hall came up with brilliant saves off Jacques Laperriere and Cournoyer with Gary Sabourin off for slashing. Worsley showed why he was Vezina Trophy winner by doing the splits to turn back a shot by Jimmy Roberts that was headed for the corner.

The Canadiens dominated the second period, outshooting the Blues 14-8. Only excellent goaltending by Hall and some erratic shooting that saw Rousseau, Cournoyer and Duff misfire on great chances kept St. Louis close. At 16:24 Cournoyer rang a shot off the post and the game remained scoreless through two periods.

The final period was 1:55 old when Dick Duff took an elbowing penalty. An injury to Gilles Tremblay forced Montreal coach Toe Blake to use Serge Savard as a penalty killer alongside Claude Provost. Provost lugged the puck down the right side deep into Blues territory before shooting in the direction of the opposing goal. The puck was stopped by Jimmy Roberts, who lost it in his skates. Savard barged in full tilt and leveled Roberts who knocked over goaltender Hall. Somehow the puck found its way into the net. The task of playing catchup was made all the more difficult when Red Berenson of St. Louis drew a five-minute major for cutting Bobby Rousseau with his stick. Montreal forechecked the Blues to a standstill, outshooting them 12–3 in the third period. Rousseau drew a holding penalty at 18:05 and Hall was pulled for an extra attacker at 18:52 but the tying goal did not come. The Canadiens held on to win 1–0 and take command of the series heading back to the Montreal Forum. Glenn Hall was superb despite the loss, turning away 35 shots. Worsley blocked 19 in posting his fourth career playoff shutout.

Montreal won both games in the Forum to capture the Stanley Cup. Both games were one-goal victories, and Glenn Hall was named the Conn Smythe Trophy winner as the playoff MVP. Toe Blake announced his retirement after a brilliant 13–year coaching career with the Canadiens that saw him behind the bench for eight Stanley Cup championships.

The Minnesota North Stars had finished the 1968–69 season with the NHL's worst record, winning only 18 games. With victories almost as hard to come by the following year, the North Stars were in a fight with Oakland and Philadelphia for the final playoff spot. St. Louis had already clinched first place in the West Division with 86 points, while the Pittsburgh Penguins had guaranteed their first visit to postseason play with 64 points.

Heading into the final weekend of the regular season, the North Stars had 56 points, placing them just two behind the Flyers and Oakland Seals. If Minnesota could beat Philadelphia on the Flyers' home ice on Saturday afternoon, they would nail down a playoff berth by virtue of having a greater number of wins. Philadelphia had played poorly in the final three weeks of the season, dropping 15 of their last 20 games, including the last five in a row.

The North Stars had some real firepower on their squad. Danny Grant had won the Calder Trophy as the league's top rookie the previous year while equaling a goal scoring mark for freshmen with 24 tallies. J.P. Parise was trying to catch St. Louis Blues' Red Berenson for the scoring leadership in the the West Division with both men among the NHL's top ten in scoring. Bill Goldsworthy had tied the North Star record for goals in a season with 35 and was hoping to surpass this mark in the final weekend of the season.

The North Stars had swung a few deals to strengthen their club, obtaining defenseman Barry Gibbs and Minnesota-born forward Tommy Williams from the Boston Bruins for future considerations. In a dispute with management, Lorne "Gump" Worsley had retired from the Montreal Canadiens in December and general manager Wren Blair had coaxed Worsley out of retirement to tend goal for the North Stars at the end of the season.

In spite of Philadelphia's losing streak, 14,606 Flyers fans turned up at the Spectrum to cheer their team on, encouraged by the quality of play of defenseman Ed Van Impe, goaltender Bernie Parent and a 20–year-old rookie sensation named Bobby Clarke.

Both the North Stars and Flyers tied a lot of games, as the two teams had 22 and 24 ties respectively. Sixteen-year

J.P. Parise, left, was a top scorer in the NHL's West Division. Barry Gibbs, right, got the big goal that pulled the North Stars into the playoffs.

Bill Goldsworthy

veteran Gump Worsley got the start in the Minnesota goal. Worsley had to be sharp in the first period, as the Flyers outshot the Stars 9 to 7. The two teams split six penalties and settled nothing as the score remained deadlocked at zero after one period.

Minnesota moved to the attack in the second period, firing 13 shots at Bernie Parent and killing off two minor penalties to Danny O'Shea. Both goalies remained unbeatable and the match was scoreless after two periods.

In the third, Tommy Williams won a faceoff at center with 7:48 left to play. Barry Gibbs coralled it and fired a shot at the Flyer net 80 feet away. Parent must have been screened as he did not even react to the high drive until it was

by him. The North Stars played tight defensive hockey the rest of the way, killing a penalty in the last three minutes of the game. The shutout victory eliminated the Flyers from the playoffs for the first time in their short history, for while they finished the season tied with Oakland at 58 points, the Seals had won five more games.

The North Stars also won their final game of the season and captured third place. J.P. Parise finished the season with 72 points, tied with Red Berenson for the scoring lead in the West Division. Bill Goldsworthy bagged his 36th goal, establishing a club record. The North Stars were eliminated by St. Louis in a six-game West Division semi-final.

---

April 8, 1971
Game Two      East Division
             Quarter-Final
Montreal 7         Boston 5

The defending Stanley Cup champion Bruins were the hottest team in hockey in 1970–71, establishing 37 scoring records en route to first place in the East Division. Among the many single-season records set by Boston were most wins (57) and most points (121). The Habs rebounded from missing the playoffs the previous season to finish in third place with 97 points. Late in the regular season, Montreal promoted goaltender Ken Dryden from their Nova Scotia farm club to the Canadiens. Dryden responded by going undefeated

as the Habs won their last six regular-season games.

With Boston heavily favored, the Bruins won the series opener 3–1 in the Boston Garden. It appeared that Dryden would taste defeat for the second time in game two as the Bruins built a comfortable 5–1 lead by the midway point in the second as Bobby Orr had a goal and a record-tying three assists in the period. Late in the middle stanza, Henri Richard stole the puck from Orr to score an unassisted marker. The Bruins still led by three.

Henri Richard (16) stole the puck from Bobby Orr to score an unassisted goal that launched the Montreal Canadiens to a comeback win and eventually, an upset semi-final victory. Jean Beliveau, pictured above left, during a later game in the series, played strongly in winning his tenth and final Stanley Cup.

Jean Beliveau, still a fierce competitor at age 39, was not about to bring the curtain down on his brilliant career without making every effort to win. At the start of the third period, the Bruins, confident of victory, decided to forego their normal strong forechecking and heavy hitting. The Canadiens capitalized on this change in strategy as Beliveau fired career playoff goals number 74 and 75 within two minutes of each other early in the final period. The Habs were back in the contest. Jacques Lemaire intercepted a blind Boston pass back to the point and went the length of the ice on a breakaway to deadlock the encounter at 5–5. At 15:23, Beliveau held the puck

behind the net until John Ferguson bulled his way into the open in front to redirect the pass over a sprawling Ed Johnston in the Bruin goal. Frank Mahovlich added an insurance marker with 80 seconds left in the game.

This stunning defeat was the Bruins' first in their last twelve playoff games. Henri Richard best summed up the victory when he said, ''It is games like this one that make you feel younger.'' This proved to be a prophetic statement, as the veteran-laden Habs, with Beliveau, Richard and Frank Mahovlich leading the way, went on to eliminate the mighty Bruins in six games.

April 29, 1971
Game Six          Semi-Final
New York 3        Chicago 2

In 1969 two new franchises that would begin play in the 1970–71 season were added to the NHL. The Buffalo Sabres and Vancouver Canucks would join the East Division, and the Chicago Blackhawks — who at the time of the expansion had the worst record of any of the original six teams — moved to the West Division. Despite their poor showing in 1968–69, the Hawks led the East Division the following year, backstopped by the brilliant 15-shutout season of rookie goaltender Tony Esposito. In 1970–71, the Hawks' first season playing in the West Division, they dominated, finishing 20 points ahead of second-place St. Louis while recording 107 points in the standings. In the East, the Rangers established a team record with 109 points, but finished second to the record-shattering scoring machine from Boston which set a new NHL single-season record with 121 points in the standings.

This was the first year that the playoffs adopted an inter-divisional format, with semi-finalists from each division competing against one another. Chicago blasted the Philadelphia Flyers in four straight games to move on to the semi-finals, while the Rangers dispatched the Toronto Maple Leafs. The Hawks led the New York/Chicago semi-final series 3–2 in games as the Rangers prepared to make a last stand at Madison Square Garden. The series had seen two games already go into overtime, with Bobby Hull ending one encounter and Pete Stemkowski making his first playoff goal of the season the important one in a Ranger victory. Game six pitted last year's Vezina Trophy winner, Tony Esposito, against the current co-winner Ed Giacomin, who shared the award with his netminding partner, Gilles Villemure.

The Rangers were urged on by a packed house of 17,250 supporters at the Garden and came out flying in the first period. Good saves by Tony Esposito kept them off the scoreboard. Dennis Hull opened the scoring, converting passes from Cliff Koroll and Stan Mikita to beat Giacomin at 10:19 of the opening period. It looked bleak for the home side at 1:44 of the middle stanza when Chico Maki upped the margin to 2–0 with

Pete Stemkowski and the joy of a goal in triple overtime.

assists by Bobby Hull and Pit Martin. The Rangers got one back before the end of the period when Rod Gilbert finally beat Esposito at 7:07 on a set up from Brad Park and Vic Hadfield. Hadfield's assist enabled him to establish a team record with 12 points in a playoff year. The marker was Gilbert's 17th career playoff goal which was another Ranger team record. Despite outshooting the Hawks 10 to 6 in the first period and 14 to 3 in the second, the Rangers were 20 minutes from elimination.

The Goal-A-Game Line rose to the occasion as Jean Ratelle took a short feed from Vic Hadfield, who had in turn been set up by Rod Gilbert. Ratelle's short shot evened the score at 2–2. Nothing was settled in regulation time and the series moved to overtime for the third time. The first overtime period resulted in no change in the score, although the Rangers held a wide margin in the play. In the first minute of the second overtime, Stan Mikita flattened Giacomin with a rising drive off the face mask. Hawk defenseman Bill White pounced on the rebound and drilled the puck off the left post. Mikita recovered the rebound and with Giacomin still sprawled flat on the ice, fired a shot that rang off the right post and somehow stayed out of the net. The Rangers were forced to weather a penalty to 41-year-old defenseman Tim

Horton midway through the second overtime period. Pat Stapleton of the Hawks took a penalty at 19:25 of the session, but the game was still tied when the players adjourned to the dressing room for a brief intermission. Between gulps of oxygen, Brad Park stated that he was sick and tired of coming in and going out between periods.

The Garden was warm and humid and the ice was close to melting as both teams started a third overtime period. The Rangers had the man advantage for the first minute and 25 seconds of the session. The penalty to Stapleton had just expired when Tim Horton lugged the puck down the ice and fired a shot that took a strange carom off the boards. Ted Irvine found the puck on his stick perfectly set up for a drive from the left side. Esposito kicked out the shot but the rebound rolled to centerman Pete Stemkowski who jammed the puck into the open right side of the net. Pandemonium reigned in Madison Square Garden as Pete Stemkowski made his second playoff tally of the season another instant winner.

The Rangers could not duplicate their heroics of game six back at the Chicago Stadium and bowed out in seven games. The Chicago Blackhawks went on to face the Montreal Canadiens in the Stanley Cup finals.

---

**May 18, 1971**
**Game Seven     Stanley Cup Final**
**Montreal 3          Chicago 2**

Twenty thousand avid Blackhawks fans crammed into ancient Chicago Stadium, sweltering in 80 degree heat inside the building, to watch the seventh and deciding game of an excellent series between two fine clubs. The soft ice with its occasional fog haze was not what the already exhausted combatants had hoped for.

Throughout the series, a much publicized squabble between veteran Henri Richard and Canadiens coach Al MacNeil had been conducted through the media. Richard had denounced MacNeil after being benched in the later stages of a game earlier in the series. Outwardly the Canadiens were all business as usual, but there was no telling what effect this rift was having on the team.

Only the brilliance of Ken Dryden kept the Habs in the contest in the opening period. He robbed Stan Mikita from point-blank range and then turned away Eric Nesterenko on the rebound. He darted out a pad to deflect a screened shot from the point by Keith Magnuson. The Habs could not get in gear and managed little sustained action in the Hawks' end. At 17:35 Rejean Houle was sent off for holding Bobby Hull and the Hawks laid siege to the Montreal net. Again Dryden rose to the occasion, withstanding a close-in shot from Jim Pappin and turning aside a Bobby Hull slapper from the point. Finally, Dennis Hull opened the scoring with under a minute left in the period with the Hawks still enjoying a man advantage. Dryden had faced 12

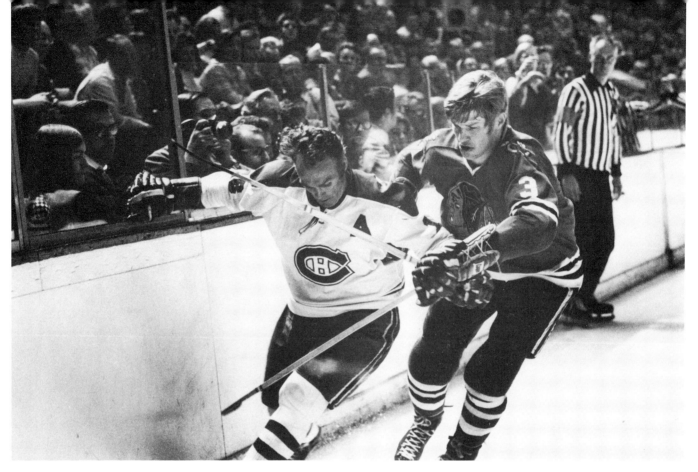

Henri Richard's third period goal clinched the Cup for the Canadiens. Chicago's Keith Magnuson logged extra ice-time throughout much of the contest.

shots in the opening frame, many of them difficult, but as the 23-year-old law student had proven throughout the playoffs, he thrived on pressure situations.

It was Tony Esposito's turn to sparkle in the second period. With the Hawks two men down, he made a remarkable leg save off a backhand by Jacques Lemaire. After these penalties expired, the Hawks surged into the Montreal zone and applied intense pressure. Finally, their patience was rewarded following a Doug Jarrett shot from the point. Pit Martin outduelled two Montreal defenders to feed a pass into the slot to Danny O'Shea who put the puck behind Dryden. Shortly thereafter, Bobby Hull unleashed his patented slapshot only to ring it off the crossbar. In the 14th minute of the period, Jacques Lemaire skated leisurely over center and unleashed an 80-foot shot at the Chicago net. Esposito dropped in his normal butterfly fashion, but the puck kept rising and caught the top of the net over his shoulder. This goal at 14:18 devastated the Hawks. At 18:20 Henri Richard took a pass from Lemaire, who was stationed behind the net, and beat Tony Esposito from in close.

At 2:34 of the third period, Richard took a pass from Houle, walked around

Keith Magnuson and fired a shot over Esposito's right shoulder to give the Habs their first lead. The Hawks sagged visibly after the goal, but Bobby Hull twice drew penalties as he barged toward the Montreal net. Dryden was called upon for further heroics and rose to the occasion with a remarkable sliding save off of Pappin from the lip of the crease. The Hawk player went from raising his stick in exultation to slamming it on the ice as Dryden came out of nowhere to get a pad on his shot. Frank Mahovlich, though best known as a goal scorer, excelled in the third period killing penalties, enabling the Canadiens to skate off with their sixteenth Stanley Cup.

Their 1971 Cup win was marked by a number of highlights for the Canadiens. Richard and MacNeil hugged each other following the victory, but MacNeil was not behind the Canadiens bench the following year. It was learned that veteran defenseman Jacques Laperriere had been playing with a broken left forearm since the second game of the series. Frank Mahovlich established a record for goals in the postseason with 14. Ken Dryden was named playoff MVP and Jean Beliveau announced his retirement after his tenth Stanley Cup victory.

September 26, 1972
Game Seven
Team Canada vs. Soviet Nationals
Team Canada 4    Soviet Union 3

When the eight-game challenge series between a team of Canadian NHL all-stars and the Soviet Nationals had been proposed, hockey experts predicted a one-sided NHL victory. Though the Soviet team was the Olympic gold medal winner and winner of nine of the previous ten world championships, conventional wisdom held that the toughness and skill of the Soviets' first NHL oppponents would prove too much for them. Of course, the Soviets were a more than credible opponent for Team Canada, winning games one and four in Canada as well as game five in Moscow. As one game had ended in a tie, Team Canada faced the unenviable task of having to win three straight games in Moscow to salvage a narrow 4–3–1 series victory. In game six, Team Canada emerged with a hard-fought 3–2 victory.

Throughout the series, Team Canada players and officials were highly critical of the European referees who worked the games. In the aftermath of the game six victory, an irate Team Canada coach Harry Sinden complained bitterly, insisting that two West German referees be dropped for the remaining two games of the series. Valery Kharlamov, the Soviets' top scorer, did not dress, having suffered a cracked ankle compliments of a wicked slash from Team Canada centerman Bobby Clarke. From the outset of the game, it was evident that the Russian intensity level was high. Never known for their willingness to lay on the body, the Soviets came out hitting to start game seven. Team Canada's Phil Esposito managed to open the scoring, picking the corner from the slot despite having Soviet defenseman Vladimir Lutchenko draped all over him. Team

Bobby Clarke and Alexander Maltsev

Canada's lead was short-lived as Soviet stars Alexander Yakushev and Vladimir Petrov beat goaltender Tony Esposito. Phil Esposito tied the game with his second goal of the period at 17:34.

The second period was scoreless and featured spectacular goaltending by Tony O. Team Canada's offense sputtered, as the line of Bobby Clarke, Ron Ellis and Paul Henderson could not seem to click on their passes. Speedster Yvan Cournoyer remained mired in a slump, as he patroled the right side on a line with J.P. Parise. The Soviets' short passing game still seemed to mystify Team Canada.

Team Canada broke through to get the all-important fifth goal early in the third period, as Rod Gilbert scored with assists going to his Ranger linemate Jean Ratelle and Chicago's Dennis Hull. The Soviets bounced right back when their leading scorer, Alexander Yakushev, scored on the powerplay. A tie in this contest would have eliminated any chance for Team Canada to win the series. Two minutes remained when Paul Henderson took a pass from Serge Savard at his own blue line. At top speed he broke in on Soviet defenseman Gennady Tsygankov and attempted to push the puck through the defender's legs. Tsygankov was fooled by Henderson's move, letting the Canadian player dance around him. In all alone, Henderson picked the top corner on Soviet goaltender Vladislav Tretiak as he was chopped down from behind. Crashing into the boards, Henderson didn't know if the puck had gone in. The goal judge was slow turning on the light that indicated a goal, but slowly the referee's arm rose to signify that the puck had gone in. Assistant coach John Ferguson, borrowing a bit of gamesmanship from his old coach Toe Blake, sent the Team Canada players clambering over the boards to congratulate Henderson, thinking that their exuberance would aid the referee in deciding that the puck had entered the net.

In a move very uncharacteristic of the Soviet concept of team play, coach Vsevolod Bobrov reproached Tsygankov for costing his team the game. The stage was set for a dramatic finale to the 1972 Super Series as both teams required a win in the final game to claim a series victory.

---

September 28, 1972
Game Eight
Team Canada vs. Soviet Nationals
Team Canada 6     Soviet Union 5

---

The organizers of hockey's first challenge series could not have hoped for a more dramatic finish than the eighth game between Team Canada and the Soviet Nationals in 1972. After game five in Moscow, Team Canada trailed the Soviets 3–1–1 in games and required three straight wins. The Miracle of Moscow was two-thirds completed as Team Canada had won two games in a row, evening the series. Paul Henderson had emerged as the squad's trigger man, netting the winner in each of the last two games. In the deciding contest, Ken Dryden got the start in the Canadian net. The game featured the return of Josef Kompalla, the West German referee whom Team Canada had complained bitterly about following game six.

The match was played at a high emotional pitch from the outset. J.P. Parise received an interference penalty in the game's fifth minute, despite the fact that his check, Alexander Maltsev, had the puck. An enraged Parise was given a misconduct and then was tossed out of the game for overstating his case. The situation turned ugly when Team Canada coach Harry Sinden hurled a stool onto the ice, followed by a metal chair compliments of trainer John Forristall. The 2,000 Canadian supporters who had followed Team Canada to Moscow repeatedly chanted, "Let's go home! Let's go home!"

The Russians opened the scoring with Alexander Yakushev's goal at 3:34 of the first period with both Bill White and Pete Mahovlich in the penalty box. Phil Esposito, who had emerged as the club's spokesman and inspirational leader, let his play speak for itself as he converted Brad Park's rebound to tie the game on a powerplay. Powerplay goals continued as Vladimir Lutchenko restored the home team's lead while skating with the man advantage. Jean Ratelle was set up by Ranger teammate Brad Park and netted the equalizer to end the first

Phil Esposito (7) had two goals and two assists as he controlled the area in front of Soviet goaltender Tretiak.

period at 2–2.

The second period got off to a disastrous start for Team Canada when Vladimir Shadrin scored after only 21 seconds. A hard rising shot by Yakushev caromed off the trampoline-like netting that replaced the conventional plexiglass above the end boards behind Ken Dryden. Unfortunately for Dryden, the puck ricocheted right in front of the net and Shadrin put it home. Defenseman Bill White burst into the offensive zone to deflect a Rod Gilbert shot that tied the game at the mid-way point of the period. Later in the period, Dryden was superb, making a remarkable save on a shot from Boris Mikhailov. This forced a faceoff in the Team Canada zone. Phil Esposito won the draw and the Canadians moved hurriedly up ice. Somehow a Soviet player managed to corral the puck and slip it to a wide-open Yakushev who easily beat Dryden. The situation became dire as Valeri Vasiliev upped the Soviet advantage to two goals with a powerplay marker late in the the second period.

Even the most ardent of Team Canada's supporters felt their hopes waning with the team trailing by two goals at the start of the final period. Early in the

period, big Pete Mahovlich spotted Phil Esposito all alone in the slot. Esposito knocked down the knee-high pass with his glove and with two whacks of his stick, had Team Canada back in the game. Soviet defenseman Victor Kuzkin earned himself a notation in coach Bobrov's notebook for being nowhere to be seen on the play. At 12:56 Yvan Cournoyer took a pass from Esposito and lifted it over a prone Tretiak to tie the game. The goal judge's light did not come on and Alan Eagleson tried to fight his way down to the timekeeper's bench. An international incident nearly ensued, as the Team Canada players left their bench to rescue Eagleson from a skirmish with the Soviet police. When the smoke cleared, the referee was at center ice signifying a goal and Eagleson was huddled in the safety of the Team Canada bench.

Team Canada continued to press and, with 34 seconds remaining, Paul Henderson converted a pass from Phil Esposito for his third game-winning goal. Team Canada had won the first of hockey's international super series by the narrowest of margins: four wins, three losses and one game tied.

May 19, 1974
Game Six            Stanley Cup Final
Philadelphia 1            Boston 0

Though most expansion franchises were doing well at the gate, in the early 1970s none of the new teams were considered to be among the better clubs in the NHL. But in 1973–74, the Philadelphia Flyers shocked the hockey world when they edged the perennial West Division champion Chicago Blackhawks for first place over the regular season. The Flyers compiled an excellent record, with 50 wins and 112 points, the second-best record in the NHL. The Boston Bruins, whose style of play the Flyers had tried to emulate, led the East Division with 113 points. While the Bruins were led by two of the game's top players, Phil Esposito and Bobby Orr, the Flyers had a few stars of their own.

The previous season, Bobby Clarke had won the Hart Trophy as the league's MVP when he became the first player from an expansion team to have a 100-point season. Teammate Rick MacLeish

had become the first expansion player to reach 50 goals in a season. Bernie Parent had returned from a brief sojourn in the WHA to establish himself as one of the NHL's premier goaltenders, fashioning a brilliant 1.89 goal-against average with 12 shutouts while appearing in goal for 70 games with the Flyers. Parent's superb season enabled him to share the Vezina Trophy with Tony Esposito as the league's top netminders during the 1973–74 season.

The Flyers continued their robust yet effective play in the postseason, eliminating the Atlanta Flames and the New York Rangers. The victory over the Rangers marked the first time that an expansion team had defeated one of the established teams in the playoffs. Boston trounced the Toronto Maple Leafs in four straight and had taken six games to sideline the stubborn Chicago Blackhawks.

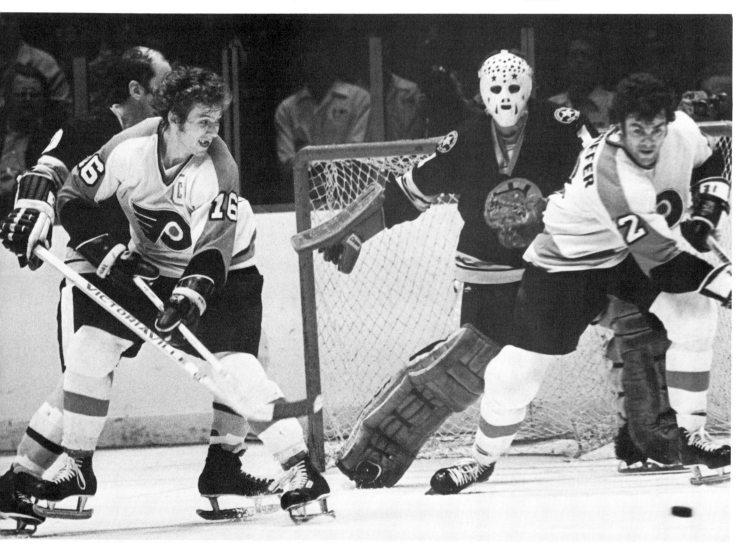

Bernie Parent, above, was unbeatable as the Flyers won their first Stanley Cup. Boston goaltender Gilles Gilbert, at left, stopped everything except a Rick MacLeish deflection in the first period.

attempt to exhaust Orr and prevent him from freewheeling on his patented end-to-end rushes. The move worked to perfection as the Bruins' on-ice general was frustrated by all the added attention. At the 14-minute mark of the opening period, he threw his glove at Bobby Clarke and the two players were banished after a skirmish in front of the Bruins' net. Rick MacLeish won a face-off from Greg Sheppard and drew the puck back to the point to Andre Dupont. As MacLeish broke for the net, he lost sight of the puck only to have it glance off his stick and go past a startled Gilles Gilbert.

The Bruins came to life in the second period, peppering 14 shots at Parent. The Flyers were without the services of hardnosed forward Gary Dornhoefer and defenseman Barry Ashbee, but their depth on the bench enabled them to continue to play a forechecking game. The Flyer defense, led by Ed Van Impe, aided Parent tremendously by keeping the front of the net clear. A team that had garnered widespread publicity for its brawling tactics played sound defensive hockey in nursing a one-goal lead. The Bruins relied almost exclusively on their big guns, Orr, Esposito and Hodge, while the Flyers played as a team. Bobby Orr logged 14 minutes and 28 seconds of ice time in the second period alone.

The close checking became contagious in the third period as neither team mounted much in the way of offense. Parent was tested, and made sparkling saves throughout the period. The turning point in the contest came at 17:38 when an exhausted Bobby Orr was forced to take a penalty for pulling down Bobby Clarke as he skated toward the Boston net. It would be the closest thing that Orr got to a rest, as he logged 35 minutes of ice time during the game. The upstart Philadephia Flyers defeated the Boston Bruins for the first Stanley Cup win by an expansion club.

Rick MacLeish paced all postseason scorers with 13 goals and 22 points. When Bernie Parent was awarded the Conn Smythe Tropy for his postseason heroics, the goalie stressed that the Flyers' disciplined defensive style required him to make only four or five big saves a game.

In the final, the Flyers gained a split in the first two games of the series at the Boston Garden when Bobby Clarke fired in the winner at 12:01 of overtime in game two. Backstopped by the magnificent goaltending of Bernie Parent, the Flyers won both games at the Spectrum to lead the series three games to one. The gritty Bruins ground out a 5–1 victory in the Boston Garden to stay alive and force a sixth game.

The genius of Flyer coach Fred Shero was at work in game six. Shero had the Flyers dump the puck into Bobby Orr's side of the defensive zone at every opportunity. The rationale was to put constant pressure on the Bruins' defenseman and lay on the body whenever possible in an

October 5, 1974
Game 7
Team Canada vs. Soviet Nationals
Team Canada 4    Soviet Union 4

Bobby Hull and Gordie Howe

The WHA was keen to establish its new hockey league as being the equal of the NHL. To this end, it undertook to play the Soviet Nationals in an eight-game series that invited comparison with the NHL-Soviet series of 1972. However, the challenge series was poorly marketed and very few fans watched the competition. The 1974 version of Team Canada was coached by Billy Harris, a student of the Russian style of play and the coach of the Swedish national team during the 1971–72 season. Harris's squad did not lack for experience as their roster read like an NHL all-star team from the mid-1960s. The team featured Gordie Howe, fresh from a two-year retirement and back in hockey with the WHA's Houston Aeros; Bobby Hull, whose defection to the WHA

two years earlier had prevented his playing for Team Canada '72; and the hero of the previous series, Paul Henderson, now skating for the Toronto Toros. There were three former NHL rookies of the year: Frank Mahovlich (1958), Ralph Backstom (1959), and Dave Keon (1961). The team's two best defensemen were 37-year-old J.C. Tremblay and 34-year-old Pat Stapleton.

Despite concern that Team WHA was too old to keep up with the superbly conditioned Soviets, the WHA contingent fared better than their illustrious predecessors during the Canadian portion of the tournament. The teams were all even with a win apiece and two ties. Had Frank Mahovlich not missed a glorious opportunity in the last minute of a 3–3 tie in the first game of the series, and had Team Canada not blown a 5–2 lead in game four, the team could have headed to Moscow in command of the series.

An ugly incident marred game five when Rick Ley punched Soviet star Valery Kharlamov after the final whistle in a 5–2 Soviet triumph. The Soviets earned a 3–2 decision in game six despite the superb goaltending of Gerry Cheevers. Two victories could only give Team Canada a tie in the series but even this would have been seen as a tremendous accomplishment as no one in North American hockey underestimated the skills of the Soviets any longer.

The Soviets came out flying to start game seven. Vyacheslav Anisin opened up the scoring at 3:34 with Shadrin adding a second goal for a 2–0 Soviet lead. Andre Lacroix set up Tom Webster to cut the margin in half late in the first.

Team Canada played an inspired second period, outshooting the Soviets 15 to 8. Coach Billy Harris had been impressed with the play of Ralph Backstrom throughout the series, commenting that a team with his spirit and drive could not be beaten. Backstrom, displaying the style that had made him an integral part of great Montreal Canadiens teams, notched the equalizer on a pass from Gordie Howe. Team Canada jumped into the lead for the first time on a powerplay goal by Mark Howe, but Gusev came back to tie the score on a Soviet powerplay. The marvelous line of Kharlamov, Petrov and Mikhailov was clearly the

Soviets' best during the series, and within a minute of the Gusev marker, Boris Mikhailov had the Soviets back in front.

Team Canada carried the play once again in the final period. Backstrom put the game on even terms with a goal at 6:38. Knowing that a tie in the contest was enough to guarantee a series win, the Soviets went into a defensive shell. Cheevers headed for the bench with a minute to go in an all-out effort for victory. Just before Cheevers was lifted for a sixth attacker, he had protested that the Soviet timekeeper allowed four seconds to tick off on the clock after a stoppage in play. After bitter protests by the Canadians, two seconds were added back to the time remaining. These two seconds would prove to be crucial, costing Team Canada a victory. As time expired, Paul Henderson set up Bobby Hull who blistered a shot past Tretiak for what appeared to be the winning goal. The red light went on to signify a goal, but referee Tom Brown of Canada, acting on the advice of a Soviet linesman, said that time had expired and the goal was disallowed.

With the series no longer in doubt, Team Canada dropped a listless 3–2 verdict in the eighth game. Gordie Howe and Bobby Hull led the scorers for Team Canada while Alexander Yakushev paced the Soviet squad, despite being hobbled by a knee injury.

December 31, 1975
Montreal Canadiens 3
Soviet Central Red Army 3

Many hockey fans have called this the greatest game they have ever seen. Two Soviet club teams, the Soviet Wings and Central Red Army, were in North America to play a series of eight exhibition games against NHL club teams. The Soviet clubs were faring very well against their NHL opponents, but it was felt that if any team could skate with the speedy Russians, it would be the Habs. This match would feature a renewal of acquaintances for many players who had opposed each other in the Team Canada '72 series. Pete Mahovlich, Serge Savard, Yvan Cournoyer and Ken Dryden all faced the Russians in 1972 while Petrov, Kharlamov, Mikhailov, Vasilyev and Tretiak had all been with the Soviet Nationals that year. As the game was played in the middle of the NHL season, it eliminated any concern that the NHLers would not be in top shape.

The Canadiens roared into an early lead when Steve Shutt beat Tretiak with a screened drive from the top of the right-wing face-off circle at 3:16. Yvon Lambert bulled his way into the slot to cash in Doug Riseborough's shot and shovel it home at 7:25 and the Habs had a two-goal bulge. The Canadiens forechecked beautifully in the game's opening ten minutes, confusing Red Army and forcing them into uncharacteristic giveaways. They held an 11–4 edge in shots and prevented the Soviets from getting a shot on goal on two powerplays. Statistics are for losers, and although the Soviets fired only three shots at Ken Dryden during the second period, they scored twice. It was the Russian style not to waste any opportunity with low-priority shots, and when they did work a man into position the results were generally lethal. Boris Mikhailov put his team on the board with a 20-foot drive that handcuffed Dryden at 3:54. Dryden managed to get the heel of his glove on the shot, but its momentum carried the puck over the line. Cournoyer restored the Habs' two-goal advantage on the powerplay, but Valery Kharlamov managed to sneak in behind the Montreal defense and beat Dryden late in the period to cut the lead in half. Montreal coach Scotty Bowman felt that inactivity may have hurt Dryden on the two goals.

Montreal held a wide territorial edge in the final stanza, but Red Army scored the only goal. Habs defenseman Don Awrey fell at center ice, allowing Boris Aleksandrov and Victor Shluktov to wheel out on a two-man break with only Larry Robinson back. Robinson slid to block Shluktov's pass, but he feathered it by him to Aleksandrov who steered the puck at the net. Dryden, no stranger to the Soviet style of short passes and quick shots, lunged across the net. He managed to get a good portion of the shot, but it trickled into the net for the equalizer at 4:04. Nothing was settled in the

It's in! Montreal's first tally is just visible between Red Army defenseman Tsygankov's legs.

remainder of the period and the teams skated to a classic 3–3 verdict.

Central Red Army coach Konstantin Loktev praised the disciplined positional play of the Canadiens. Scotty Bowman could find no fault in his team's performance. The Soviets had not played a strong game in their own end, as the 38–13 shots on goal total indicated, but Vladislav Tretiak confirmed his position as hockey's greatest goalie. Serge Savard stated that it was a pleasure to

be playing a team of Red Army's caliber that relied on ability instead of intimidation tactics. There were only eight minor penalties called throughout the contest. The Soviets completed a successful tour with five wins, the tie against Montreal and two losses in eight games. The Soviet Wings were outgunned by the Buffalo Sabres 12–6, and the Stanley Cup champion Flyers beat Red Army 4–1 in the last game of the tour.

---

**April 29, 1978**
**Game Seven          Quarter-Final**
**Toronto 2  New York Islanders 1**

---

The Islanders had improved at a dramatic rate after their first two seasons in the NHL. In 1977–78, they led the Patrick Division with 111 points, paced by the emergence of Bryan Trottier as an NHL superstar. Trottier was runner-up in the scoring race to Guy Lafleur, firing 46 goals and 123 points. Mike Bossy established a record for rookie goal scorers with 53 tallies and Denis Potvin became the first defenseman since Bobby Orr to score 30 goals. The Leafs finished third in the Adams Division with 92 points and had not threatened in postseason play since their glory days of the 1960s. Over the course of the season, Darryl Sittler established

a team record for points with a fine 117-point season and linemate Lanny McDonald scored 47 goals, providing the Leafs with some much-needed firepower.

The Islanders won the first two games of the series at home only to have the Leafs bounce back with two victories of their own at Maple Leaf Gardens. Cocky little Mike Palmateer played strongly in the Leaf net as the home-ice advantage continued through game six. The series returned to the Nassau County Coliseum for the seventh and deciding game. It was a tough series, and by game seven, both teams were without one of their star players. The Leafs' brilliant defenseman, Borje Salming, was felled by an eye injury in game three while the Isles' rookie sensation, Mike Bossy, had been injured after a hard bodycheck from Jerry Butler. Bryan Trottier was sporting a broken jaw, but it was not enough to keep him out of the line-up.

From the outset of the game, Leaf forwards Tiger Williams and Dan Maloney threw themselves at everything in an Islanders jersey. Palmateer continued to provide the Leafs with acrobatic goaltending until Denis Potvin opened the

Lanny McDonald

scoring on a 35-foot screened blast. The Islanders controlled a wide territorial edge in the first period, but Palmateer kept Toronto in the contest.

Ian Turnbull, playing particularly well in the absense of Salming, took a perfect feed from Jimmy Jones and tied the score in the second period. The game then settled into an old-fashioned goaltenders' duel between Mike Palmateer and Glenn Resch. At one point, Palmateer strayed from the Leaf net while trying to clear the puck and was caught totally out of position when a funny bounce sent the puck directly in front. A wide-open net greeted the onrushing Islander shooter, but Palmateer vaulted from behind the net to somehow deflect a certain goal. Nothing was decided in regulation time even though Islander general manager Bill Torrey counted 15 good scoring chances for his club, compared with only five for the Leafs.

Islanders forward Billy Harris had not recorded a single point in the series. Early in overtime he had a chance to make amends, walking in cold on Palmateer only to be robbed by the goaltender. Lanny McDonald had been the Leafs' hardluck story, hitting a number of goalposts while playing much of the series with the discomfort of a broken nose. In the fourth minute of overtime Ian Turnbull burst out of his own end and up the left side. McDonald swung over from the right wing and veered toward the middle, hoping to split the defense. In a move that the Leafs had worked on in practise, Turnbull sent a waist-high pass in McDonald's direction. He gloved the puck and it bounced off his pads, landing directly in front of him. As Resch rushed out to meet him, McDonald shot, finding the corner on the glove side just beyond the goaltender's reach. In retrospect, the series was recognized as hardhitting playoff hockey at its finest.

The Leafs went on to meet the Montreal Canadiens, rekindling memories of some of the great playoff encounters between the two clubs. The 1978 series pitted the reigning master tactician of the NHL, Scotty Bowman, against the Leafs' creative rookie coach, Roger Nielson. The Canadiens, en route to the Stanley Cup, turned out to be just too powerful, skating off with a four-game sweep.

**M**ontreal, winner of the previous three Stanley Cups, finished another fine season at the top of the Norris Division with 115 points. Boston led the Adams Division with 100 points and was eager to avenge back-to-back defeats in the finals at the hands of the Habs. The 1979 semi-final series had been dominated by the home team, as both clubs recorded three victories with the home-ice advantage. Game seven was set for Montreal by virtue of the Canadiens finishing with more points than the Bruins in the regular season.

Doug Risebrough of Montreal was playing with a cage protecting his face because of a broken nose sustained in a scrap with Boston's Terry O'Reilly in the fifth game. Rejean Houle returned to the Montreal line-up after a lengthy layoff due to a groin pull. Despite dominating the game territorially, the Habs found themselves trailing 3-1 after two periods.

Wayne Cashman had a pair of goals for the Bruins, with a single going to Rick Middleton. Jacques Lemaire had replied for Montreal.

The potent Montreal offense came to life in the third period when Mark Napier, set up neatly by Guy Lafleur, cut the deficit in half. Guy Lapointe restored the Habs to even terms with a goal on the powerplay, but was later carried from the ice on a stretcher after suffering stretched knee ligaments. Momentum had definitely shifted in favor of the home team when Rick Middleton silenced the crowd by stealing the puck behind the Montreal goal and stuffing it into the net at 16:01. Time was running out when referee Bob Meyers called the Bruins for too many men on the ice. It would prove as costly a penalty as any taken that season. With this gift of a powerplay opportunity, the Canadiens had one last shot at prolonging their season. A glimmer of

Yvon Lambert eliminated the Bruins with his seventh-game overtime goal.

hope was all that Guy Lafleur needed. Taking a pass from Lemaire in full stride, he unloaded one of his bullet-like drives from just inside the blueline. This shot caught a puck-sized opening on the far side of Bruin goaltender Gilles Gilbert, tying the game and bringing forth a sustained ovation from the Montreal crowd.

The Canadiens swarmed all over the Bruins in the overtime period, but the feisty Gilbert turned away every volley that came his way. Finally at 9:33, Mario Tremblay fed a pass out from the corner to Yvon Lambert who, driving to the front of the net, converted it into a goal. After the game, Guy Lafleur was quick to lavish praise on Gilles Gilbert for his

gritty performance in the Bruins' goal. Montreal had tested him 52 times during the contest, with 8 shots in the overtime alone.

The 1979 Stanley Cup final paled in comparison to this series. The long-anticipated showdown between Montreal and the New York Islanders, who sported the NHL's best record, failed to develop when the Isles were ambushed by their crosstown rivals, the New York Rangers. The Rangers featured Swedish stars Anders Hedberg and Ulf Nilsson and had former Philadelphia coach Fred Shero behind the bench, but the Canadiens went on to win the final and their fourth straight Cup in just five games.

Don Cherry's Bruins were caught with too many men on the ice late in the third period.

---

May 24, 1980
Game Six          Stanley Cup Final
New York Islanders 5
Philadelphia 4

---

Beginning in 1980, the NHL playoff format was changed to accommodate the four former WHA franchises that had merged with the NHL. Under the new rules, the top 16 teams based on points in the regular-season standing would make the playoffs, regardless of division. Matchups would have the team with the best regular-season record playing the team with the 16th best. The second-best would play the 15th, the third the 14th and so on. The Philadelphia Flyers boasted the NHL's best record with 116 points. The Islanders had finished fifth overall and second in the Patrick Division with 91

points, down from the previous year's franchise high of 116 points. But in the postseason, the Islanders had shown an uncommon knack for winning in overtime, recording five wins against just one loss in the early rounds of the playoffs.

In the final, Denis Potvin had won game one for the Isles with an overtime victory in the Spectrum. The Flyers rebounded to gain a split by defeating New York 8–3 in the second game. Back in the friendly confines of the Nassau Coliseum, the Isles parlayed the fine goaltending of Billy Smith into back-to-back wins of 6–2 and 5–2, giving them a 3–1 lead in games. The Flyers extended the

side, but nevertheless the marker stood. It took a late goal by Brian Propp to even the encounter after one stanza.

Mike Bossy and Bob Nystrom, a pair of tireless performers for the Isles throughout the series, counted the only goals of the second period and the crowd could sense victory within its grasp. But the Flyers had not won the Stanley Cup twice by wilting under pressure. They came up with an inspired third period, tying the score at 4–4 and forcing overtime.

The Islanders had become masters of overtime in 1980, as five different players—Morrow, Gillies, Bourne, Potvin and Nystrom—had scored goals in sudden death. With seven minutes gone in the extra session, Nystrom and John Tonelli wheeled up the ice on a two-on-two break. Tonelli carried the puck over the Philadelphia blue line and made a nifty move to step around Flyer defenseman Bob Dailey. Nystrom went to the front of the net for a pass which worked to perfection. Nystrom and the puck arrived in front of goaltender Pete Peeters at precisely the same time. All that remained was for him to deflect the shot over the goalie. Nystrom was one of the few remaining "original" Islanders and, over the years, had established himself as a steady performer who saved some of his biggest goals for the playoffs. This biggest of all goals was his fourth overtime winner, placing him second on the all-time list behind the legendary Rocket Richard, who accomplished the feat six times.

"Original" Islander Bob Nystrom brought the Cup to Long Island with an overtime goal in game six against the Flyers.

series with a 6–3 victory that set the stage for game six before a packed house of 14,995 fans in Long Island. A New York team had not won the Stanley Cup since the Rangers had done the job in 1940.

The Flyers put a damper on the festivities when Reggie Leach scored while his team enjoyed a two-man advantage at 7:21 of the first period. Denis Potvin brought the Islanders back to even terms with a powerplay tally and Duane Sutter scored to put the home team ahead. Sutter's goal was a tarnished effort as replays showed that he was clearly off-

April 10, 1982
Game Three     Smythe Division
                         Semi-Final

Los Angeles 6      Edmonton 5

Despite allowing five goals Kings' goal-tender Mario Lessard made important saves as his club upset the Edmonton Oilers.

T he Oilers had been the surprise team of 1981–82, finishing first in the Smythe Division and compiling the second-best record in the NHL with 111 points. Their cast of young stars had another season under their belts and, paced by the brilliant 92-goal 212-point performance of Wayne Gretzky, seemed a safe bet to eliminate the Kings who had finished fourth in the Smythe with 63 points. The series was tied at one game apiece when the two teams took to the ice before a sellout crowd in the Kings' home rink, the Forum in Inglewood, California.

The Forum crowd had little to cheer about in the game's early stages, as the Oilers took an early lead. A long slapshot by Mark Messier eluded Mario Lessard midway through the opening period and Wayne Gretzky added a short-handed tally late in the first.

Gretzky put on a hockey clinic in the second period, as he set up defenseman Lee Fogolin for the Oilers' second straight short-handed marker early in the frame. He then fed Risto Siltanen, who launched a 30-foot blast to put the Oilers up by four goals before the game reached the halfway point. Gretzky added a goal of his own on a tap-in from the lip of the crease with time winding down in the second period. The general chatter in the Kings' dressing room was to try and play tough, outscore the Oilers in the third period and establish some momentum for game four.

Kings' owner Jerry Buss left the Forum secure in the knowledge his team would not be shut out when Jay Wells scored to make it 5–1 for Edmonton. Doug Smith's marker did not give rise to optimism by the Forum crowd, but at least the Kings were not rolling over for the Oilers. Charlie Simmer's goal, jamming the puck in from behind the Oiler net, made the score 5–3. Still, with only five minutes left in the game, the task ahead of the Kings appeared monumental.

But Edmonton's Garry Unger drew a five-minute major penalty for highsticking. With a long powerplay, the Kings came back. A 40-foot blast from defenseman Mark Hardy drew Los Angeles to within a goal at 15:59. After Oiler penalty-killer Pat Hughes missed a breakaway with 90 seconds left in the game, Steve Bozek of the Kings fell heir to a Fuhr rebound and tucked a backhand upstairs. The tying goal was scored with just five seconds remaining in regulation time.

While this miraculous comeback was taking shape, Los Angeles rookie Daryl Evans sat in the Kings' dressing room listening to the game on the radio. Evans had been banished from the game with ten minutes remaining for fighting. League rules stipulate that a player kicked out of a game can return for the overtime, and Evans listened to the comeback and prepared to play.

The Oilers had a glorious opportunity to end it early in the extra session, but

Mark Messier lifted a backhand over the net with Lessard down. The overtime period was nearly three minutes old when Doug Smith won a faceoff and pulled the draw cleanly back to Evans.

"I saw the puck laying there and broke for it," he said, "I had a vague idea where the net was and just shot and prayed. It was an unreal feeling when the puck went in."

The series followed its script when the Oilers won the fourth game to force a fifth and deciding match back at the Northlands Coliseum. But 1982 was the year of the upset, and the Kings eliminated the Oilers in Edmonton. The Kings went down to defeat in the division final as the astonishing Vancouver Canucks, with sizzling hot goaltending from Richard Brodeur, baffled the experts by making it all the way to the Stanley Cup final.

March 24, 1984
NCAA Final
Lake Placid, New York
Bowling Green 5
Minnesota-Duluth 4

The Bowling Green Falcons capped a fine 34-8-2 season by advancing to the final four in the National Collegiate Athletic Association hockey championships for the second time in the school's history. The Falcons had never won a national title, but had inched closer to their goal with a 2-1 overtime victory in the semi-finals against Michigan State. Their opponents, the Minnesota-Duluth Bulldogs, had experienced an equally difficult task in the semis, turning back the North Dakota Fighting Sioux by an identical 2-1 overtime score. Some observers felt that because the Bulldogs had clinched their berth in the final on Thursday and had been afforded a day of rest, they might be the fresher of the two clubs.

The 7,918 spectators in the Olympic Arena were treated to a remarkable display of goaltending by the Bulldogs' rookie netminder Rick Kosti. Despite being inundated with shots through the first two periods, Kosti held his ground and, with the third period half over, the Bulldogs led 3-2. Minnesota-Duluth fans were relieved when Tom Herzig fired a wrist shot just under the crossbar and beyond the reach of Falcon freshman netminder Gary Kruzich, making the score 4-2. A two-goal advantage appeared safe, but the Falcons continued their tight checking and stormed the Bulldog zone. Kosti could not control the rebound from a slapshot from Mike Pikul, allowing Peter Wilson to cut the lead in half at 12:42. Then, with time running

A goal after 67 minutes of overtime determined the winner of the 1984 NCAA Division I hockey championship.

Goaltender Gary Kruzich (30), NCAA tournament MVP, races the length of the ice to congratulate overtime goalscorer Gino Cavellini.

out, the Falcons fell heir to a lucky break. A clearing shot by a Bulldog defenseman bounced off the backboards and appeared about to carom in front of the net. Kosti stepped out to block the puck only to have it slither through his legs and onto the stick of John Samanski, who tipped home the equalizer. The two teams prepared for overtime.

Both coaches, Jerry York of the Falcons and Mike Sertick of the Bulldogs, used three forward lines throughout the game. Their fourth lines were relegated only to spot duty. The larger ice surface of the Olympic-sized rink in Lake Placid had both squads playing bone-tired. The Falcons held the advantage in play through the first two overtime periods, but could not beat Kosti.

The ice was resurfaced after the second overtime, and this seemed to inspire Minnesota-Duluth. Bowling Green goaltender Gary Kruzich was forced to come up with five game-saving stops. The fans were on their feet in a standing ovation as the two teams prepared for a fourth overtime period. Only the brilliance of Gary Kruzich kept the Falcons in the contest, as he came up with a pair of great saves on two-on-one breaks by Minnesota-Duluth. Both teams had solid scoring chances on powerplays, but neither could net the winner. Finally, the Falcon defense repelled a dangerous Bulldog rush. The Bowling Green forwards sped

up ice on a three-on-two break with center Dan Kane lugging the puck. Gino Cavallini, then a big sophomore left winger, was able to sneak in behind the Minnesota-Duluth defense and take a perfect feed from Kane. Cavallini swept in alone and put a short backhand shot past Kosti for the game winner at 7:11 of the fourth overtime period. This was the type of contest that no one deserved to lose. Rick Kosti had been spectacular, facing 55 shots, equaling an NCAA record. Gary Kruzich, who turned away 32 shots, was named the tournament's most valuable player.

Tom Kurvers, a Minnesota-Duluth senior defenseman who amassed 149 goals in his college career, was named the Hobey Baker Award winner as college hockey's best player. Kurvers currently plays for the Buffalo Sabres and was a member of the 1986 Stanley Cup champion Montreal Canadiens. Bowling Green rearguards Dave Ellet and Garry Galley play for the Winnipeg Jets and Washington Capitals respectively, while their former college teammate, Cavallini, skates for the St. Louis Blues. Bulldog goaltender Rick Kosti is between the pipes for the Canadian Olympic team. Bill Watson provided Minnesota-Duluth with its second consecutive Hobey Baker Award winner in 1985 and currently plays with the Chicago Blackhawks.

Nine minutes of overtime were needed to decide 1984's "Battle of New York". Bryan Trottier seems to be leading a joyous chorus of Islanders fans.

The last major realignment of the NHL's divisional structure took effect with the 1981–82 regular season. The new set-up took advantage of natural rivalries between neighboring cities. In Alberta, the cities of Calgary and Edmonton were long-time competitors in sports, culture and business. The realignment of 1981–82 put both cities' hockey teams in the Smythe Division. In Quebec, Montreal, the cosmopolitan center, and Quebec City, the seat of government, had a rivalry best measured in centuries rather than years. Now, both the Canadiens and the Nordiques were part of the NHL's Adams Division and played each other eight times a year.

These rivalries were at least equaled by that between the New York Rangers from Manhattan and the New York Islanders from Long Island. The Rangers were the original game in town, but the Islanders had built a pleasing team that, by 1983–84, was aiming for a

record-tying fifth consecutive Stanley Cup win. The two teams were matched up in the five-game Patrick Division semi-final series of 1984. After four games both teams had won twice, with the deciding fifth game set for the Nassau Veterans' Memorial Coliseum on Long Island.

Mike Bossy and Ron Greschner exchanged goals in the first period. The second was scoreless, though the Rangers held a substantial edge in play, repeatedly forcing Islanders' goaltender Billy Smith to make acrobatic saves. In stopping the Rangers, Smith demonstrated the skills that had earned him a reputation as a goaltender who plays his best hockey in the most important games.

Despite constant pressure by the Rangers, it was the Islanders who got the tie-breaking goal as defenseman Tomas Jonsson connected on a 35-foot wrist shot at 7:56 of the third period. A 2–1 Islander victory appeared likely until

Don Maloney of the Rangers scored his only goal of the playoffs with less than one minute to play and the Rangers' net empty to ice a sixth attacker. The "Battle of New York" would be decided in overtime.

The Rangers continued to put pressure on Billy Smith in the extra session. After several fine saves, he made what was perhaps his best and certainly the biggest save of the evening off the stick of the Rangers' Bob Brooke, who was in close. Immediately following this stop, the Islanders worked the puck into the Rangers' end of the ice and defenseman Ken Morrow won the game for the Islanders with a slapshot from just inside the right point at 8:56 of overtime. Morrow had led a charmed life in hockey, playing for the US Olympic gold medal team in 1980 and then joining the Islanders in time to win four consecutive Stanley Cups.

In what was perhaps his finest performance, Billy Smith stopped 42 shots and held the Islanders in the game until Morrow scored the winner.

---

September 13, 1984
Canada Cup                    Semi-Final
Team Canada 3    Soviet Union 2

---

Western Canada won the right to stage the third Canada Cup tournament in September, 1984. Hockey fans were skeptical of this series, as the recent domination exhibited by the Soviets in games against NHL opponents demonstrated the shortcomings of all-stars being assembled to play against a true national team that worked and trained together. In 1979, the NHL All-Stars played the Soviet Nationals in a three-game series in New York City. The NHLers had won game one, but the Soviets took charge in the middle of game two, won that match and then embarrassed the NHL Stars 6–0 in the deciding game. Team Canada 1981 had fared little better, being humiliated 8–1 by the Soviets and failing to qualify for the finals of the tournament.

Team Canada had an indifferent start in the round-robin portion of the tournament, as the club tied Team USA 4–4, lost to the Swedes 4–2 and was whipped by the Soviet Union 6–3. The ensuing negative response from the press and the public did more to unify Team Canada than any amount of practice. The disgruntled players decided to play the remaining contests for themselves and not fulfill any notion of national pride. As luck would have it, the normally strong Czech team fared very poorly in the tournament and Canada was able to qualify for the playoff round.

A relatively small but vocal crowd of 13,307 turned up at Calgary's Olympic Saddledome to view the second meeting between the Soviets and Team Canada. This was a semi-final match, with the winner advancing to the deciding game of the tournament. The first period was scoreless, although the Soviets had the better of the play. Team Canada scored first on the powerplay when Paul Coffey made one of his few forays into the offensive zone, where he shovelled a one-handed pass to John Tonelli. The big Islander winger fired a rising shot that soared past Vladimir Myshkin in the Soviet goal and put Team Canada ahead 1–0 at 7:18 of the second period. This lead stood up throughout the middle stanza.

Early in the third period, Larry Robinson was sent off for hooking. Sergei Sveltov broke in off the left wing and uncorked a backhand that hit Pete Peeters in the shoulder and snuck into the net just under the cross bar. The Soviets came right back with a brilliant individual effort from Sergei Makarov. Makarov, one of the most exciting players in the Soviet lineup, made a brilliant move that turned Larry Robinson inside out at the Team Canada blueline. He faked to the outside and then cut back sharply into the middle. In alone on Peeters, he deked left then moved to the right, slipping the puck into the net.

These two quick Soviet tallies threw Team Canada into a seven-minute tailspin that saw them play poorly without giving up any additional goals. As the third period wore on, Team Canada started to exert some pressure in the Soviet end. Following two minutes of sustained hard work in the corners of the Soviet end of the rink, Wayne Gretzky passed the puck out in front of Myshkin.

Team Canada trailed the Soviet Nationals 2–1 in the final period, but rallied to win in overtime. Brent Sutter challenges goaltender Vladimir Myshkin.

Doug Wilson unloaded a blast that made its way through a maze of players into the net. No other goals were scored in the remaining six minutes of regulation time.

A fired-up Team Canada held a territorial edge in the extra session, but needed a brilliant defensive play by Paul Coffey who stopped the Soviets on a two-on-one break. Coffey immediately sent the puck up ice, trapping the two Soviets out of position. Mike Bossy cruised in front of the Soviet net, inadvertently knocking the goal stick out of Myshkin's hand just prior to being levelled from behind by a Soviet defender. John Tonelli, always at his best in the heavy

going along the boards, freed the puck and got it back to Coffey at the point. Bossy, still somewhat dazed by the force of the hit he had taken, saw Coffey leaning into a shot and jumped to his feet, breaking for the front of the net. He never saw the puck carom off his stick and into the net.

In the game's aftermath, Wayne Gretzky called the triumph more satisfying than the Oilers' recent Stanley Cup victory. Tonelli put the win on a par with his four Stanley Cup championships with the Islanders. In the best-of-three final, Team Canada defeated Sweden in two straight games for their second Canada Cup triumph in three tournaments.

The Montreal Canadiens had finished fourth in the Adams Division with only 82 points, but defeated division leader Boston in five hard-fought games in the division semifinal. The Nordiques had finished third in the division, but turned aside second-place Buffalo in five games. The final series between the two bitter provincial rivals was everything hockey fans hoped for. The Canadiens had easily handled the Nordiques during the regular season, holding a 6-1-1 record in matches between the two clubs. The playoffs were quite a different story, as Quebec won twice in the Montreal Forum and the series stood dead even at three games each. The games were hardhitting and the action was beginning to take its toll as both clubs were hobbled by injuries. The Nordiques' Dale Hunter played the seventh game with a painful hand injury while Michel Goulet's status was questionable due to a bad back. Montreal defenseman Rick Green had a painful shoulder injury and young Chris Chelios was still dragging a twisted knee that had plagued him since game one of the Boston series.

The first period saw little in the way of offense. The Habs' penalty killers had just turned aside the powerful Quebec powerplay when Bruce Bell's 40-foot drive beat Montreal goalie Steve Penney. The marker stood up throughout the first period and the Nords took a 1-0 lead to the dressing room.

Steve Penney would probably rather forget Quebec's second goal. Diminutive J.F. Sauve, normally a powerplay specialist, took what appeared to be a routine shot from 50 feet out. The puck somehow managed to squeeze through Penney's pads and trickle into the net.

A tough man to stop: Peter Stastny, pursued by Montreal's Mario Tremblay, scored the series-winning goal in overtime in game seven.

Nordiques supporters were alarmed when goaltender Mario Gosselin dropped to the ice after being hit in the throat by a blast from the stick of Mario Tremblay. Gosselin, who had performed brilliantly throughout the series, lay motionless for several minutes. Struggling to regain his breath and fighting off dizziness, he remained in the game spurred on by the knowledge that many of his teammates were playing hurt. The Habs regrouped after the stoppage and stormed back to even the contest on goals by Pierre Mondou and Mats Naslund. The encounter was deadlocked at 2–2 after the second period.

Both teams struggled in the third period as the cumulative aches and pains of a very rugged series claimed their victims. Dale Hunter could not continue after a brief appearance in the first period while Rick Green looked on from the bench from the midway point of the third period. Nothing was settled in the third, although Montreal defenseman Craig Ludwig tested Gosselin from the slot late in the session.

Guy Lapointe, a long-time defensive stalwart for Montreal, was an assistant coach with the Nordiques. Lapointe noticed that Penney was playing too far back in the net and was prone to giving up rebounds. His failure to challenge the shooter made him vulnerable, and Lapointe's advice to the Quebec shooters was to put the puck on net whenever possible. Early in the overtime Peter Stastny won a draw against Montreal's best face-off man, Guy Carbonneau, deep in the Montreal zone, and fed the puck back to defenseman Pat Price. Stastny broke for the front of the net just as Penney kicked out Price's shot. Pouncing on the rebound, he fired a quick shot that Penney turned aside, but, when the puck rolled free a second time, he buried it behind Penney for the winning marker at 2:17 of overtime.

A decimated Quebec squad went on to face the Philadelphia Flyers in the Wales Conference final. The Nordiques would go no further in the playoffs that year, as the young Flyers went on to be surprise participants in the Stanley Cup final.

---

April 30, 1986
Game Seven     Smythe Division Final
Calgary 3     Edmonton 2

---

The Edmonton Oilers led the Smythe Division with 119 points and the best record in the the NHL in 1985–86, while Calgary finished a distant second with 89 points. After eliminating Vancouver and Winnipeg in two division semi-final series, the Flames and the Oilers hooked up in a spirited renewal of their Alberta rivalry. Edmonton, the highest-scoring team in NHL history, was highly favored to win. Given the record-breaking single-season performances of Paul Coffey and Wayne Gretzky, the Oilers seemed destined to skate to their third straight Stanley Cup final. Neither team gave an inch in the first six contests of the series, which were ruggedly played. The Flames demonstrated an extremely close-checking style of play and were understandably reluctant to get into a freewheeling skating series with the Oilers. A sellout crowd at the Northlands Coliseum hoped that home-ice advantage would turn the series in Edmonton's favor.

Calgary scored the only goal of the first period when Hakan Loob beat acrobatic Oiler goalie Grant Fuhr while the Flames were playing a man short. Calgary had benefited from magnificent goaltending by Mike Vernon, who had been called up from Moncton of the AHL during the regular season's stretch drive.

The Flames upped the lead to 2–0 when Jim Peplinski's long shot took a crazy bounce and fooled Fuhr. Momentum shifted as the Flames reverted to a defensive shell and neglected their strong forechecking in the Edmonton zone. Once able to wheel out of their own end, the Oilers had room to invade the Calgary zone and create the chances required to get back into the contest. Glenn Anderson halved the Flames advantage with a goal at 10:47 of the second period. It appeared that Calgary would escape the second period still clinging to a one-goal lead, but Edmonton's Mark Messier broke clear to pot the equalizer with 51 seconds to play in the period.

A tie heading into the third period certainly seemed to favor the Oilers. But

one of those unpredictable breaks that add to the fascination of sports went in Calgary's favor. Flame forward Perry Berezan fired the puck into the Oiler zone and headed off for a line change. Steve Smith, a rookie on the Edmonton defense who picked the puck up behind the Edmonton goal, attempted to pass up-ice only to have the puck glance off Fuhr's left goal pad and ricochet into the net. A startled Berezan, with his back to the play, had to be told about the goal he was credited with scoring. Still, with 15 minutes remaining in the game, the contest was far from over and the Oilers moved to the attack. Mike Vernon was repeatedly tested in the Calgary goal but continued to thwart the Oilers. In the final minutes of regulation time, with Grant Fuhr already lifted for an extra attacker, the Flames were penalized for having too many men on the ice. The Calgary end of the ice looked like it was under siege, but try as they might, the Oilers could not get the equalizer.

The tight checking principles of de-fense that former Wisconsin Badger coach Bob Johnson had drilled into his players paid off. The size, strength and strategy of the Flames succeeded in keeping the game's most potent offense off-balance. As the game neared its final stages, the Flames kept four players back and forced the Oilers to dump the puck in, disrupting the crisp passing and flow of their offense. No additional goals were scored and the defending champion Oilers were eliminated on a goal they had scored into their own net.

The Flames were involved in an equally thrilling seven-game series series with the surprising St. Louis Blues in the match-up to decide the Campbell Conference's representative in the Stanley Cup. Calgary prevailed by the narrowest of margins, winning the seventh and deciding game 2–1. The Cup final turned out to be a showdown that no one could have predicted, with the Montreal Canadiens defeating the Flames in five games to capture their 23rd Stanley Cup championship.

The Calgary Flames played Edmonton perfectly in engineering a seven-game upset of the defending champion Oilers in the 1986 Smythe Division final. John Tonelli (27) battles with Kevin Lowe in front of the Edmonton net.

April 18, 1987
Game Seven

Patrick Division
Semi-Final

NY Islanders 3

Washington 2

Rod Langway congratulates goaltender Kelly Hrudey who faced a 75-shot barrage.

How many of you diehard hockey fans use the Stanley Cup playoffs as a mooring point when grinding the old memory back to your childhood days? Over the years, postseason play has produced some epic sudden death overtime confrontations. I can vividly recall, as a nine-year-old, being furious with my father when he ordered me to go to bed at the end of the first overtime period in a classic semi-final contest between the Toronto Maple Leafs and the Detroit Red Wings in 1960. Granted, it was a school night, but the Leafs were *my team*, and here they were with a legitimate shot at the Cup for the first time in my short lifetime.

Just as I was about to fall off into a sulking slumber my dad stuck his head in my door to tell me that the Leafs had won and that my favorite player Frank Mahovlich had scored the game winner in the third overtime period.

I don't imagine that too many youngsters were around for the finale of the seventh game of the New York Islanders–Washington Capitals Division semi-final. After four games, the Capitals owned a stranglehold 3–1 lead in the series. To make matters worse for the Islanders, injuries had severely depleted their roster. Rugged centerman Brent Sutter saw no action in the series, while Mike Bossy was out from the second game on. Denis Potvin was lost to the club after game four. But the Islanders rallied in game five, and took a 4–2 victory out of the Capital Centre in Landover, Maryland, then again dodged elimination with a 5–4 victory at home in game six.

The Capitals, too, had suffered injuries — Craig Laughlin had been lost to the team since the first game, and Alan Howarth played the first six games with a damaged leg, and was scratched for the seventh game. Playing with the support of their home crowd, the Caps opened briskly, and Islander goalie Kelly Hrudey had to be brilliant to stop 15 first-period shots. Only Mike Gartner, the Caps best triggerman during the regular season, was able to beat Hrudey during the period, by diving for a loose puck and batting it into the net as he lay sprawled on the ice.

During the first two periods, Bob Mason of the Capitals faced only 10 shots, and the inactivity was evident when New York's Pat Flatley put a rather weak shot through Mason's legs to tie the score part way through the second frame. But the Caps' wide advantage in play continued, and with just over a minute remaining in the second, Grant Martin, playing in place of the injured Howarth, scored his first goal as Cap, skating out of the corner and beating Hrudey. By the end of the second period, the Capitals had outshot their opponents 25–10, but led only 2–1.

During the third period, the momentum began to shift, and the Islanders played their best hockey of the contest. Hrudey continued to frustrate the Caps, and late in the third period Bryan Trottier converted a pretty set-up from Steve Konroyd and Alan Kerr, backhanding a trickler through Mason's pads to deadlock the score. The Washington goalie would have loved a second chance at the

shot.

Regulation time decided nothing, and, during the first overtime period, with the referee intent on letting the teams, not penalties, decide the outcome of the game, play was punctuated by several flagrant tackles by both sides. The period summary showed 11 shots for each team.

During the second overtime period, however, the Caps turned up the heat and outshot New York 17–9.

It was during the third overtime that the Isles displayed their first offensive advantage of the contest, outshooting Washington 11-10.

But by the end of the period, with the teams tiring severely, there was still no Patrick Division champion. The overtime periods had produced some marvelous play, however — especially by the goaltenders. Kelly Hrudey had robbed Bobby Gould several times and had stood up to Lou Franchescetti on a partial breakaway. Bob Mason had made game-salvaging stops on Duane Sutter and Pat LaFontaine.

Between overtime periods, LaFontaine promised his teammates that he was going to score the winner. His words proved prophetic when, nearly half-way into the fourth overtime frame, Islander defenseman Gord Dineen circled the Capitals' net and fired a shot from the circle. The puck hit the stick of Caps rearguard Kevin Hatcher and rolled out to the right point where LaFontaine fired a slapshot through a forest of players. The puck glanced off the goalpost and into the net before goaltender Bob Mason caught so much as a glimpse of it. The division championship belonged to the Islanders.

Just before the final tally, the Capital Centre organist had been playing the theme from the "Twilight Zone," and Kelly Hrudey, who had faced 75 shots, said he could readily relate to the tune. It was past 2 a.m. in Washington, and the rival teams had played a gruelling six-and-a-half hours, making the game the fifth longest in NHL history and the longest since Jack McLean scored for Toronto to beat the Red Wings in 1943.

It was 2 a.m. Sunday when more than 68 minutes of overtime ended mid-way through the seventh period.

Designed by Jean Lightfoot
Production Management by Paula Chabanais & Associates Ltd.
Typesetting by Compeer Typographic Services Ltd.
Printed and bound in Canada by Friesen Printers

**Canadian Cataloguing in
Publication Data**
Main entry under title:
Hockey
ISBN 0-385-25120-3
1. National Hockey League — History.
I. Diamond, Dan.  II. Stubbs, Lew.
GV847.8.N3H62  1987  796.96′2′06
C87-094114-3

Library of Congress Cataloguing in
Publication Data
Diamond, Dan.
  Hockey: twenty years.
  1. Hockey — History.  I. Stubbs, Lew.  II. Title.
GV846.5.D52 1987 796.96′2′09
86-32856
ISBN 0-385-25120-3

**ACKNOWLEDGEMENTS**
*Photo Credits:* Bowling Green State University Sports Information Office, Bruce
Bennett Studios, Frank Prazak, NHL Services, New York Rangers.

*Special thanks to* Stu Hackel, Gary Meagher, John Halligan, Bob Butera, Steve
Ryan, Charles Wilkins.

*In appreciation* of the efforts of players, coaches, on-ice officials, front office
personnel, scouts, trainers, reporters, and broadcasters whose endless hard work
won fans for hockey throughout the expansion years.